Studio Studies is a much needed work of enquiry: the studio is by turns an obvious and an unknown thing today. They are far more common and influential spaces than the laboratories about which we know so much – and yet no such signature volume has existed until now. It will be a defining collection by extraordinary contributors.

Chris Kelty, *Associate Professor, Institute of Society and Genetics & the Department of Information Studies, University of California, Los Angeles*

This book offers an excellent introduction to one of the defining projects in social studies today: the performative analysis of creative practice. Combining case studies and interviews by outstanding scholars in the study of science, technology and culture, it shows how the studio enables the assembly and negotiation of relations between art, design, markets, publics and social studies themselves. It thereby offers a welcome empirical handle on an especially complex contemporary phenomenon, the valuation of creativity across domains.

Noortje Marres, *Associate Professor, Centre for Interdisciplinary Methodology, University of Warwick*

In this sophisticated and theoretically astute collection, the authors make a case for the studio as a rewarding site for ethnographic research. But more profoundly, the studio is offered up – in its ad hoc procedures and modes of emergent organization – as an empirical model for social life and creativity more generally. It makes the studio mundane while showing how the worlds outside – factories, firms and so much more – share in the 'studio-ness' that makes things happen.

Harvey Molotch, *Professor of Sociology and Metropolitan Studies at New York University*

Studio Studies

Consider the geography of artefacts arrayed around you, from the building you are in to the lights illuminating the interior, the computational devices mediating your life, the music in the background, even the crockery, furniture and glassware. Common to all these objects is that their concrete, visual and technological forms were invariably conceived, modelled, finished and tested in sites characterized as studios. Remarkably, the studio remains a peculiar lacuna in our understanding of how cultural artefacts are brought into being and how 'creativity' operates as a located practice. *Studio Studies* is an agenda-setting volume presenting a set of empirical case studies that explore and examine the studio as a key setting for aesthetic and material production. As such, *Studio Studies* responds to three contemporary concerns in social and cultural thought: first, how to account for the situated nature of creative and cultural production; second, the challenge of reimagining creativity as a socio-materially distributed practice rather than the cognitive privilege of the individual; and finally, how to unravel the parallels, contrasts and interconnections between studios and other sites of cultural–aesthetic and technoscientific production, notably laboratories. By enquiring into the operations, topologies and displacements that shape and format studios, this volume aims to demarcate a novel and important object of analysis for empirical social and cultural research, as well to develop new conceptual repertoires to unpack the multiple ways studio processes shape our everyday lives.

Ignacio Farías is an Assistant Professor at the Munich Center for Technology in Society and the Department of Architecture of the Technische Universität München.

Alex Wilkie is a Senior Lecturer in Design at Goldsmiths, University of London.

CRESC
Culture, Economy and the Social
A new series from CRESC – the ESRC Centre for Research on Socio-cultural Change

The *Culture, Economy and the Social* series is committed to innovative contemporary, comparative and historical work on the relations between social, cultural and economic change. It publishes empirically-based research that is theoretically informed, that critically examines the ways in which social, cultural and economic change is framed and made visible, and that is attentive to perspectives that tend to be ignored or side-lined by grand theorising or epochal accounts of social change. The series addresses the diverse manifestations of contemporary capitalism, and considers the various ways in which the 'social', 'the cultural' and 'the economic' are apprehended as tangible sites of value and practice. It is explicitly comparative, publishing books that work across disciplinary perspectives, cross-culturally, or across different historical periods.

The series is actively engaged in the analysis of the different theoretical traditions that have contributed to the development of the 'cultural turn' with a view to clarifying where these approaches converge and where they diverge on a particular issue. It is equally concerned to explore the new critical agendas emerging from current critiques of the cultural turn: those associated with the descriptive turn for example. Our commitment to interdisciplinarity thus aims at enriching theoretical and methodological discussion, building awareness of the common ground that has emerged in the past decade, and thinking through what is at stake in those approaches that resist integration to a common analytical model.

Series titles include:

The Media and Social Theory
Edited by David Hesmondhalgh and Jason Toynbee

Culture, Class, Distinction
Tony Bennett, Mike Savage, Elizabeth Bortolaia Silva, Alan Warde, Modesto Gayo-Cal and David Wright

Material Powers
Edited by Tony Bennett and Patrick Joyce

The Social after Gabriel Tarde
Debates and assessments
Edited by Matei Candea

Cultural Analysis and Bourdieu's Legacy
Edited by Elizabeth Silva and Alan Ward

Milk, Modernity and the Making of the Human
Richie Nimmo

Creative Labour
Media work in three cultural industries
Edited by David Hesmondhalgh and Sarah Baker

Migrating Music
Edited by Jason Toynbee and Byron Dueck

Sport and the Transformation of Modern Europe
States, media and markets 1950–2010
Edited by Alan Tomlinson, Christopher Young and Richard Holt

Inventive Methods
The happening of the social
Edited by Celia Lury and Nina Wakeford

Understanding Sport
A socio-cultural analysis
By John Horne, Alan Tomlinson, Garry Whannel and Kath Woodward

Shanghai Expo
An international forum on the future of cities
Edited by Tim Winter

Diasporas and Diplomacy
Cosmopolitan contact zones at the BBC World Service (1932–2012)
Edited by Marie Gillespie and Alban Webb

Making Culture, Changing Society
Tony Bennett

Interdisciplinarity
Reconfigurations of the social and natural sciences
Edited by Andrew Barry and Georgina Born

Objects and Materials
A Routledge companion
Edited by Penny Harvey, Eleanor Conlin Casella, Gillian Evans, Hannah Knox, Christine McLean, Elizabeth B. Silva, Nicholas Thoburn and Kath Woodward

Accumulation
The material politics of plastic
Edited by Gay Hawkins, Jennifer Gabrys and Mike Michael

Theorizing Cultural Work
Labour, continuity and change in the cultural and creative industries
Edited by Mark Banks, Rosalind Gill and Stephanie Taylor

Comedy and Distinction
The cultural currency of a 'good' sense of humour
Sam Friedman

The Provoked Economy
Economic reality and the performative turn
Fabian Muniesa

Rio de Janeiro
Urban life through the eyes of the city
Beatriz Jaguaribe

The Routledge Companion to Bourdieu's 'Distinction'
Edited by Philippe Coulangeon and Julien Duval

Devising Consumption
Cultural economies of insurance, credit and spending
By Liz Mcfall

Industry and Work in Contemporary Capitalism
Global models, local lives?
Edited by Victoria Goddard and Susana Narotzky

Lived Economies of Default
Consumer credit, debt collection and the capture of affect
By Joe Deville

Cultural Pedagogies and Human Conduct
Edited by Megan Watkins, Greg Noble and Catherine Driscoll

Unbecoming Things
Mutable objects and the politics of waste
By Nicky Gregson and Mike Crang

Studio Studies
Operations, topologies and displacements
Edited by Ignacio Farías and Alex Wilkie

Studio Studies

Operations, topologies and displacements

Edited by
Ignacio Farías and Alex Wilkie

First published 2016
by Routledge
2 Park Square, Milton Park, Abingdon, Oxon OX14 4RN

and by Routledge
711 Third Avenue, New York, NY 10017

First issued in paperback 2018

Routledge is an imprint of the Taylor & Francis Group, an informa business

British Library Cataloguing in Publication Data
A catalogue record for this book is available from the British Library

Library of Congress Cataloging in Publication Data
Studio studies : operations, topologies & displacements / edited by Ignacio Farías and Alex Wilkie.
pages cm
Includes bibliographical references.
1. Cultural industries. 2. Creative ability. I. Farías, Ignacio, 1978- II. Wilkie, Alex.
HD9999.C9472S78 2015
338.4'77–dc23
2015014099

ISBN 13: 978-1-138-59637-5 (pbk)
ISBN 13: 978-1-138-79871-7 (hbk)

Typeset in Times New Roman
by Taylor & Francis Books

Contents

List of figures

List of contributors

Tomás Ariztía is Associate Professor at the Sociology department of Diego Portales University, Chile. His research is concerned with consumption studies, particularly marketing studies and sustainable consumption, and the sociology of methods. Tomás is currently interested in researching how consumers are mobilized in marketing knowledge practices, and has done fieldwork in advertising agencies and marketing departments. He is currently involved in a three-year research project comparing big data, design thinking and market research as different knowledge grammars through which social entities are enacted in markets. He recently edited the book *Produciendo lo social: usos de las ciencias sociales en el Chile reciente* (Ediciones UDP, 2011) which explores the connections between social sciences and the production of social worlds.

James Ash is a geographer researching the relationship between technology, design and embodiment, with a particular interest in digital interfaces, games and mobile media. He is a Lecturer in Media and Cultural Studies at Newcastle University, UK. James is author of *The Interface Envelope: Gaming, Technology, Power* (Bloomsbury, 2015). He has also published a number of articles on technology and video games in a range of international journals including *Theory, Culture and Society*, *Body and Society* and *Environment and Planning D: Society and Space*. You can learn more about James' research on his website: http://www.jamesash.co.uk.

Ariane Berthoin Antal is a Senior Fellow at the WZB Berlin Social Science Center, and honorary professor at the Technical University of Berlin in Germany, as well as Distinguished Research Professor at Audencia Nantes School of Management in France. Her research interests include business and society, organizational learning and culture, and, since 2008, artistic interventions in organizations. Recent books include the *Oxford Handbook of Organizational Learning and Knowledge* (co-edited with M. Dierkes, J. Child and I. Nonaka, Oxford University Press, 2001); *Learning Organizations. Extending the Field* (co-edited with P. Meusburger and L. Suarsana, Springer, 2014); *Moments of Valuation. Exploring Sites of Dissonance* (co-edited with M. Hutter and D. Stark, Oxford University Press, 2015);

and *Artistic Interventions in Organizations: Research, Theory and Practice* (co-edited with U. Johannson Skolberg and J. Woodilla, Routledge, 2015).

Georgina Born is Professor of Music and Anthropology at Oxford University, Visiting Professor at Oslo University and McGill University, and was 2014 Bloch Distinguished Visiting Professor, U. C. Berkeley. Her books are *Rationalizing Culture: IRCAM, Boulez, and the Institutionalization of the Musical Avant-Garde* (University of California Press, 1995); *Uncertain Vision: Birt, Dyke and the Reinvention of the BBC* (Vintage, 2005); *Western Music and its Others: Difference, Representation, and Appropriation in Music* (co-edited with D. Hesmondhalgh, University of California Press, 2000); *Interdisciplinarity: Reconfigurations of the Social and Natural Sciences* (co-edited with A. Barry, Routledge, 2013,); and *Music, Sound and Space* (Cambridge University Press, 2013). The collection *Improvisation and Social Aesthetics* will be published by Duke in 2015. Georgina is an anthropologist whose work is highly interdisciplinary, building dialogues with musicology, art history, and science and technology studies. From 2010–15 she is directing the ERC-funded research programme 'Music, Digitization, Mediation: Towards Interdisciplinary Music Studies'.

Ignacio Farías is an Assistant Professor at the Munich Center for Technology in Society and the Department of Architecture of the Technishe Universität München. He has held Visiting Fellowships at Harvard University, Goldsmiths, University of London and New York University. Farías has conducted ethnographic research on studio processes in three creative fields: architecture, video games and visual arts, and done extensive research in urban issues such as tourism and disaster reconstruction. He is co-editor of *Urban Assemblages. How Actor-Network Changes Urban Studies* (Routledge, 2009) and author of several articles in journals including *Economy and Society, European Journal of Social Theory, Sociological Review* and *Space and Culture.*

Emmanuel Grimaud is a Research Fellow at the National Center for Scientific Research (CNRS), France. He has conducted ethnographic research in various fields related to the anthropology of technology, including film studios and robotic labs. He is also the coordinator of Artmap (www.artmap-research.com), an interdisciplinary research platform gathering researchers and artists to design experimental protocols in order to work on frontier objects of the human sciences. He received the Bronze Medal of the CNRS in 2011.

Antoine Hennion is Research Director at MINES-ParisTech and Professor and former Director of the Centre for the Sociology of Innovation (CSI). He has written extensively in the sociology of music, media and cultural industries (radio, design, advertising), and on amateurs and the taste for music. With colleagues from the CSI, he participated in a new problematization of mediation (in the field of science, technology and society, and the sociology of the arts and culture). Developing a pragmatist approach, he is now studying diverse forms of attachment and detachment from taste and sports to issues about care, aging or disability. Some recent books are *The Passion for Music. A Sociology of Mediation* (Ashgate, 2015 [2007, 1st edn 1993]); *La Grandeur de Bach* (with J.-M. Fauquet, Fayard, 2000); and *Figures de l'amateur* (with S. Maisonneuve and É. Gomart, La Documentation française, 2000).

Sophie Houdart is a Research Fellow at the National Center for Scientific research (CNRS), France and is a member of the Laboratory of Ethnology and Comparative Sociology. Trained in social anthropology, she has been focusing on various practices within the field of innovation studies, in the realm of science as well as art, especially in Japan. She is the author of several books including *Kuma Kengo. An Unconventional Monograph* (Éditions Donner Lieu, 2009) dedicated to the studio practice of the eminent Japanese architect; and *Humains, non humains. Comment repeupler les sciences sociales* (with O. Thiery, La Découverte, 2011).

Mike Michael is sociologist of science and technology, and a Professor at the Department of Sociology and Social Policy at the University of Sydney. His interests have included the relation of everyday life to technoscience, and biotechnological and biomedical innovation and culture. He is currently developing a 'speculative methodology' through an engagement with mundane technology, design practice and big data. Recent publications include *Innovation and Biomedicine: Ethics, Evidence and Expectation in HIV* (co-authored with Marsha Rosengarten, Palgrave, 2013); and *Accumulation: The Material Politics of Plastic* (co-edited with Jennifer Gabrys and Gay Hawkins, Routledge, 2013).

Erin O'Connor is an Associate Professor of Sociology at Marymount Manhattan College in New York City. Erin specializes in the fields of ethnography, culture, art, work, body and knowledge. She is currently completing her book *Firework: Art, Craft and Self among Glassblowers*, which, drawing from four years' field research at a glassblowing studio during which she became a glassblower, unpacks the intrigue of craftwork and provides an account of how glassblowers problem-solve with and through their bodies to learn to blow glass and thereby gain material knowledge, practise self-expression and build community. Erin has also conducted ethnographic analysis of creativity in interdisciplinary scientific research as a researcher at the Social Science Research Council, and is expanding her research to include environment-crafts. Her work has appeared in the journals *Thesis Eleven, Qualitative Sociology Review, Qualitative Sociology* and *Ethnography*, as well as in edited volumes such as *Craftwork as Problem Solving: Ethnographic Studies of Design and Making* (edited by Trevor Marchand, Ashgate, 2016).

Laurie Waller is a Lecturer in Sociology at Goldsmiths, University of London. His work addresses the relations between science and culture, and his PhD research examined the proposition of the exhibition as an experimental format. Current research interests include the empirical study of public experiments and the social and political theorizing of materiality. He is also a Visiting Fellow at Technische Universität Berlin.

Alex Wilkie is a Senior Lecturer in Design at Goldsmiths, University of London, and he is a sociologist. His research interests combine aspects of science and technology studies with practice-based design research that bear on conceptual, methodological and substantive areas such as data and algorithmic practices, energy-demand reduction, healthcare and information technologies, human–computer interaction design, inventive and performative methods, user-centred and participatory design, process theory, and speculative theory and practice. Alex set up and runs the MA in Interaction Design and is Director of the PhD programme in Design Studies, both at Goldsmiths. He is currently preparing a monograph based on an ethnographic study of user-centred designers, and he is also co-editor of *Inventing the Social* (with Michael Guggenheim and Noortje Marres, Mattering Press, forthcoming 2016); and *Transversal Speculations* (with Jennifer Gabrys, Marsha Rosengarten and Martin Savransky, forthcoming 2016).

Acknowledgements

This book came about by way of an encounter between the editors at Goldsmiths, University of London. Ignacio Farías was a British Academy Visiting Scholar at the Department of Sociology at Goldsmiths, and Alex Wilkie, a member of the Interaction Research Studio, a Research Fellow in Sociology and a Lecturer in Design. For enabling this meeting, we would like to begin these acknowledgements by thanking Nina Wakeford, also a member of Sociology Department at Goldsmiths.

Next, we would like to say thank you to the contributors to this book for their enthusiasm for this project and their patience with the process of editing and publication. We would also like to thank them for participating in two events that we organized in order to explore the viability of this programme and its traction with the interests of scholars of social and cultural research. The first event was the double session 'Studio studies – creative production' at the Joint Conference of the Society for Social Studies of Science (4S) and the European Association for the Study of Science and Technology (EASST) entitled 'Design and displacement: social studies of science and technology' that was held in Copenhagen in 2012. The second was a two-day author workshop held at WZB Berlin Social Science Center, which was generously funded by the WZB and the Department of Design, Goldsmiths, University of London. For their involvement in the second workshop, and the zeal with which they worked with the contributions and the problematic of the studio-as-site, we would again like to thank Nina Wakeford as well as Noortje Marres and Alvise Mattozzi.

This book features interviews with two notable scholars whose work, we believe, plays a formative role in acknowledging and addressing the studio as a requisite element of 'social' life and cultural production. We would like to extend our thanks to Georgina Born and Antoine Hennion for kindly being interviewed and collaborating on the production of the interview texts, and in so doing enthusing the project of the empirical study of studio practices and processes. Ignacio Farías would like to extend a special thanks to Michael Hutter at the WZB for his continuous support with this and other academic endeavours and making possible the research visits of Antoine Hennion, Noortje Marres and Alvise Mattozzi to our former research unit 'Cultural

Sources of Newness'. Likewise, Alex Wilkie would like to acknowledge his appreciation of an indebtedness to members of the Interaction Research Studio at Goldsmiths, notably Bill Gaver, Andy Boucher and Tobie Kerridge.

For her trust and enthusiasm from the very first moment we suggested the possibility of a volume on the studio, we would like to thank Penny Harvey, Professor of Anthropology at Manchester University and one of the editors of this CRESC Book Series. For her enormous and painstaking support in proofreading the manuscript for this book, we would like to thank Barbara Schlueter at the WZB and also Alyson Claffey, editorial assistant at Taylor & Francis, for her patient and kind support with the production process.

1 Studio studies

Notes for a research programme

Ignacio Farías and Alex Wilkie

Introduction

This edited collection approaches the 'studio' as a key site for the production of cultural artefacts, and in doing so it aims to open up a novel and underdeveloped topic for social and cultural research. As the chapters of this book demonstrate, studios play an essential role in bringing into being all manner of aesthetic, affective and reflexive objects including, but not limited to, artworks, brands, buildings, crafted artefacts, concepts, designed products and services, live action and animated films, information technologies, music, software and video games. Even government policy is being conceived and incubated in 'social' and 'service' design studios, continuing the intervention of design into democratic procedures (e.g. SEE Platform 2013). The list is seemingly endless. Studios, it appears, have become the principle resource for what are, after Theodor Adorno and Max Horkheimer (1979), commonly known as 'culture industries' where so-called 'creativity' is heralded as the driving factor in the revitalization of contemporary capitalist economies. The premise of this collection, however, is that despite the key role played by the studio in cultural production, its importance has been, and remains, largely overlooked by anthropologists, sociologists, cultural theorists, historians, policy makers and so forth. In short, the studio remains a peculiar and remarkable lacuna in our understanding of how cultural artefacts are brought into the world and how creativity operates as a situated practice.

So where to begin and how to proceed? If social and cultural researchers want to study the studio, where might they start? What traditions and disciplines might provide the techniques, analytical tools and concepts for exploring, examining and analysing what a studio is, what happens in a studio, what is made in a studio, and what other sites, processes and actors the studio is connected to? For readers familiar with the programme of ethnomethodology as well as Science and Technology Studies (STS), one particular precedent acts as a cue to approaching sites where knowledge, material entities and practices come together in an organized, routinized and managed way to produce new phenomena and new knowledge: namely, the research tradition known as 'laboratory studies' (e.g. Knorr Cetina 1995). Such studies provide inspiration and instruction in how to address situated and coordinated work environments that are organized and maintained in order to support creative practices, invention and the making of cultural artefacts. Rather than understanding studio processes as the practical expression of an individual's creativity, the chapters brought together in this collection variously view creation as a situated process wherein new cultural forms are made, without assuming an *a priori* distinction between supposedly creative acts and routine activity, or between creative actors as opposed to assistants, equipment and tools.

As we detail in this introduction, there is no easy access to the studio since the obstacles come in both empirical and theoretical form. That is to say, not only are studios challenging sites to gain access to, but 'access' also involves circumventing decades of sociological and anthropological assumptions about creativity in order to delineate an alternative approach to making as a situated and distributed process. Once this is achieved, we can begin to imagine the studio as the laboratory's cultural analogous: a space that harbours and manifests the conditions in which prototypes, models, designs, media and visualizations are conceived, planned, tested, and synthesized into coherent, bounded and affective forms. But, as we will suggest, this is not enough. Paying attention to the specific epistemic–ontological problems configuring studio work requires us to start exploring alternative conceptual repertoires that take us beyond analogies with scientific experimentation and into questions of invention, intimacy and attachment. This is a task that this introduction can only begin to realize, and one that is further explored in the chapters of this book.

Creative work: towards a situated approach

Since the 1990s, creativity has emerged as a central category in public discourses about economic prosperity as well as social and individual wellbeing (Osborne 2003, Nelson 2010), as shown by its proliferation in notions such as 'creative industries' (DCMS 1998, Caves 2000, Howkins 2001), 'creative class' (Florida 2002), 'creative cities' (Landry and Bianchini 1995, Hall 2000) and 'creative economy' (UNCTAD 2008). It has also come to be seen as an obligatory point of passage for the cultural production of the new (e.g. Osborn 1957) – a necessary ingredient for stimulating and provoking novelty. For governments, the notion of creative industries has become a key instrument in policy frameworks across Europe, North America and around the world in attempts to harness cultural production for the restructuring of urban and national economies (Banks and O'Connor 2009). A prime example of this is the first *World Report on the Creative Economy* published by the United Nations, which entrusts the creative industries with the capacity to forge 'a new development paradigm' (UNCTAD 2008: 3). Most policy frameworks construe the creative economy by means of industrial classification systems, which typically include categories such as the visual and performing arts and crafts; service-oriented sectors such as architecture and advertising; and technology-intensive sectors including film, TV, radio, social media and video game industries. Underlying such classifications are vague definitions pointing to creativity as a human faculty, to expressive or experiential aspects of creative products characterized as 'values', or to the creation of intellectual property. Despite discussions about the distinctiveness of these industries (Banks and O'Connor 2009, Potts et al. 2008), the sense in which such industries are 'creative' remains largely ignored or undeveloped.

Clearly, then, the very notion of 'creativity' has become a black box – a process the contents of which remain unknown and unproblematic (Callon 1986, Latour 1987) – hindering empirical enquiries into actual creative practices and sites in the various 'sectors' of cultural production. Typically, creativity is imagined in two ways. On the one hand, by drawing on psychological definitions that point to original, divergent thought processes leading to new ideas (Csikzentmihalyi 1996, Boden 1994), creativity is located in an individual's mind as a cognitive capacity acquired prior to, and the cause of, a person's creative processes or 'behaviour'. This understanding of creativity, for instance, leads urban policy advisors such as Richard Florida (2005) to recommend orienting urban policy strategies towards attracting members of the creative class. Notably, these formulaic approaches have been criticized for their misleading association of creativity with homogeneous occupational groups with high educational achievement (Markusen 2006) and the contradictory use of a microeconomic category ('creativity') to justify a macroeconomic construction (an industrial sector) nonexistent from a microeconomic perspective (Potts et al. 2008). On the other hand, scholarly research in sociology and geography has focused on the contexts and conditions that enable creativity to unfold and flourish, and on how creative industries can be nurtured. Here, studies place emphasis on the role played by creative milieus (Meusburger 2009, Hall 2000), creative neighbourhoods and urban spaces (Grabher 2001, Lloyd 2004), creative industry clusters (van Heur 2009, Sunley et al. 2008), and governance tools for the creative industries (Pratt 2004). Furthermore, scholars in the social sciences have also focused on the impact of the creative economy on the individual, in terms of both the constitution of new 'creative' subject positions (Reckwitz 2012) and the precarization of creative workers (McRobbie 2002). In examining the political economy of creative labour, critical scholars (Hesmondhalgh and Baker 2010) have pointed to the market and institutional arrangements that allow firms in the media and cultural sector to extract the surplus value of creative work, such as exploiting unpaid labour time or deploying aggressive copyright regimes (Cohen 2012). Thereby, however, social scientists tend to overlook the very settings where the products of the creative industries are brought into being by focusing on the urban contexts as well as and inter-institutional conditions in which creativity is achieved.

This, then, is precisely the challenge presented to the contributors of this book: how can socio-cultural research overcome individualistic and contextualist explanations of 'creativity' and how might the situated and concrete dynamic of creative production be grasped? Evidently, this involves jettisoning the endemic correlation between creativity and innovation. As mentioned above, creativity is commonly understood as a thought process leading to a novel idea (Boden 1994). Apart from the problematic reduction to cognitive activity, the reference to novelty only allows for *ex-post* accounts of creativity, since whether a (thought) process is deemed creative depends on the future valuation of its upshot as being new; something that is not just uncertain, but also varying in space and reversible in time, as innovation studies have clearly shown (e.g. Akrich et al. 2002a, 2002b). An equally important problem with the notion of innovation is the way in which it works to amalgamate creativity and invention to the logics, rationalities and temporalities of market economics (Godin 2006), thus historically naturalizing the connection between the two.

With *Studio Studies*, our purpose, then, is to change the very register through which creativity is understood by bringing into focus creation processes understood as processes of both inventing and making cultural artefacts. In our view, creation processes do not deal primarily with the problem of *interessement* and enrolment of actors as new objects circulate through (and in doing so, fashion) space and time, that is, the problem of innovation. The fact that 'nobody knows' in advance whether an invention will become an innovation requires us to approach creation processes as more than just a prelude to innovation, that is, as processes imbued and shaped by other practical and, indeed, more pressing problems, such as how to produce knowledge about not-yet-existing things, how to engage in form-giving processes, how to stabilize new forms and artefacts, or how to model attachments to future users and consumers. By focusing on such fundamental problems of creation processes, *Studio Studies* sets out a redescription of creative work – an overhaul of how we understand and appreciate the emergence of new cultural artefacts.

It is important to note that creation has been classically understood as a process of imposing a form (*morphe*) onto matter (*hyle*) (cf. Ingold 2010); an understanding intimately related to that of creativity as a thought process leading to the generation of new immaterial forms. Such notion of creation bears similarities to the Kantian notion of cognition, which also posits an isolated 'mind-in-the-vat', grasping the world and producing knowledge in terms of its own synthetic categories (Latour 1999). In both cases there is a passive material world open to mental designs and categories and an individualized understanding of the 'creator' or the 'cognizer'. But at least since sociologists of scientific knowledge discovered the laboratory as a site for studying 'science-in-the-making' (Latour and Woolgar 1986, Knorr-Cetina 1981), there has been a major move away from such a conception of cognition towards a notion of 'distributed cognition' (Gieri and Moffat 2003, Hutchins 1995). This shift has led researchers to study how the production, manipulation and circulation of material inscriptions through different media, technologies and bodies makes possible cognitive processes that no single person can perform. Moreover, in laboratory studies equal attention is paid to all the activities undertaken by scientists and lab technicians, whether routine informal talk, strategic career decisions or fact-making efforts. All such practices are considered part of knowledge-making processes, debunking the myth of scientific method and rationality, while furnishing it with a stronger objectivity.

The prospect of *Studio Studies* is predicated on a similar move made by introducing the notion of 'distributed creation' in its widest sense. Such a notion has, in our view, two key interrelated advantages. First, distributed creation allows one to account for the active and enabling role played by the materials and technologies participating in creation processes, undermining the distinction between form and matter that informs traditional understandings of creativity. Or, to paraphrase Latour (1987: 258), we have to be undecided as to what actors to follow and what creation is made of. Second, this mode of empirical accounting involves closely describing all the activities performed by all actors involved in creation processes, and not assuming an *a priori* distinction between creative acts and routine activity. Assuming that creation occurs in all manner of human and non-human configurations and thus, much like actor–network theory's (ANT) methodological dictum to follow the actors, the study of creativity requires an appreciation and sensitivity to non-human processes and entities. Thus, the notion of distributed creation emphasizes creativity as a socio-material and collective process, in which no single actor holds all the cards (e.g. Farías 2015); a view that is somewhat sympathetic to and commensurate with ANT and its developments (Law and Hassard 1999).

Notably, taking distributed creation to its extreme brings us 'back' to Whitehead's (1927 [1926]) original coining of creativity (Ford 1986, Meyer 2005, Halewood 2005: 35) as a metaphysical concept to describe processes by which entities and phenomena, human and non-human alike, come into being and change. The implication of this view is that creativity is a basic feature of existence, a generic, mundane and fundamental feature of all ontological processes, not just of persons endowed with special cognitive abilities. Thus understood, creativity is linked to the notion of 'event' (see Wilkie 2013, also Wilkie and Michael, chapter 2 in this volume) as a process of becoming. The principle of process is foundational for the emergence of all new entities and phenomena: '*how* an actual entity *becomes* constitutes *what* that actual entity is … Its "being" is constituted by its "becoming"' (Whitehead 1978 [1929]: 23, emphasis in original). Going back to Whitehead requires the ethnographer of creativity to attend to actual, specific and situated becoming of studio phenomena.[1] This approach also opens a view of the studio as a site productive of what, following Isabelle Stengers (2005), could be called 'cosmopolitical' events – events at which the possibility of new social and cultural arrangements, and the kinds of common worlds that studios are part of speculating on and constructing, are at stake.

One might reasonably assume that this has long been a major research focus in studies of cultural production. Yet, ever since Adorno and Horkheimer (1979) described the subordination of culture to an industrial logic based on rational standardization, commodification and capital accumulation, the study of cultural production has focused on its determination by 'broader' social, industrial and institutional contexts. Here, the prominence of Richard Peterson, Pierre Bourdieu and Howard Becker is unmistakable. Peterson's influential 'production of culture' perspective, drawing on Merton's sociology of science, focuses on the systemic and institutional configurations of cultural production by looking at six essential features: technology, law and regulations, the industry structure, the organizational structure of the dominating firms, occupational careers, and market structure (Peterson 1976, Peterson and Anand 2004). Bourdieu's sociology of the 'field of cultural production' addresses how social spaces condition cultural production through competitive yet complementary relationships among individual producers, artistic genres, cultural intermediaries and cultural institutions. He thereby charges against the 'ideology of creation' and the individual artist as an 'apparent producer' (Bourdieu 1980). Bourdieu also refuses to address cultural objects, which he views as mere effects of the producers' 'agonistics of position-taking', as Georgina Born (2010: 179) notes. Becker's work on art as collective activity (1974) and art worlds (1984) is perhaps the most relevant and promising for our purposes, as it focuses on the interactive and cooperative practices and networks of people who participate, directly or indirectly, in the production of artworks. However, and somewhat disappointingly, instead of looking at how art world actors actually engage in creative activity in the actual sites of cultural production, Becker concentrates on shared knowledge and conventions, while attempting the classification of different social types, such as 'integrated professionals', 'mavericks', 'naïve artists' or 'folk artists' for producers (1976), and 'well-socialized people', 'experienced audience members' or 'art students' for audiences (1984).

Antoine Hennion presents a sobering and substantial charge against such perspectives in that they have 'only attempted the study of milieu, professions, institutions, markets, policies – that is, everything "around" the object itself' (Hennion 1989: 401). Since this critique was expressed, various 'turns' to the object have occurred in studies of cultural production and the sociology of art. Hennion himself (1993) has pioneered the study of the material 'mediators' of music, such as instruments, bodies, notation systems, sheet music, recording technologies, reproduction devices, music halls etc., arguing that these 'are neither mere carriers of the work, nor substitutes which dissolve its reality; they are the art itself' (2003: 84). Alfred Gell (1998) describes cultural objects (or 'indexes') as condensing and mediating relations between persons and things, and even changing in their physical form as they mediate among different entities. More recently, Scott Lash and Celia Lury (2007) propose following cultural products, this time through global circuits, describing how media, especially films, become thing-like, and how things, including shoes or watches, are mediatized. Freed from the identities imposed by producers and the logic of the commodity, these cultural media-things operate as brand environments open to different experiences, interpretations and doings.

Contemporary studies of cultural and creative production, as exemplified by the above, have thus moved from the analysis of contexts and conditions of cultural production to the cultural artefacts that come into being in such processes. However, while such perspectives make it necessary to turn our gaze to the actual sites in which practitioners engage in conceiving, modelling, testing and finishing cultural artefacts (Dubuisson and Hennion 1995, Hennion et al. 1993), the studio, although a preoccupation in the visual arts (e.g. Jacob and Grabner 2010), has not been an object of systematic and intensive analysis for the social sciences (e.g. Zembylas 2014). The most notable exception is possibly Born's (1995) ethnography of the Institut de recherche et coordination acoustique/musique (IRCAM), which brings together an institutional analysis focused on status relationships, subject positions and power conflicts with a socio-technical analysis of the practices and mediations of experimental music creation.

Taking this into account, this edited collection brings into sharp focus the specificity of the studio as an empirical site for the study of the 'distributed' creation, making and invention of cultural artefacts. It is important, though, to emphasize that our understanding of the studio does not prescribe a homogeneous space that can be characterized by physical or organizational features, such as size, location, labour division, conflicts over status or institutional discourses. Studios have assumed very different forms, not just throughout the history of art (Hughes 1990, Alpers 1998, Jones 1996), with some closer to factories and ateliers, others to offices and shops, as well as self-declared post-studios, but also in fields of practice beyond the visual arts. As the chapters in this volume show, the studio is a key configuration in advertising, various genres of design (architectural, interactive, product and service), film and television production, experimental music, video game development, and even post-studio visual arts.

In all cases, though, the studio designates a more-or-less contained and bounded space shaped by, and shaping, distributed creation processes. Furthermore, it is possible to describe our object of enquiry as 'studio life' (cf. Latour and Woolgar 1986). This reference to life obviously points to the more routinized aspects of workplace activities occasioned in these sites, to the studio as a humdrum and habitual workplace, rather than the domain of individual genius. But the notion of studio life also has a more specific sense, a more specific purpose. It designates a vitality: a generative capacity that inheres in the human–material arrangements and circulations taking place in studios and converging in the creation of new cultural artefacts. Approaching studio life as one major aspect of processes of distributed creation, we advocate paying attention to the variegated events in which the potentialities of materials, artefacts, bodies, images and concepts unfold empirically, taking into consideration the properties and constraints of phenomena and entities that enter into the studio. Turning to studio life therefore involves rejecting approaches based on an external causation of creative processes and closely studying the situations in and through which distributed creation processes take place.

Studio life: invention, intimacy and aesthetics

As mentioned above, this volume draws inspiration from a key research tradition in STS, namely the field of laboratory studies which emerged in the late 1970s shaped by a commitment to the participant observation of scientific practices as an approach for understanding the production and contents of scientific knowledge and objectivity.[2] The key lesson we draw from this is that an emphasis on the creation of cultural artefacts cannot be separated from the settings in which such entities are brought into existence. Clearly, then, this places studio studies firmly in a particular lineage marked by Garfinkel's (1967) influential programme of ethnomethodology, where the minute observation of situated accomplishments of 'members' in organized everyday settings discloses the reflexive accountability of routine practical activity. Accordingly, it also betrays our interest in bringing the insights and methods associated with ANT to bear on the studio as a centre for the production of cultural artefacts. It is necessary to describe in more detail how laboratory studies can inform the study of studios and to what extent the latter entails new problematizations and novel conceptual repertoires.

We cannot fail to notice a marked tendency to imagine and shape studios as laboratories in different fields of creative practice. Michael Century (1999) has described the 'studio laboratory' as a post-Manhattan project trope characterizing art–technology innovation engagements. In the field of design, for example, 'living labs' (Björgvinsson et al. 2010) and 'culture labs' (see Born and Wilkie, Chapter 9 in this volume) are imagined as settings for the design and innovation of computational technologies, whilst the label 'design lab' is indicative of an epistemic flinch in which the term 'lab' or 'laboratory' affords legitimacy and authority to institutional milieus for knowledge production and innovation practices involving design. Also in the contemporary visual arts, artists are increasingly conceiving and configuring their studios as experimental systems akin to laboratories (see Farías, Chapter 12 in this volume). In the context of new institutional arrangements redefining art and design as practice-based research, the analogy with the laboratory allows the studio to be viewed as a key site of knowledge production. The key, however, is less a discursive leveraging of experiences and knowledges assembled in studio products than the qualification of studio processes as experimental, something noted by several scholars. In an early contribution to the study of studios, Hennion et al. (1993) describe advertising agencies as 'laboratories of desire' – sites in which experimental answers are sought in response to one of the most fundamental questions in social sciences and humanities alike, such as what makes individuals desire certain objects. In their view, advertising experiments with human desires in a mode resembling 'the more chancy tinkering of laboratories [where t]he subject–object model [...] becomes a laboured product that on the laboratory bench reacts to the way in which advertising deals with it' (1993: 172). Similarly, the art historian Svetlana Alpers relates how laboratories and studios are the twin descendants of the rise of an experimentalist spirit in the seventeenth century. From this perspective, the historical departure of the artist's studio from the artisan's workshop did not lie just in the search for originality understood as *poiesis* (Sennett 2008), but above all in the experimentation with the socio-environmental conditions affecting human perception and visual cultures (see Farías, Chapter 12 in this volume).

Taken in a stricter sense, however, the notion of experiment can only describe some highly specific studio processes and is far from offering a more general heuristics. Indeed, as Hans-Jörg Rheinberger (1997) has shown, experimental systems involve entanglements of epistemic things – the objects about which knowledge is to be produced – and the technical objects, apparatuses and systems shaping the experimental practice. Aimed at producing reproducible discoveries, experimental systems require a high stabilization of the socio-technical assemblages of experimental work and the epistemic things at stake. Even if the latter are by definition unknown, they need to be clearly identified, at least in the form of the research question or hypothesis, as bounded objects of inquiry. According to Rheinberger, experimental systems 'allow, to put it paradoxically, to create new knowledge effects in a regulated manner and yet one that transcends our capacities of anticipation' (2004: 8). Whereas an analogy could be made here to conceptualize some techniques and methods deployed in studios to foster creativity, such as brainstorming (Osborn 1957, Wilkie and Michael forthcoming), studios mostly feature less formalized modes of inquiry. Thus, whilst experimental systems are designed to produce new answers to well defined problems, studio processes consist to a large extent in actually finding and defining a problem. In different fields of cultural production, architects, artists and advertising professionals consistently describe their explorations as open inquiries, in which neither the work-to-be-made, nor the technical apparatus of inquiry, nor the actual problem is well defined or at all stabilized. Arguably, then, a typical studio situation is one in which practitioners do not quite know what they are searching for.

Moreover, in contrast to the lab, where the obligation is to produce new knowledge, newness does not offer a sufficient criterion for the shaping of studio products. A short visit to any studio or, even better, to their storage rooms, where piles of sketches, models, prototypes and other half-baked ideas and propositions are stacked up to the ceiling, is enough to discover that the problem is not to come up with new variations, alternatives and possibilities. The fundamental studio challenge is rather the production of necessity (Farías 2013), that is, establishing conditions and constraints to close down the infinite span of possibilities, discard alternatives and make decisions. Producing necessity is thus crucial for bringing cultural artefacts into being, making them consistent, coherent and stable, that is, to put it with Latour (2013), for their instauration as beings. The studio problem is thus a fundamentally ontological one, very well grasped by notions of expressing (Dewey 2005 [1934]), making (Ingold 2013) and prototyping (Wilkie 2013). This, however, should be carefully understood, as it does not mean that scientific experimentation is shaped by epistemic concerns only. At both sites, labs and studios, we encounter practices of knowing and constructing new objects, not-yet existing objects, that is, epistemic–ontological achievements. The difference we are pointing to is that, to the extent that such processes are framed as discovery or creation, they entail different styles, methods and modes of inquiry.

Hence, and as Lucy Suchman has pointed out, if the major challenge for laboratory studies was to demonstrate that scientific facts are made, not discovered, the challenge for what we call studio studies lies in showing 'the historical anteriority of even the most innovative objects' (2012: 55). The notion of invention in the Tardean sense is helpful here, as it imagines invention not as a *poiesis ex-nihilo*, but as a potential contained in every act of imitation (Barry and Thrift 2007). Taking this as a cue, we can start to reimagine the studio as a site, where invention is reverse engineered, so to speak, as it necessitates connecting new cultural artefacts to existing settings and arrangements. Taking into account that in the studio every sketch, every model, every new material arrangement, every conversation potentially implies a new ontological proposition, the key challenge for studio practitioners lies in discovering and reflecting on the capacity of such propositions to become part of existing histories of human–non-human attachments and reconfigurations.

Paying attention to these existing histories enables us to address another important issue related to the relationship between the studio and its outside; between the sites where a cultural artefact is assembled and where it encounters and possibly attaches itself to its users, consumers or publics. Here too we can see how the studio takes a shape fundamentally different from that of the lab. One of the most powerful insights of laboratory studies conducted in the tradition of ANT was that the laboratory has no outside. In other words, scientific facts produced in a laboratory are not simply validated in and by other laboratories, rather the very condition of their success is the laboratorization of the world, or at least of those milieu in which facts enact their power. The prime example of this process is what Latour (1988) dubs the 'Pasteurization of France' – the fact that Pasteur's laboratory construction of microbes succeeded in ensuring the quality of milk was due to the fact that French dairies had to be configured to reliably reproduce the conditions under which microbes come into existence. As such, milk could only be pasteurized if dairies became laboratories. Pasteur's laboratory thereby became an 'obligatory point of passage' (Callon 1986) for those wanting to understand epizootics and epidemics. The lab is thus one of the fundamental truth spots of science (Gieryn 2002): an enhanced site within which facts (and science) hold their shape, and thus a key site grounding the power of science to shape the social.

Arguably, and especially in the context of this volume, studios could not be more different. Studios are, by definition, *not* the place in which inventions are validated, evaluated and valorised: homes, galleries, museums, cars, cinemas and offices are just some obvious examples of the sites where the cultural artefacts conceived and shaped in studios are exhibited, installed, appropriated, experienced, transformed, discarded. In contrast to the laboratory, the world persists here as an uncontrollable and irreducible outside to which cultural artefacts and forms devised in the studio are ultimately delivered, and where they have to impose themselves once more. Such an insurmountable gap between the studio and its outsides, constitutive of cultural artefacts, has two major consequences for studio cultures that we need to address briefly, before presenting the chapters of the volume.

First, to the extent that studios are not sites of validation of cultural artefacts, they can remain withdrawn from the audience's eye, exempted from the obligation to publicly disclose studio practices and arrangements. In most cases, there is indeed no need to painstakingly record every studio operation in what would then probably be called a 'studiolog' – a word that doesn't even exist. Even if some recording takes place, this is never done for public accounting, but for keeping a studio memory. The point here is that studio memory, as well as the variegated studio life we have been calling attention to, defines a workspace that is not just private, but intimate. As cultural historians and sociologists have suggested, the modern invention of intimacy did not just involve an interpersonal space protected from the public view, but also one in which individuals engage with each other in a comprehensive manner, not reducing each other to specific public roles. This has particular methodological implications for ethnographers of studio life, who often cannot restrain themselves from becoming 'native' members of studio collectives and thus actively involved in creation processes. Beyond this, it is possible to think the studio as a space of 'material intimacy' (Farías forthcoming); a space in which an intensive and comprehensive engagement with non-human entities as complex things that cannot be reduced to some of its qualities, properties or figurations takes site. The studio appears thus as a site in which one lives with objects and materials, and where tinkering and invention result from the long-term engagement with them. More importantly, the concept of intimacy describes a situation in which 'a clear cut attribution of duties and responsibilities [...] is [...] no longer possible' (Luhmann 1998: 57). Conceptualizing the studio as a site of interpersonal and material intimacy thus allows us to underscore the view that creation processes are not just radically distributed, but it is also practically impossible to establish which human and non-human actors contribute what to the assembling of a cultural artefact. Authorship appears from this perspective less grounded in studio life than in the process of deciding which studio products leave the studio and how.

Second, and following on from the above, the question arises as to how studio practitioners work towards strengthening the reality of their cultural artefacts. This is a key practical issue as the studio is separated from the sites where the reality effects of their newly created cultural artefacts are put to test – where the artefact–'public' (user, consumer, audience, spectator etc.) assemblage coheres. To approach this, the idiom of laboratory studies, and for that matter innovation studies, is not very helpful as it emphasizes the practical construction of strong assemblages, stable configurations and powerful alignments of people and things. What is curious and perhaps idiosyncratic about cultural artefacts is that it often requires just a weak attachment to take hold, unfold and shape the real. No matter how much testing, repetition and so on goes on in advance in the studio, the practical problem is that the source of that weak attachment simply cannot be reliably anticipated. It could be anything: the colour, the finish, a certain weight, a name, a reference to X, etc. There is no way to know or to model such things, for the studio does not scale down the world; rather, it involves taking the risk of assembling alternative relationships between objects, people and spaces, introducing alternative propositions, imagining a different world. Studio practices are always a risky bet, the success of which relies less on probabilistic practices or the 'studioification' (c.f. Guggenheim 2012) of the world than on the aesthetic capacities of the artefacts invented to affect – or 'concrese' with, to return to a Whiteheadian terminology – its users and recipients.

Aesthetics, as the elephant in the room, can be addressed in this context. That is, away from the old disputes in the sociology of arts on whether the contents of art and issues of aesthetics and style can be explained by the historical, political and social contexts in which art works are produced, or whether the sociological imagination is irrelevant since art works involve evaluative criteria autonomous from social contexts and conditions and should be left to the practices of art theory and history (Fowler 2003, Zangwill 2002, Bourdieu 1993). Such ways of demarcating the boundary between the social and aesthetics are not useful (Born 2010). Instead, following Latour's (1996) iconophilic lead, the key seems to be grounding the aesthetic in the series of transformations and mediations shaping certain objects and experiences. Studio work therefore involves a form of aesthetics-in-action, of assembling, improvising and manipulating cultural artefacts in view of producing affective attachments to future users, audiences, spectators and publics. Such a perspective requires overcoming the 'critical' mode of debunking (Latour 2004) the practices and beliefs of what might be termed 'aesthetic' publics as extant and passive collectives (c.f. Rancière 2009). It is by paying attention to the iconophilic proliferation of mediators in the studio that the ethnographer can start piecing together how studios wrought their own 'implicated actors'. From such a perspective, the classic definition of aesthetic experiences as those in which the sensorial perception and experience becomes an end in itself (Dewey 2005 [1934], Reckwitz 2012) can only be accepted as a possible accomplishment of studio tinkering with the aesthetic qualities of cultural artefacts. Thus, and by way of an opening to the studio as an empirical object for social and cultural research, this volume presents detailed descriptions of how the aesthetic is assembled in the studio.

The structure of the book

The bulk of this volume is organized into three sections, each consisting of three chapters. Throughout the process of preparing this book we have explored the capacities of different ordering strategies to relate and reinforce some of our main tenets for a research programme in studio studies. The three concepts proposed here have been chosen to stress two key messages. First, that studios are not architectural types housing creative processes, but emergent topologies resulting from the execution of specific form-giving operations. Second, and as a consequence of the first, the studio as an emergent topology can be radically displaced and studio studies needs to follow such displacements.

The first section of the book – 'Operations' – radically expands and enriches some of the tentative steps made in this introduction regarding the operations of reconfiguration, invention and attachment shaping the studio. Three key studio operations are discussed here in detail: synthesizing, referencing and taking points of view. Alex Wilkie and Mike Michael's exploration (Chapter 2) of three distinctive design studios, including a university-based research unit, a user-centred design group in a multinational IT corporation, and a 'service design' consultancy, addresses – both ethnographically and conceptually – the combination of radically heterogeneous things coming into being through processes of becoming. Synthesis in their account is not dialectically thought of as the overcoming of difference and contradiction, but in terms of events crystallizing coherent socio-technical propositions and thus performing both a closing and an opening of the design process. Compared with other epistemic domains, the design studio exhibits a radical version of synthesis, as what enters into design events is particularly heterogeneous. Tomás Ariztía's chapter (Chapter 3), on the 'reference' as a valuation device, also addresses the heterogeneity of elements brought together in creating an advertising concept, but, instead of the synthesizing process, he underscores the uses and transformations of the bits and pieces qualified as references. Ariztía shows that references are not just inspirational devices, departure points for creating new advertising concepts and campaigns, but they retain a key role throughout the creative process as devices through which creative worth is mobilized and assessed. Somewhere between referencing to an already existing form and synthesizing heterogeneous elements into a new form, we encounter what Emmanuel Grimaud (Chapter 4) describes as the key operation constituting the film studio: taking someone's or something's perspective. Grimaud, however, is not just interested in the socio-technical arrangements and filmic conventions of the classical studio setup to take someone's point of view. His main concern is to what extent the current proliferation of mounted cameras, attached to all types of non-human entities, is leading to a studioification of the world. Grimaud's chapter makes apparent one of the key claims of this volume, that the studio is the spatial configuration resulting from the realization of specific operations. The analysis of such operations by no means ends with the first section, as the chapters in the following two sections offer further descriptions to expand our conceptual repertoire for analysing studio operations.

The second section – 'Topologies' – explores the relational spaces of various studio processes, complementing the move initiated in the first section beyond an architectural understanding of the studio. The three chapters in this section explore spatial configurations that can be extrapolated to a variety of other cases. James Ash's analysis in Chapter 6 of the spheres and atmospheres of a video game design studio describes key spatial arrangements shaping collaborative work across studio locations. Mobilizing Peter Sloterdijk's concepts of spheres and atmospheres, Ash explores the socio-technical underpinnings of studio spaces and the extent to which these are stabilized in spheres that do not coincide with architectural divisions. Thus, whereas headphones and servers allow for the emergence and ongoing enactment of shared spheres for teams working in different building stores, they also produce clear atmospheric boundaries within open-plan offices. Erin O'Connor (Chapter 7) provides a rich historical and ethnographic account of the contemporary glassblowing studio as different from the pre-industrial glassblowing workshops and the industrial glass factory, focusing on the inter- and intra-corporeal configuration of the 'hotshop' as its key site. In O'Connor's account, studio spaces are shaped not just by specific socio-technical arrangements allowing the team to work in a coordinated manner with certain tools, techniques and materials, but also by pre-individual intensities, such as heat or pressure, that circulate across the human and non-human bodies involved in glassblowing. Finally, Sophie Houdart (Chapter 8) engages with one fundamental topological configuration of any studio: the articulation of an inside/outside boundary. In her detailed description of the comings and goings of architects engaged in designing a contemporary glassblowing studio, Houdart demonstrates that crossing this boundary in different directions, leaving and entering the architectural studio, is crucial to expanding the space of conception. The studio as a space of conception is not a mental space, but the result of concrete socio-material arrangement and practices taking place both inside and outside the office. From this perspective, the studio is not simply an amalgamation of the inside and the outside, but the performance of the difference from its constitutive outside.

The third section – 'Displacements' – explores some of what could be called studio para-sites (Marcus 2013). It offers historical and ethnographic descriptions of the constitution of studios in unconventional and unexpected sites, such as the home, the corporation and extreme landscapes; that is, sites that seem to diverge in every sense from what the studio is often expected and imagined to be. The three chapters comprising this section explore these para-sites, paying particular attention to the processes of displacement of conventional studio configurations and the ensuing transformations. This is particularly evident in Laurie Waller's archival research about electronic music composer Daphne Oram's home-studio and how the domestic shaped it as a setting of invention (Chapter 10). The contrast with Oram's experimental practice at the BBC's Radiophonic Workshop, traced by Waller, is helpful to grasp the home-studio as a domestic site grounding an experimental practice less geared to success. Stressing the failure of the Oramics machine allows Waller to question the contemporary 'rediscovery' and appreciation of Oram's home-studio practice. Over the past decade, Ariane Berthoin Antal has studied the proliferation of artist residency programmes in corporate settings, paying attention to their impact on organizational cultures as well as the temporary reconstruction of an artistic topology, of studios and exhibition spaces, within firms and corporations. Her chapter (Chapter 11) features four distinct studio configurations in a French consulting company, showing how activities involving research, production and exhibition can be differently placed and linked to the organization's everyday routines. By emphasizing the plurality and plasticity of studio configurations, Berthoin Antal's chapter demonstrates the need for a relational understanding of the studio. Finally, Ignacio Farías' chapter (Chapter 12) on the mobile studio of artist Mirja Busch aims at undoing the studio/site bifurcation in contemporary art discourses. By analysing how studio operations, such as manipulation and storage, are performed under the precarious conditions of a road trip, this chapter links back to the first section and closes the circle proposed by the editors.

Interspersed between the three sections of this volume are interviews with Georgina Born (Chapter 9) and Antoine Hennion (Chapter 5), two eminent scholars who have played an instrumental role in the study of cultural production and offered formative studies of studio settings. In both cases, the status and role of the 'object' or cultural artefact is foregrounded, as well as the intellectual milieu out of which each emerges. In chapter 5, Antoine Hennion speaks with Ignacio Farías about his work that cuts across advertising, amateurs, consumption, design, popular music and passion. Here, we get a sense of the studio as a multiplicity in which connections are sought and forged between heterogeneous entities including, but not limited to, users, publics, aesthetics, taste and so on. Crucially, such things are combined, and emerge from the making of what Hennion describes as *maquettes* or 'empirical materializations of a plurality of things' – temporary stabilizations reminiscent of Michel Serres' (2007 [1980]) 'quasi-object' as a kind of intermediary between the studio-produced entity and its users, markets, publics and producers. In Chapter 9, Georgina Born recounts her intellectual biography to Alex Wilkie, and in so doing describes her post-Bourdieuian approach to the mediation of art works, notably musical works. Born's ethnographic engagement with prominent cultural institutions as well as local outfits points to the distributedness of studio setups and their multiple products, not least the finished 'work'. Here, Born points to how studios are productive of multiple temporalities mediated by the work, by the genre, by aesthetics, as those times through which publics are sought and constructed. In both interviews, ANT and STS are acknowledged, but you will also see dissatisfaction in the capacity of these approaches, honed on the sciences and technological innovation, to adequately dissect cultural practices and the studio. In this volume we believe there are the makings of the practico-theoretical tools for such work.

Finally, the afterword (Chapter 13), written by Mike Michael, who has been at the forefront of design/STS studio-based collaborations for some years now, offers three provocative ways to think through the contributions in this book as well as presenting challenges for further work. First, pointing to phenomena of risk and consumption as shaped by the products of both studios and labs, Michael emphasizes the need to follow studio products outside the studio, paying attention to how they become mediators in processes of aesthetization and epistemization in everyday life. It is important to stress that *Studio Studies* does not attempt to leave behind the valuable traditions of studies that focus on the mediation of cultural artefacts (e.g. Hennion, Born, Gell, Lash and Lury), but to expand the settings of this research and thus to explore related but distinct practices and processes. Second, Michael draws on Whitehead's notion of 'satisfaction' to characterize how particular creative moments concrese and how such moments are resourced – or 'grasped', to use Whiteheadian terminology – by prepositional actors, such as 'users' or *maquettes*, that reside productively between the actual and the virtual – between what is and what is to come. Here, we are asked to identify the variety of prepositional actors and reflect on their peculiar capacities for novelty. A number of candidates are present in this volume. Artistic practices, marketing campaigns and glassblowing processes, to name just a few, become apparent as creation processes that articulate a variety of implicated or putative actors who trouble or expand our understanding of 'users'. In so doing, we glimpse the actual–virtual presence of large audiences, of critics, of consumers and of clients, shaping studio practice in significantly different ways. Finally, Michael asks whether studio-based interdisciplinary practice can itself become a feature of social and cultural research rather than an object of enquiry. For Michael, drawing on the work of Stengers (2010), this necessitates exploring the prospects for collaboration among social scientists and studio practitioners, and reimagining joint work as occurring in an 'ecology of practice' in which collaboration occurs through difference. While little discussed in the book, many of the chapters, especially those resulting from ethnographic engagements, are the upshot of collaboration across difference, of putting oneself 'in the presence of' others to learn from and think with them. The written accounts collected need to be read less as neutral descriptions, and rather as committed attempts to thicken the reality of the studio practices we have had the opportunity to explore.

Notes

1 We thank Michael Halewood for his clarifications regarding the work of A.N. Whitehead, especially the precise provenance of the concept of 'creativity'.
2 Knorr-Cetina (1983) provides an overview of the early wave of laboratory studies and Lynch (1993) presents a sober analysis of the field and a searing appraisal of *Laboratory Life* (Latour and Woolgar 1986).

References

Adorno, T. W. 1991. *The Culture Industry. Selected Essays on Mass Culture.* London, New York: Routledge.

Adorno, T. W. and Horkheimer, M. 1979 [1944]. *Dialectic of Enlightenment*. London: Verso.

Akrich, M., Callon, M. and Latour, B. 2002a. The key to success in innovation. Part I: The art of *interessement*. *International Journal of Innovation Management*, 6(2), 187–206.

Akrich, M., Callon, M. and Latour, B. 2002b. The key to success in innovation. Part II: The art of choosing good spokespersons. *International Journal of Innovation Management*, 6(2), 207–225.

Alpers, S. 1998. The studio, the laboratory, and the vexations of art. In: Jones, C. A. and Galison, P. eds, *Picturing Science, Producing Art*. New York, London: Routledge.

Banks, M. and O'Connor, J. 2009. Introduction. After the creative industries. *International Journal of Cultural Policy*, 15(4), 365–373.

Barry, A. and Thrift, N. 2007. Gabriel Tarde: imitation, invention and economy. *Economy and Society*, 36(4), 509–525.

Becker, H. 1974. Art as collective action. *American Sociological Review*, 39(6), 767–776.

Becker, H. 1976. Art worlds, and social types. *American Behavioral Scientist*, 19(6), 703–718.

Becker, H. 1984. *Art Worlds*. Berkeley, Los Angeles, CA and London: University of California Press.

Björgvinsson, E., Ehn, P. and Hillgren, P.-A. 2010. Participatory design and 'democratizing innovation'. In: PDC '10, Proceedings of the 11th Biennial Participatory Design Conference, 41–50.

Boden, M. A. 1994. What is creativity? In: Boden, M. A. ed., *Dimensions of Creativity*. Cambridge, MA and London: MIT Press, pp. 75–118.

Born, G. 1995. *Rationalizing Culture: IRCAM, Boulez, and the Institutionalization of the Musical avant-garde*. Berkeley: University of California Press.

Born, G. 2010. The social and the aesthetic: for a post-Bourdieuian theory of cultural production. *Cultural Sociology*, 4(2), 171–208.

Bourdieu, P. 1980. The production of belief: contribution to an economy of symbolic goods. *Media, Culture & Society*, 2(3), 261–293.

Bourdieu, P. 1993. *The Field of Cultural Production*. New York: Columbia University Press.

Callon, M. 1986. Some elements of a sociology of translation: domestication of the scallops and the fishermen of St. Brieuc Bay. In: Law, J. ed., *Power, Action and Belief: A New Sociology of Knowledge?* London: Routledge, pp. 196–223.

Caves, R. 2000. *Creative Industries: Contracts between Art and Commerce*. Cambridge, MA and London: Harvard University Press.

Century, M. 1999. *Pathways to Innovation in Digital Culture*. Montreal: McGill University, Centre for Research on Canadian Cultural Industries and Institutions.

Cohen, N. 2012. Cultural work as a site of struggle: freelancers and exploitation. *tripleC: Communication, Capitalism & Critique*, 10(2), 141–155.

Csikzentmihalyi, M. 1996. *Creativity. Flow and the Psychology of Discovery and Invention*. New York: Harper Collins.

DCMS 1998. *Creative Industries Mapping Document*. London: Department of Culture, Media and Sport.

Dewey, J. 2005 [1934]. *Art as Experience*. London: Perigee Books.

Dubuisson, S. and Hennion, A. 1995. Le design industriel, entre création, technique et marché. *Sociologie de l'Art*, 8, 9–30.

Farías, I. 2013. Heteronomie und Notwendigkeit. Wie Architekt/innen Wettbewerbsbeiträge entwickeln. In: Tauschek, M. ed., *Kulturen des Wettbewerbs. Formationen kompetitiver Logiken*, 10th edn. Münster, New York, Berlin and München: Waxmann.

Farías, I. 2015. Epistemic dissonance: reconfiguring valuation in architectural practice. In: Berthoin Antal, A., Hutter, M. and Stark, D. eds, *Moments of Valuation. Exploring Sites of Dissonance*. Oxford: Oxford University Press, pp. 271–289.

Farías, I. forthcoming. Städtisches Leben von und mit Schadstoffen. Materielle Intimität als Einschränkung urbaner Dingpolitik. *Berliner Blaetter*, 69 (Sonderheft 'Urbane Aushandlungen. Die Stadt als Aktionsraum'), in press.

Florida, R. 2002. *The Rise of the Creative Class. And How It's Transforming Work, Leisure and Everyday Life*. New York: Basic Books.

Florida, R. 2005. *Cities and the Creative Class* . New York, London: Routledge.

Ford, L. S. 1986. Creativity in a future key. In: Neville, R. C. ed., *New Essays in Metaphysics*. Albany: State University of New York Press, pp. 179–197.

Fowler, B. 2003. A note on Nick Zangwill's 'Against the sociology of art'. *Philosophy of the Social Sciences*, 33(3), 363–374.

Garfinkel, H. 1967. *Studies in Ethnomethodology*. Cambridge: Polity.

Gell, A. 1998. *Art and Agency*. Oxford: Oxford University Press.

Gieri, R. D. and Moffat, B. 2003. Distributed cognition: where the cognitive and the social merge. *Social Studies of Science*, 33(2), 1–10.

Gieryn, T. 2002. Three truth-spots. *Journal of the History of the Behavioral Sciences*, 38(2), 113–132.

Godin, B. 2006. The linear model of innovation: the historical construction of an analytical framework. *Science Technology Human Values*, 31(6), 639–667.

Grabher, G. 2001. Ecologies of creativity: the village, the group, and the heterarchic organisation of the British advertising industry. *Environment and Planning A*, 33, 351–374.

Guggenheim, M. 2012. Laboratizing and de-laboratizing the world changing sociological concepts for places of knowledge production. *History of the Human Sciences*, 25(1), 99–118.

Halewood, M. 2005. A.N. Whitehead, information and social theory. *Theory Culture Society*, 22(6), 73–94.

Hall, P. 2000. Creative cities and economic development. *Urban Studies*, 37(4), 639–649.

Hennion, A. 1989. An intermediary between production and consumption: the producer of popular music. *Science, Technology and Human Values*, 14(4), 400–424.

Hennion, A. 1993. *La passion musicale*. Paris: Métailié.

Hennion, A. 2003. Music and mediation: towards a new sociology of music. In: Clayton, M., Herbert, T. and Middleton, R. eds, *The Cultural Study of Music: A Critical Introduction*. London: Routledge, pp. 80–91.

Hennion, A., Méadel, C. and Libbrecht, L. 1993. In the laboratories of desire. Advertising as an intermediary between products and consumers. *Réseaux*, 1(2), 169–192.

Hesmondhalgh, D. and Baker, S. 2010. *Creative Labour: Media Work in Three Cultural Industries*. Abingdon and New York: Routledge.

van Heur, B. 2009. The clustering of creative networks: between myth and reality. *Urban Studies*, 46(8), 1531–1552.

Howkins, J. 2001. *The Creative Economy: How People Make Money From Ideas*. New York: Penguin.

Hughes, A. 1990. The cave and the stithy: artists' studios and intellectual property in early modern Europe. *Oxford Art Journal*, 13(1), 34–48.

Hutchins, E. 1995. *Cognition in the Wild.* Cambridge, MA and London: MIT Press.

Ingold, T. 2010. *Bringing Things to Life: Creative Entanglements in a World of Materials*, Working Paper 15. Southampton: ESRC National Centre for Research Methods, University of Southampton, pp. 1–14.

Ingold, T. 2013. *Making: Anthropology, Archaeology, Art and Architecture.* London and New York: Routledge.

Jacob, M. J. and Grabner, M. 2010. *The Studio Reader: On the Space of Artists.* Chicago, IL: University of Chicago Press.

Jones, C. A. 1996. *Machine in the Studio. Constructing the Postwar American Artist.* Chicago, IL: University of Chicago Press.

Knorr Cetina, K. 1995. Laboratory studies: The cultural approach to the study of science. In: Jasanoff, S., Markle, G. E., Peterson, J. C. and Pinch, T. eds, *Handbook of Science and Technology Studies.* Thousand Oaks, CA: Sage, pp. 140–167.

Knorr-Cetina, K. 1981. *The Manufacture of Knowledge: An Essay on the Constructivist and Contextual Nature of Science.* Oxford: Pergamon.

Knorr-Cetina, K. and Mulkay, M. 1983. The ethnographic study of scientific work: towards a constructivist interpretation of science. In: Knorr-Cetina, K. ed., *Science Observed: Perspectives on the Social Study of Science.* London: Sage, pp. 115–140.

Landry, C. and Bianchini, F. 1995. *The Creative City.* London: Demos.

Lash, S. and Lury, C. 2007. *Global Culture Industry: The Mediation of Things.* Cambridge: Polity Press.

Latour, B. 1987. *Science in Action.* Cambridge, MA: Harvard University Press.

Latour, B. 1988. *The Pasteurization of France.* Cambridge, MA: Harvard University Press.

Latour, B. 1996. How to be iconophilic in art, science and religion? In: Jones, C. A. and Galison, P. eds, *Picturing Science Producing Art.* London: Routledge, pp. 418–440.

Latour, B. 1999. *Pandora's Hope: Essays on the Reality of Science Studies.* Cambridge, MA: Harvard University Press.

Latour, B. 2004. Why has critique run out of steam? From matters of fact to matters of concern. *Critical Inquiry*, 30(2), 225–248.

Latour, B. 2013. *An Inquiry into Modes of Existence.* Cambridge, MA: Harvard University Press.

Latour, B. and Woolgar, S. 1986. *Laboratory Life. The Construction of Scientific Facts.* Princeton, NJ: Princeton University Press.

Law, J. and Hassard, J. 1999. *Actor Network Theory and After.* Oxford: Blackwell.

Lloyd, R. 2004. The neighborhood in cultural production: material and symbolic resources in the new bohemia. *City & Community*, 3(4), 343–372.

Luhmann, N. 1998. *Love as Passion: The Codification of Intimacy.* Stanford, CA: Stanford University Press.

Lynch, M. 1993. *Scientific Practice and Ordinary Action: Ethnomethodology and Social.* Cambridge: Cambridge University Press.

Marcus, G. 2013. Experimental forms for the expression of norms in the ethnography of the contemporary. *HAU: Journal of Ethnographic Theory*, 3(2), 197–217.

Markusen, A. 2006. Urban development and the politics of the creative class: evidence from a study of artists. *Environment and Planning A*, 38, 1921–1940.

McRobbie, A. 2002. From Holloway to Hollywood? Happiness at work in the new cultural economy. In: Du Gay, P. and Pryke, M. eds, *Cultural Economy: Cultural Analysis and Commercial Life.* London: Sage, pp. 97–114.

Meusburger, P. 2009. Milieus of creativity: the role of places, environments, and spatial contexts. In: Meusburger, P., Funke, J. and Wunder, E. eds, *Milieus of Creativity.* Berlin: Springer, pp. 97–154.

Meyer, S. 2005. Introduction. *Configurations*, 13(1), 1–33.

Nelson, C. 2010. The invention of creativity. The emergence of a discourse. *Cultural Studies Review*, 16(2), 49–74.

Osborn, A. F. 1957. *Applied Imagination: Principles and Procedures of Creative Problem-Solving*. New York: Scribner.

Osborne, T. 2003. Against 'creativity': a philistine rant. *Economy and Society*, 32(4), 507–525.

Peterson, R. 1976. The production of culture: a *prolegomenon*. *American Behavioral Scientist*, 19(6), 669–684.

Peterson, R. and Anand, N. 2004. The production of culture perspective. *Annual Review of Sociology*, 30, 311–334.

Potts, J. D., Cunningham, S. D., Hartley, J. and Ormerod, P. 2008. Social network markets: a new definition of the creative industries. *Journal of Cultural Economics*, 32(3), 166–185.

Pratt, A. 2004. Creative clusters: towards the governance of the creative industries production system? *Media International Australia*, 112, 50–66.

Rancière, J. 2009. *Aesthetics and its Discontents.* Cambridge: Polity Press.

Reckwitz, A. 2012. *Die Erfindung der Kreativität.* Frankfurt am Main: Suhrkamp.

Rheinberger, H.-J. 1997. *Toward a History of Epistemic Things: Synthesizing Proteins in the Test Tube.* Stanford, CA: Stanford University Press.

Rheinberger, J. 2004. Experimental systems. *The Virtual Laboratory.* Berlin: Max Planck Institute for the History of Science. http://vlp.mpiwg-berlin.mpg.de/references?id=enc19.

SEE Platform. 2013. *Design for Public Good.* Cardiff: Sharing Experience Europe Platform.

Sennett, R. 2008. *The Craftsman.* New Haven, CT: Yale University Press.

Serres, M. 2007 [1980]. *The Parasite.* Minneapolis and London: University of Minnesota Press.

Stengers, I. 2005. The cosmopolitical proposal. In: Latour, B. and Weibel, P. eds, *Making Things Public.* Cambridge, MA: MIT Press, pp. 994–1003.

Stengers, I. 2010. *Cosmopolitics I.* Minneapolis: University of Minnesota Press.

Suchman, L. 2012. Configuration. In: Lury, C. and Wakeford, N. eds, *Inventive Methods.* London, New York: Routledge, pp. 48–60.

Sunley, P., Pinch, S., Reimer, S. and Macmillen, J. 2008. Innovation in a creative production system: the case of design. *Journal of Economic Geography*, 8(5), 675–698.

UNCTAD2008. *Creative Economy Report 2008. The Challenge of Assessing the Creative Economy: Towards Informed Policy-Making*. New York: United Nations Conference on Trade and Development.

Whitehead, A. N. 1927 [1926]. *Religion in the Making.* Cambridge: Cambridge University Press.

Whitehead, A. N. 1978 [1929]. Process and reality: an essay in cosmology. In: Griffin, D. and Sherburne, D. eds, *Gifford Lectures of 1927–8*, corrected edn. New York: Free Press.

Wilkie, A. 2013. Prototyping as event: designing the future of obesity. *Journal of Cultural Economy*, 7(4), 476–492.

Wilkie, A. and Michael, M. forthcoming. Doing speculation to curtail speculation. In: Gabrys, J., Rosengarten, M., Savransky, M. and Wilkie, A. eds, *Transversal Speculations.* Ann Arbor, MI: Open Humanities Press, in press.

Zangwill, N. 2002. Against the sociology of art. *Philosophy of the Social Sciences,* 32(2), 206–218.

Zembylas, T., ed., 2014. *Artistic Practices. Social Interactions and Cultural Dynamics.* London and New York: Routledge.

Part 1

Operations

2 The design studio as a centre of synthesis

Alex Wilkie and Mike Michael

Studio one: a meeting in a studio located in a London University Design Department. The 'Interaction Design Studio' (IDS) undertakes enquiries into human–computer interaction (HCI) and is recognized as a leading centre of 'practice-based' research. The meeting has been convened to resolve the specification of a five-core shielded cable, resembling a common telephone coil, that connects a microphone handset to the main enclosure of a sound-based and interactive research device called the 'Babble'. The role of the handset is to allow users to contribute spoken messages to the sound output of the device – a talk radio-like internet appliance that vocalizes energy and environmental related online content drawn from a variety of sources, notably Twitter. The intended users of the appliance are members of UK-based energy communities who are expected to assimilate the device into their everyday lives in the deployment phase of the research project. The aim of the deployment is to explore the issues at stake in energy demand reduction, how local communities enact low-carbon living, and how these enactments can be communicated and potentially reconfigured.

At the centre of the discussion, on a meeting table, sits a prototype. This is frequently invoked – verbally and tangibly – as members of the design team present and materially demonstrate their views on the cable. At the time of the meeting, the cable fitted to the prototype was grey, wound in a coil like a telephone cable and, due to its length, it rested partly on and partly off the enclosure of the device. The team compared different coil samples whilst speculating on the precise aesthetics of the final design. It became apparent that the central issue was the length and colour of the cable: some team members viewed the hang of a shorter cable as aesthetically key, whereas others believed the length was primarily a matter of ergonomics rather than aesthetics (a shorter cable would result in the device being yanked out of place). Neither faction could agree. Central to the discussion was the notion of 'aesthetics' and how this was deployed to prioritize certain visual and material aspects of the design. Here was a shared concern with a modelling of the 'aesthetic-user', even if this differed in its details over the course of the discussion. Wrangling over the cable colour concerned the question of whether to use grey, or a yellow cable that would match certain 3D printed components. Here, the lead 'product' designer had selected a yellow (RAL 1016 Sulfur Yellow) from a pre-specified list. Selection was made possible by visually approximating the stated colour with a pantone colour chart, and ensuring this approached the yellow colour of the 3D printed ABS components produced by a high-resolution FDM printer installed in a separate studio workshop, alongside a laser cutter, a MakerBot, circuit board fabrication equipment, a water bath, various dedicated computing terminals and all manner of hand-tools for metal, plastic and woodwork. Amidst all this lay an orderly mess of components, fixings, materials, off-cuts, glues, solvents and polishes etc.

A solution emerged during the meeting, when a designer proposed specifying a coil with a far larger diameter, thereby downplaying ergonomic concerns by producing a longer cable that would dangle pleasantly within the geometry of the enclosure boundary whilst simultaneously achieving an aesthetic of scale. In short, the coil would become a noticeable and idiosyncratic feature of the design rather than a mere functional and ergonomic component.

Studio two: an interaction designer is sitting at a cubicle in a low-rise facility of a multinational microprocessor manufacturer in the Pacific Northwest of the USA. The designer is a member of a 'user-centred' design group (UCDG) that is responsible for designing computing enclosures as well as providing design expertise on strategic projects, often in collaboration with other work groups, such as research scientists engaged in the fields of computer science and HCI, also working at company facilities around the world. The cubicle is one amongst thousands in the building and butts up against motherboard, graphic processing and basic input/output system (BIOS) engineering teams, and is encircled by various testing laboratories and engineering workshops. To demarcate their space within the facility and to embody a 'design studio', members of the design team have, quite noticeably, reconfigured their space by removing cubicle dividers and bringing in beanbags and various other domestic furnishings.

The designer is working at his computer on a graphical user interface (GUI) for the second stage prototype of a wearable healthcare technology that incorporates a novel body-worn 'multi-modal' sensor (pedometer, barometric pressure, accelerometer, humidity, infra-red and visible light, temperature and sound) with a GUI to enable the user to monitor, manage and reflect on their daily activities. The design team explicitly envisioned the prototype as a computational solution to the pandemic threat of obesity, where individuals use the activity-monitoring device to avoid the onset of, or to manage, the disease. To that end, the brief for the design stipulated that the GUI must: run on the Windows Mobile OS; provide glanceable data on fitness activities; act as the home screen; translate the data into an abstracted visualization so as to ensure the privacy of the user; and visually depict daily and weekly activity and progress. After various design proposals, such as correlating the wearer's activities with real-world mountain treks, the design team chose to employ a garden metaphor where different activities (walking, running, cycling etc.)

would be symbolized by flowers, the growth of which would plot the user's accumulated activity and progress.

To get to a functioning piece of software from the proposal, the work on the GUI included the visual design by the interaction designer and its implementation by software engineers. For the designer, this included the wireframe definition of the application and the visual detailing of discrete screens, including backgrounds, sprites, typography and transitions. Having realized and obtained approval for the wireframe, the designer sets about the detailing work using a combination of Adobe Illustrator and Photoshop, ubiquitous graphic editing software. The designer is fluent with both applications and editing is a two-handed activity: the left hand swiftly invokes keyboard shortcut operations such as changing the precise behaviour of the cursor's editing capabilities, constantly saving the document, switching between adding or deleting vector anchor points; and the right hand constantly positions and repositions the cursor, drags and transforms sprites, drags the artboard and zooms to focus on and amend a particular graphical object. All these operations are done frequently, perhaps 10 or 20 in a given minute, in combination with constant visual judgments about line weight, length and form. Once the artworks are completed – the sprites and individual page illustrations – the files are emailed (as PDFs) for review to the project manager on the other side of the studio and to other team members located in a research laboratory in another city in the Pacific Northwest.

Studio three: at the central London offices of a sanitary ware manufacturer, two designers, employees of a small service design studio (SDS), are presenting to senior executives the results of a short piece of market research conducted on behalf of the manufacturer. Three months previously, the SDS had been reappointed by the manufacturer to envision domestic bathroom uses. The brief, agreed by client and contractor, prescribed a study to identify and describe emerging and future domestic sanitary trends, with a description of the deliverables and schedule of work. In this case, as in many other contracts undertaken by the SDS, the product of the studio's work consisted of a presentation to the client's senior management alongside an illustrated report in which recommendations are made as to how the organization can improve its various 'touchpoints' with consumers: for example, how a healthcare company can enter into the childcare market; setting up a 'social innovation lab' with a UK council as a site for local policy experimentation; or optimizing customer relationships with various organizations including, but not limited to, energy suppliers, broadcasting and media organizations, car manufacturers, financial and insurance companies, and government. The 'designs' produced by the SDS were varied, but typically included the detailed and visual orchestration of 'customer journey' including evocative propositions, such as the portrayal of a customer facing elements of a service (architectural, branding, print, employee uniforms and behaviour, in-store experiences, management processes, web presence etc.) or the rationalization of an organizational process.

In the months leading up to the presentation, work on the design had taken place at the studio of the SDS. Their space is a small, one-room office rented from and located in the building of a larger architectural practice. The expectations of the studio and the manufacturer had been set by the apparent success of the previous project – a set of playing card-like visual and narrative descriptions of sanitary prospects. The SDS set about the project by devising an in-house brief redescribing the tasks and project schedule according to studio resources and estimated task durations. The design work, as with other engagements undertaken by the studio, was conducted under principles and practices explicitly but loosely modelled around user-centred design, where 'customer-centric' and 'co-design' approaches result in emphasis being placed on the imagined service user. Thus the designers speculated on and represented the imagined identity, capacity and competencies of people carrying out domestic hygiene within novel sanitary settings. Services, so the thinking goes, should be modelled around the (service) designer's understanding of the 'needs' and 'requirements' of customers. With the deadline approaching, however, and the need to finalize plans for the completion of the deliverable to the client, including the presentation, it was decided that the work would be presented in a format similar to the first project.

Given the timing and resources, the project proceeded by way of desk-based research – thus avoiding the practical complexities of involving research subjects in the design process. Here, the designer began to work up various propositions, describing bathroom practices and fittings, including material technologies, engineering installations and interventions, providing, for instance, the infrastructure to allow small bathrooms to accommodate multiple practices, such as the *ad hoc* conversion of the toilet cistern and pan into table and bench surfaces, or fittings that could easily be installed by tenants and thus moved into new rentals; bathroom designs that support self-monitoring and self-care, as well as environments to support recreation. What emerged through this was the definition of a set of categories, ordering a series of substantive propositions concretizing the theme through visual and narrative representation and communicated by succinct titles such as 'Care of the self', 'Relaxation', 'Adaptability' etc.

The ensuing work consisted of preparing a PowerPoint presentation of propositions including brief narrative descriptions for each, as well as accompanying visuals. The narrative descriptions encompassed the context of use, relevance to the business and the likely market demographic, as well as the identity, interests and behaviours of putative users. To visually communicate a proposition, images were sourced from the internet or made where appropriate. Photographs were selected for their ability to quickly express multiple aspects of the proposition, for instance the visual tonality and hue of a category's aesthetic; the presence, or lack of, technology; the presence, or lack of, fittings and fixtures; the representation of a sanitary, healthcare, grooming or other practice.

Centres of synthesis and diverging events

Above, we have narrated three vignettes drawn from experience in three distinct design workplace settings. In addressing – and comparing – these we wish to explore the design studio in terms of processes of synthesis. Echoing Rheinberger (1997), we suggest that design studios can be productively understood as centres characterized by the compounding of entities, expertise and practices that are ordered and integrated through a multiplicity of processes. More specifically, we suggest that design studios entail processes wherein a heterogeneous variety of elements are brought together and combine to generate knowledge (and its accoutrements) of some sort or another.[1] On this score, the design studio sits alongside other sites – business, engineering, law, medicine, science, to state but the most obvious. What is relatively distinctive about the design studio is the *breadth* of the heterogeneity that comprises it: in the mix we can find, all at once, aesthetic/material/visual, engineering, healthcare, historical, marketing, programming, psychological, and sociological elements. Of course heterogeneity marks many sites, notably the scientific laboratory, as Latour (1988) famously insists. Further, this heterogeneity seems to be on the increase, not least as 'interdisciplinary' initiatives between science and art, for instance, take root (Barry et al. 2008). Nevertheless, we detect a qualitative, if not quantitative, difference between the design studio and other 'sites of synthesis'.

In focusing on synthesis, we also seek to move away from the 'studio as container' or 'site' – as a bounded vessel for practices (e.g. Century 1999) – and attend to the processuality and relationality of design practices. The products of design studios, as the vignettes above signal, are multiple. They bring into being any number of user figurations (Wilkie 2010), models and buildings (Yaneva 2005), prototypes (Wilkie 2013), technical inventions (e.g. Bijker 1995), intellectual property and copyrights (Raustiala and Sprigman 2006), methods and techniques (e.g. Asaro 2000), as well as linguistic practices (Fleming 1998). However, their synthesizing practices can also bring into being more interesting, or inventive, questions, and develop better and more relevant problems. Here, studio practices can be understood, following Schön (1985), as 'problem-setting' procedures where problem definition and parameters are constructed.

At this point we present another qualification. Drawing on Whitehead, Deleuze and Latour, Fraser (2010) differentiates two models of the event. On one hand, the heterogeneous elements that combine in an event – 'synthesis' in our terminology – retain their identity, their being. They *inter-act* to produce something that is new, but this newness falls within the existing problem definitions (which in the case of a design event might be a client's brief). Against this, let us call it 'being event', she contrasts what we call a 'becoming event', where the constituent elements can be said to *intra-act* (Barad 2007), and in the process of intra-action, they can be said to mutually change, to co-become. If the constituents change, so does the (design) event itself: the parameters that define it become 'unhinged' and markedly 'inventive problems' that rework the issues at stake – the very 'meaning' of the event – can begin to emerge (see also Stengers 2005, Michael 2012). However, against Fraser's ontological, qualitatively dichotomous version of the event, we would like to propose an empirical, quantitatively differentiated version of the event. That is to say, as our vignettes above suggest, and as we detail below, new inventive problems, intra-action and mutual co-becoming, *more or less*, emerge. In the events of design synthesis with which we have engaged, we notice that they vary in the '*proportion*' (to put it rather too crudely) of their 'being' and 'becoming'.

In what follows, we trace this 'eventful' variation across the three design studios. In this respect, we trace how the synthetic processes that characterize studio events are embroiled in divergent patterns of relationalities, which we tentatively and heuristically call: organization/distribution; time/temporalization; user/modelling; and 'invention'/'innovation'.

Studio processes

Organization/distribution

First, we consider the range, configuration and disposition of competencies within the three studios, which becomes apparent through the distribution of labour (DoL). As mentioned above, distinctive to design is the breadth of the heterogeneity of expertise that is called upon to realize its products Thus the synthesis of studio outputs necessarily entails differing interchanges of practices and knowledge arranged in specific ways.

The DoL within the IDS is subtly hierarchical but easily and routinely breached. The studio has a director who is responsible for agenda setting, gaining and directing funding awarded on the basis of his research expertise, interests and biography. Supporting the director is a senior research fellow who, amongst other responsibilities, acts as a studio manager by leading project planning and finances, and project teams, as well as playing a leading role in determining and supervising the visual and material aesthetics of the design work, akin to a 'creative director'. The senior researcher and research assistants carry out the day-to-day design work, ensuring the progress of project trajectories. All members, however, are responsible for, and have a say in, 'specifying' the idea or ideas of a project. The competencies of the IDS lie mainly in three-dimensional design since final designs take the form of interactive and computational appliances. Software and hardware engineering will be instigated in-house, with advance competency brought in on a freelance basis where appropriate. A recurring difficulty of the IDS is to employ and retain 'creative technologists' – engineers with formal training in the arts. However, like laboratories, the IDS operates much like an inscription device (Latour and Woolgar 1979), where designs, methods and deployments are regularly transformed into scholarly publications, codifying studio practices.

At the UCDG, the DoL is more rigid. Teams are convened as projects arise. Initial meetings typically involve the organization of team and sub-team structures where competencies (e.g. interface and interaction design, ethnography, mechanical and software engineering) are arranged below management figures. Members with domain expertise, such as healthcare or domestic technologies, with device design (industrial and interactive) expertise such as handheld or wearable technology, and/or engineering expertise such as personal-area networking technology, are designated areas of responsibilities, and clear lines of management are determined which will routinely appear as visual diagrams used in presentations and project documentation. The UCDG typically works on a variety of projects simultaneously, and members often work two or more projects simultaneously. The composition of competencies at the UCDG is tied to the 'core' business of the corporation – the development and production of microprocessors – and various forms of advanced engineering expertise are prevalent. More so than the IDS, the UCDG is able to conceive, design and realize fully working prototypes, as the corporation holds much of the necessary technical expertise and apparatus in numerous labs and workshops around the world. Ideas are also implicitly and explicitly pre-given in the light of broader corporate priorities that are fixed upon maintaining and prospecting computation markets (areas of socio-cultural life that are supported or made possible by microprocessing).

The DoL at the SDS was very rigid, perhaps the most rigid of the three studios discussed here. The two company owners micro-managed each project whilst undertaking other company duties, notably the acquisition of new business. The studio was in its infancy and regular contract income a necessity – repute, size and human resources were in the process of being established. The hierarchy of the studio was therefore overt and tied to individual project briefs which, as well as a company owner, would include one or two designers as well as freelancers where necessary. The SDS had recently refashioned itself as a service design consultancy, a genre that emerged in the early 2000s. This transformation included explicit efforts within the studio to formulate a client-facing vocabulary and to codify its design practices as billable 'ideation methods'.

So, under the motif of 'organization', we can detect a DoL that varies more or less systematically across the three studios. The IDS exhibits considerable flexibility in what individual designers can take on, and such work is often collectively determined, although publications are, by and large, the preserve of the studio director. By comparison, the DoL within the UCDG is very much organized by the corporation's priorities, management hierarchy and division of expertise, though within these there is room for some creative exchanges across different design and engineering specialisms, not least insofar as the precise shape of the products is more open. For the SDS, proximal market conditions and opportune developments mean that 'invention' is jettisoned in favour of 'service design', with the result that DoL is enforced as a necessary means of micro-resource management, meeting client briefs and enacting a normative studio model compatible with client expectations. In sum, we see how the synthetic events vary in the proportion of 'becoming' and 'being' as we move across the three studios: IDS having the greatest relative levels of 'becoming', SDS the least.

Time/temporalization

Next, we contrast how different temporal processes configure, and are configured by, the studios: how the design studios are enacted though different temporal patternings that reflect and mediate organizational demands, funding models, resources, material pliancy, and expertise relating to (often emerging) technological components and processes. Distinctive to design practices, and studios, is how futures are rendered and made manageable in the present, often invoking prior experience and assumptions, which then work to engender certain futures.

The IDS operates along temporal arcs that are influenced by the time frames of research grants, usually between one and five years. Such durations are typically determined by Research Councils, and projects and practices are organized within the limits of these durations. Projects proceed from grant application to initial engagement with putative research volunteers (user group), the design and deployment of 'cultural probes' amongst the volunteers, analysis of probe returns, the design and production of workbooks documenting existing and prospective socio-cultural-technical practices and technologies, as well as propositions for designs that are often unusual, sometimes comical and occasionally absurd. The focus of the design process then turns to the specification and design of individual, or batches of, devices, which are then deployed amongst the research volunteers for an extended period (usually more than two months). Site visits and observational work are then conducted whilst the devices are *in situ* with the volunteers. Members of the IDS are involved in all aspects of a project. The extended temporalization allowed for innovation; for example, during the development phases of the 'Babble', the project team developed and conducted a 'probe workshop' for the first time. The extended time frame also mediated and reflected the particular temporalizations of socio-material processes such as those of 3D printing, the duration of the manufacturing of the cable, the hiccups in the making of material and electronic components, and the exigencies faced by volunteer user communities. While the studio operated within, and managed, cross-cutting temporalities pertinent to each individual project, it was nevertheless embedded within the institutional temporalizations: cycles of teaching, conference-going and publication, research assessment and grant application.

Projects undertaken by the UCDG were driven by three interrelated temporalities: (i) the logistics of microprocessor development, production and global distribution; (ii) the continuity of existing markets (e.g. desktop and server chips), and the emergence of new, silicon markets (e.g. health and transportation); and (iii) organizational accounting cycles. The UCDG served corporate preoccupations both by designing conventional hardware enclosures and by undertaking more speculative projects, often in collaboration, as described above. That said, the nature of prospective projects, which raises the question of what can be done with 'computation', brought with each a novel and speculative temporality, such as the emergence of digital body-monitoring, or the capacities/performance, scheduling or availability of new hardware, such as the sensor unit on which the garden GUI relied or the battery performance of the unit, adversely affected by the power consumption of the Bluetooth wireless networking standard being used. Thus the UCDG accommodated multiple temporalities, rigid and emergent – shifted by new innovations – and its work routinely involved the interweaving of both.

The SDS, by contrast, worked to the time frames delimited by contracts and briefs. Most were relatively short – between three and twelve months – and there was no guarantee of further work from a particular client. The upshot of the SDS's reliance on contractual work meant that its timings were largely dependent on a client's agenda. That more than one project was operating simultaneously meant that the SDS was contending with multiple, sometimes conflicting schedules and had to manage resources accordingly. The project with the sanitary ware manufacturer is therefore indicative of the nature of the work conducted by the SDS. As such, the tempo of the SDS was not overly hindered by the obduracy of materials or the struggles associated with the under-determination of new technologies or technical practices. Visualization, PowerPoint and outsourced printing processes, for example, were largely known and controllable. The sanitary project, however, demonstrates how the question of innovation preoccupied the SDS. Here, the attempt at innovation concerned both the novelty of bathroom propositions (successful) and the novelty of presentational techniques by which the propositions were communicated to the client (unsuccessful). As the vignette illustrates, the practical contingencies of project work shaped the temporalization of studio practice such that, where innovation could be enacted, it was with regard to sanitary propositions rather than the means of expression.

To summarize, we can say that IDS is characterized by a synthetic process in which there is temporally both looseness and openness such that it could absorb and creatively respond to the temporal 'hiccups' of the design process. At the same time, there were outer limits of temporal constraint that reflected research funding and teaching rhythms. By contrast, SDS entails a tight temporal coupling with the client's brief (as well a strictly drawn division of labour within the studio itself). Here, even where attempts are made to find some room for inventiveness, these are only partially successful in light of the temporal the rigidity of these relations. The UCDG, again, falls somewhere in between, entailing at once fluid and rigid relations with the other elements of the corporation that mediate and reflect at once flexible and inflexible temporalizations. Put another way, these differences in temporalization across the studios also inflect the balance of 'becoming' and 'being' in the events of synthesis. Here, the actuality of 'slowing down' is crucial, according to

Stengers (2005): to slow down is to become sensitive to the *possibilities* that are present in synthetic events and to question our existing sense of 'ourselves (as) authorized to believe we possess the meaning of what we know'.

User/modelling

A key figure in design studios is the user (Wilkie 2010). Users mediate, and are shaped by, multiple relations including, but not limited to: the body and the device; the social and technological; existing practices and future use; individual preferences/requirements and collective demands; and the accountability of design work. Users are pivotal in all manner of 'design' practices and, alongside realized designs, are notable synthetic outcomes of studios.

The IDS has developed a distinctive approach to engaging with users, involving home-grown research techniques. Users are depicted as 'research volunteers', underscoring the obligations and requirements (unpaid, able to withdraw without penalty and non-directive) of their role. Users are involved and represented by way of some combination of techniques, including 'ethnographic' engagement during initial contact as well as deployment, cultural probes (Gaver et al. 1999), workshops and the use of 'cultural commentators' (Gaver 2007), where scriptwriters and documentary filmmakers are employed to elicit alternative (non-scholarly) depictions of research volunteers and the deployment of research devices. The user is emergent through extended engagements and some combination of method assemblage (Law 2004), and is assumed to be a complex and variable socio-cultural actor who can be accessed and understood through interpretivist, material and non-linguistic techniques.

In contradistinction to the IDS, the UCDG conducted user involvement by way of off-the-shelf techniques including, but not limited to, personas, 'ethnography' and 'ethnographic' in-home interviews, focus groups, field trials with sample groups, and implicit 'I-methodology' (cf. Akrich 1995) techniques, as well as more quantitative experimental setups. More often than not, users, even empirical users (e.g. mediated through ethnography), are subordinated to the emergent capacities of technological propositions and prototypes where, for example, the previously mentioned multi-modal sensor predetermines how health and fitness are introduced into everyday practices (Wilkie 2013). As an upshot, and echoing the IDS, users were mediated by some combination of research techniques; typically however, the UCDG unproblematically mixed different epistemological and ontological assumptions by way of various research techniques (quantitative and qualitative) in modelling the user. Thus, whilst the 'ethnographic user' was provoking an ontological shift in the imagination of the corporation towards the view of its products as 'socio-cultural-technical' assemblages (Barry et al. 2008), other user figurations (e.g. cognitive, task-oriented, ergonomic, demographic) and their attendant ontological assumptions persisted unproblematically.

Consumer (user) research is an essential aspect of the commercial services provided by the SDS and is haphazardly derived from various sources. Like the UCDG, off-the-shelf techniques are used, including 'ethnography' and interviews; but, unlike the UCDG, the SDS re-presents the techniques, arguably as part of efforts to legitimate their expertise. Here, interviews become 'in-home' or 'stakeholder' interviews and observation becomes 'shadowing'. Like the IDS, the SDS also coins its own techniques, such as 'expert panels', 'stakeholder interviews' – minor modifications to existing techniques. The SDS also has few qualms in combining quantitative and qualitative research as the 'user' is a reified and pre-given human-centred actor about whom 'insights' can be gleaned and whose behaviour can be changed without the complications of epistemological and ontological considerations. Thus, user research and involvement can take numerous forms, and in the case of the vignette above, can be undertaken from a studio work station without any recourse to empirical engagement with people. As in the UCDG, I-methodology makes possible the doing of 'involvement' without involvement, that is, where the 'user' is other to the designer. Arguably, the means by which the consumer–user is modelled and represented by the SDS has emerged out of dialogue with wider industry norms and client expectations as well as the emergent discourse and practices associated with service design. A technique favoured by the SDS for involving 'stakeholders' in design is to facilitate workshops (typically half- or one-day) in which user representatives and clients engage with one another, addressing the client's requirements and problem area. Such engagements are part of a broader strategy to involve clients in various aspects of the design process that ensure 'buy-in' to the techniques for involving users. In sum, the underlying model (status and capacity) of users in the SDS is static and is as much about ensuring commercial relations as informing design.

In sum, common to each studio is some explicit form(s) of engagement with people-as-users. In practice, however, users are variably enacted: as persons whose emergent complexity is to be explored through design; as persons whose characteristics are derived through a combination of methods but nevertheless subordinated to the capacities of the emergent device; as persons who are haphazardly configured through various techniques and yet remain largely static and reified. In each case, we again are witness to the changing proportion of 'becoming'/'being' in the synthetic design event. For IDS, the relations of the user are dialogic where the user is expected to generate surprise for the designer: the user is a mediator of speculation about what makes up the 'issue at stake' (around energy demand reduction in the case of the Babble). By contrast, the UCDG's user is emergent in the context of the corporation's core business. But this malleability is hard-coded to the development of the device; that is to say, different capacities of the user can be prioritized depending on the shifting features of the device. Lastly, for the SDS, the rigidity of the user reflects the rigidity of the client–designer relation in the context of service design in which a known and reified element can be literally and unproblematically implanted into service visualizations. Here we see the predominance of 'being' in the synthetic design event, which incorporates the overarching demands of the client.

'Invention'/'innovation'

As should now be clear, each studio addresses analogous but distinctive aspects of design processes and each enacts inventiveness and innovation in divergent ways; ways that synthesize differing patterns of expertise and labour, spatialization and temporalization, as well as techniques and rationales for enacting users. In this section, we draw out how each studio accomplishes 'novelty' whilst at the same time effecting stabilization and continuity by way of 'non-invention'. Here, each studio enacts a particular arrangement of novelty and preservation where certain practices, processes and becomings reproduce certain designerly repertoires, whilst others enact newness.

For the IDS, practice-based research into HCI is the primary activity. At its core, as the design of the coil illustrates, the concern is with the meticulous design and 'sympathetic' deployment of inventive and exotic research devices where aesthetics and functionality are foregrounded as the means to elicit knowledge concerning the socio-cultural possibilities of computational technology. IDS's practices involve what might be understood as 'radical' innovation, where research devices – which operate on tensions between exoticism/accessibility, playfulness/seriousness – resist the assumptions of research volunteers. Here, 'design' becomes an operator for the ways in which formal aesthetic artefacts can be incorporated into epistemic practices. The coil vignette shows how inventiveness is distributed across the various practices and human/non-human engagements of the studio, including the materiality and aesthetics of artefacts, the techniques for engaging and understanding volunteers-as-users, as well as the inventive capacities of the milieus in which the devices are deployed, i.e. what is done *with* devices during deployment. Despite the distributed multiplicity of extreme inventiveness, and the IDS's repute for producing methodological novelty, the studio repeats a now well worn project arc beginning with initial contact with volunteers, design and deployment of probes, the collation of propositions into workbooks, electronic artefact design, deployment and write-up.

Unlike the IDS, the aim of the UCDG is to define, specify and give form to functional products and appliances that align with or seek to establish, rather than question, market and end-user expectations. Here, design practices are attuned to optimizing the ease of use of (in this case) a user interface for a wearable health technology, as well as responding to user 'needs', such as continual health monitoring, management and privacy, however such needs are shaped. Arguably, the UCDG enacts a 'standardized innovation' process, in tune with corporate business and strategy, the studio's sole audience and patron. So, where is innovation and inventiveness located within the distribution of design processes and practices at the UCDG? Arguably, the studio enacts a limited and intermediate form of innovation, where (often new) markets, products and personas are introduced as, or into, 'situated' sociocultural settings, thus intervening in the industrial practices and ontological imagination of the corporation (Barry et al. 2008). Thus, whilst the 'products' of the UCDG appear typical of IT research and development, the way such products are conceived by the corporation is inventive.

As our case of sanitation design demonstrates, the SDS aligns aesthetics and functionality with client expectations. The familiarity and immediacy of the aesthetics is adaptable to the manufacturer's brand identity. In so doing, the SDS focuses on the immediacy of communicating how a 'customer experience' mediates the relationship between organization/institutions and the user-as-customer. Thus, in aiming to attune the service propositions to the client's expectations, the SDS enacts a form of non-invention in that it operates to preserve – through outsourcing – the innovation practices of the clients, and to support and maintain normative domestic sanitary practices. The enactment of non-invention in relation to the putative product and user, as well as the deployment of normative aesthetics, can be viewed against the enactment of novelty in how design, or 'design thinking', is insinuated into the efforts of SDS to develop novel understanding of the customer-as-service-user.

In this section, we have attempted to crystallize the differing proportions of 'being'/'becoming' in the synthetic events of the design studios by focusing on invention. Again, we see how this proportion varies in a fairly systematic way across our case studies. However, we have also considered how, even within the more 'becoming' synthetic events of IDS, there is 'being', not least as it is manifested in the routinization of invention, of 'becoming', and how conversely, even within the 'being' of SDS's synthetic events, there is 'becoming' in the form of inventiveness around the customer–client.

Concluding remarks: the synthetic registers of design studios

This chapter explores three case studies of design studios. These have been chosen because they illustrate aspects of the institutional variety that pertains to design practice. We suggest that design studios are peculiar in the breadth of the heterogeneity of elements that feed into the design process. However, we also argue that this breadth varies. In particular, we propose that the work of design studios entails synthesis that can be more or less 'creative' or 'inventive'. This is theorized through the lens of 'event', which can be proportionately more or less oriented toward 'becoming' or 'being'. This proportionality is explored through four heuristic parameters applied to the cases.

Needless to say, this is but one way of articulating the differences amongst design studios and design practice. It is certainly not exhaustive. In previous drafts we attempted to think of this difference with the aid of Deleuze's (e.g. 1999) notion of the diagram to highlight the studio as an arrangement embroiled in different 'economies': epistemic economies (IDS), market economies (UCDG), or service economies (SDS). The notion of the diagram also points to how studios operate to construct realities that are yet to come: each studio, then, can be said to carry its own means of diagramming design, of operating to bring into being new socio-cultural realities. As the section on invention/innovation suggests, each studio exhibits a different patterning of invention/non-invention.

Be that as it may, we can return to what is distinctive about the design studio *per se*. We began this chapter by highlighting the synthetic character of such epistemic practices as science, law, medicine etc. – each having its own 'centres of synthesis'. We suggested that design can certainly be placed on a continuum of synthesis – though situated at an extreme because the elements that enter into its synthetic processes are particularly heterogeneous. The design studio is thus a particularly 'expansive' version of a centre of synthesis. Inevitably, we must situate the idea of a centre of synthesis in relation to Latour's (1988) notion of the scientific laboratory as a centre of calculation. Our view is that calculation is part and parcel of synthesis – in the case of the design studios, calculations were made about all manner of elements: circuit boards, users, ergonomics, materials, coils, populations, health and so on. Thus we might end with two bold proposals: centres of calculation may actually be a subset of centres of synthesis; and centres of synthesis find their apotheosis in the design studio.

Acknowledgements

The authors would like to thank Ignacio Farías and Michael Guggenheim for providing insightful comments and feedback on drafts, and members of the IDS for their patience. This chapter also draws on research conducted under the grant 'Sustainability Invention and Energy-demand reduction: Co-designing Communities and Practices' funded by RCUK and led by the EPSRC (project code ES/1007318/1).

Note

1 From an epistemic perspective, the scant literature on design studios can be seen to fall into two broad camps: (i) the pedagogic studio (e.g. Schön 1985); (ii) the studio as 'laboratory' or 'studio–lab' hybrid (see Century 1999).

References

Akrich, M. 1995. User representations: practices, methods and sociology. In: Rip, A., Misa, T. J. and Schot, J. eds, *Managing Technology in Society: The Approach of Constructive Technology Assessment*. London and New York: Pinter, pp. 167–184.

Asaro, P. M. 2000. Transforming society by transforming technology: the science and politics of participatory design. *Accounting, Management and Information Studies*, 10(4), 257–290.

Barad, K. 2007. *Meeting the Universe Halfway: Quantum Physics and The Entanglement of Matter and Meaning*. Durham, NC: Duke University Press.

Barry, A., Born, G. and Weszkalnys, G. 2008. Logics of interdisciplinarity. *Economy and Society*, 37(1), 20–49.

Bijker, W. E. 1995. *Of Bicycles, Bakelites, and Bulbs: Toward a Theory of Sociotechnical Change*. Cambridge, MA: MIT Press.

Century, M. 1999. *Pathways to Innovation in Digital Culture*. Montreal: McGill University, Centre for Research on Canadian Cultural Industries and Institutions.

Deleuze, G. 1999. *Foucault*. London: Athlone.

Fleming, D. 1998. Design talk: constructing the object in studio conversations. *Design Issues*, 14(2), 41–62.

Fraser, M. 2010. Facts, ethics and event. In: Jense, C. B. and Rödje, K. eds, *Deleuzian Intersections: Science, Technology and Anthropology*. New York and Oxford: Berghahn Books, pp. 57–82.

Gaver, W. 2007. Cultural commentators: non-native interpretations as resources for polyphonic assessment. *International Journal of Human–computer Studies*, 65(4), 292–305.

Gaver, W., Dunne, T. and Pacenti, E. 1999. Design: cultural probes. *Interactions*, 6(1), 21–29.

Latour, B. 1988. *Science in Action*. Cambridge, MA: Harvard University Press.

Latour, B. and Woolgar, S. 1979. *Laboratory Life: The Construction of Scientific Facts*. Princeton, NJ: Princeton University Press.

Law, J. 2004. *After Method: Mess in Social Science Research*. Abingdon and New York: Routledge.

Michael, M. 2012. Toward an idiotic methodology: de-signing the object of sociology. *Sociological Review*, 60(s1), 166–183.

Raustiala, K. and Sprigman, C. 2006. The piracy paradox: innovation and intellectual property in fashion design. *Virginia Law Review*, 92, 1687–1777.

Rheinberger, H.-J. 1997. *Toward a History of Epistemic Things: Synthesizing Proteins in the Test Tube*. Stanford, CA: Stanford University Press.

Schön, D. 1985. *The Design Studio: An Exploration of its Traditions and Potential*. London: RIBA Publications.

Stengers, I. 2005. The cosmopolitical proposal. In: Latour, B. and Weibel, P. eds, *Making Things Public*. Cambridge, MA: MIT Press, pp. 994–1003.

Wilkie, A. 2010. User assemblages in design: an ethnographic study. PhD thesis, Goldsmiths, University of London.

Wilkie, A. 2013. Prototyping as event: designing the future of obesity. *Journal of Cultural Economy*, 7(4), 476–492.

Yaneva, A. 2005. Scaling up and down: extraction trials in architectural design. *Social Studies of Science*, 35(6), 867–894.

3 Bringing the world into the creative studio

The 'reference' as an advertising device

Tomas Ariztía

Introduction

There is a 'baptism' prank in advertising. When a new intern is introduced to a creative team, the intern is asked by a creative director to concentrate on finding a picture of a 'man showing his back' in the agency's archive of advertising magazines. Finding the specific visual might take the intern hours since the creative team has removed all such pictures. After hours of futile work, the intern is told there was never a chance of finding the picture and they are (informally) invited to join the agency.

This anecdote captures a critical aspect of advertising: creative work involves a rather open and distributed process of production mediated by creative 'references'. In fact, finding, collecting, mobilizing and evaluating references is at the core of advertising work. References are also key devices in the process within which creative ideas are qualified and evaluated at different stages of creating an advertising campaign. In looking at how references travel and operate in advertising, creative work appears as a rather open and distributed process of creation in which the boundaries between the inside and outside of the studio are dissolved. The informant who narrated this story admitted that, in spite of the corrosive humour, the prank works as an effective induction. Searching non-existent images immerses the intern in the ecology of advertising references, a key part of routine creative work in the agency.

Drawing on fifty interviews and ethnographic fieldwork conducted in advertising agencies in Santiago de Chile, this article focuses on exploring the different knowledge practices and devices mobilized during the production of creative concepts in advertising campaigns.[1] More concretely, I examine a particular device of creative work, namely 'references' – usually images, videos, advertisements, web pages or other entities used in creative processes. In doing so, I argue that references are at the core of creative work. Referencing is a practical task that precedes creative meetings and thus frames the very reality of a creative idea and process. Furthermore, references are *descriptors* (Wilkie 2010) that play a key part in the collective advertising work, which often revolves around the qualification and evaluation of creative ideas through the use and combination of references. Finally, references also travel along the process into client relations meetings, helping to define and assess what is good and desirable in creative terms.

By examining the role of references in advertising, I seek to connect creative work with two theoretical debates on epistemic practices. On one hand, I draw a comparison with the use of references in laboratory work by comparing the work of referencing in advertising studios with the role of references in scientific work, as captured by Latour's concept of circulating reference. This is done by describing advertising references as a particular type of inscription device used to make visible, and mobilize, the qualities of creative ideas. By following recent discussion on different types of inscription devices in relation to engineering design (Henderson 1991) and user-centred design (Wilkie 2010), I argue that references in advertising can be better understood as types of 'descriptors' (Wilkie 2010: 104–105). These are visual representations that help organize the creative process, the efficacy of which relies not only on their capacity to be stable in different moments of the creative process (echoing inscriptions in scientific work), but also on their ability to help organize collective agreement on campaign qualities and to generate new creative concepts that might lead to an advertisement or piece of marketing.

On the other hand, by following literature on the pragmatics of valuation in economic and cultural practices (Lamont 2012, Muniesa 2011), I propose understanding references as a particular valuation device through which creative worth is assessed and mobilized in advertising processes. Based on these reflections, and on previous studies (Ariztía 2014), I approach creative work as a distributed process that involves qualifying and evaluating creative concepts for the purpose of a creative inquiry.

The chapter is structured as follows. First, I discuss the theoretical issues regarding creativity and advertising from the point of view of a sociology of marketing practices and devices. I then move on to discuss literature on creativity and advertising, particularly work that addresses different contexts of creative production. Inspired by laboratory studies (e.g. Latour and Woolgar 1979), I propose approaching creative work by focusing on ordinary creative practices and devices, rather than describing its contexts. Following points made by Farías and Wilkie in chapter 1 of this volume, I suggest understanding creativity in advertising as a distributed and rather open process through which creative concepts/ideas are qualified and valued. Secondly, I describe the role of references in advertising agencies. I start by presenting an overview of the necessity for references in ordinary creative work, then describe the practice of referencing for advertising campaigns, focusing on the activity of collecting and ordering. Following this, I examine the practical use of references in creative meetings. Here I focus on two interrelated processes: (i) the use of references in the qualification of creative concepts and how references work as a specific inscription devices, enacting creative ideas in meetings and throughout the advertising process; and (ii) references that operate as valuation devices through which the worth of creative concepts is valued.

Mapping advertising practices

At present, there is a renewed interest within sociological thought in ordinary marketing practices and devices (e.g. Zwick and Cayla 2011). This attention to mundane marketing activities – 'marketing in action' (Grandclément and Gaglio 2011) – clarifies the multiple and rather complex strategies mobilized by market actors in order to produce market encounters (McFall 2014). In doing so, consideration has not only been given to the proliferation of multiple marketing devices oriented at capturing publics (Cochoy 2007, McFall 2009), but also to the ordinary process through which marketing professionals qualify goods and consumers (Callon et al. 2002, Dubuisson-Quellier 2010). It has been argued that marketing practices and devices involve the enactment of particular types of realities. Scholars have explored, for example, how an ordinary marketing and advertising operation involves producing and mobilizing versions of consumers (Miller and Rose 1997, Ariztía 2013), often through the use of specific devices through which consumers are enacted (Grandclément and Gaglio 2011, Muniesa and Trébuchet-Breitwiller 2010).

Against this backdrop, advertising is perhaps the marketing device that has historically received most attention from scholars in the social sciences (Malefyt and Moeran 2003, McFall 2004, Nixon 2003). While it is typically portrayed from a macro view as the iconic vehicle for the propagation of consumerist ideology (e.g. Sklair 2002), focusing on mundane advertising work has unpacked this commercial work as a rather complex collection of practices and devices through which consumers and goods are qualified, and where success in connecting and 'capturing' consumers cannot be taken for granted. Authors have noted, for example, the relative closure and self-reference of the advertising world in terms of its operation in relation to other commercial activities (see McFall 2014).

One aspect of advertising, noted by scholars, is the fact that as a marketing practice it relies on a complex (and rather paradoxical) mix of cultural and economic logics. As Slater (2011) argues, advertising can be described in terms of its hybridity – a place in which economic and cultural repertoires converge. A key dimension of the cultural dimension of advertising relates to the central role of creativity and creative practices as defining features of advertising work. Creativity seems to embrace the more 'artistic' side of advertising work, in contrast to account management and planning, which are perceived as embodying a more commercial dimension. In spite of these differences, the fact remains that advertising companies often place creativity and creative work at the centre of their efforts to capture publics and clients (Moeran 2009). At the same time, creativity is understood as a key aspect of the self-definition and identity of advertising professionals (Nixon 2003).

Despite the significance of creativity, most of the work on advertising creativity tends to focus on exploring the social and cultural 'contexts' in which creativity takes place, rather than the creative work itself. Some authors have explored how advertising involves dealing with specific cultures of production mediated by gender and/or specific professional cultures (Nixon 2003). Attention has been paid to the organizational and occupational structures that frame the creative work in agencies, pointing at how 'Creativity is enabled, outlined and constrained, then, by various aesthetic (or representational), economic, material/technical, social, spatial, and temporal factors, none of which is entirely independent of the others' (Moeran 2009: 980). Similarly, others have explored how tacit knowledge mobilized in creative advertising work often relates to the cultural capital and class cultures of advertising professionals (McLeod et al. 2009). In sum, while some of this work has given serious attention to the ordinary practices that structure advertising work, it is mainly concerned with identifying how creative practices in advertising are mediated or framed by some particular social or cultural factors (e.g. class, gender or the professional fields).

In this chapter I take a different standpoint to unpack creative work in advertising agencies. Following the premises set out in the introduction, I examine routine creative advertising practices as situated and material processes. Creative work is thus understood as a particular type of knowledge-making practice (Camic et al. 2012), which plays a key role in the production of advertisements as marketing devices. In doing so, I take as a point of departure the visual and audiovisual entities that are used during the process of producing a new advertising campaign, namely advertising references. Exploring references as traces of creative work has several strengths. First, focusing on the uses of references enables the analyst to traverse creative practices across the (often artificial) edges between creative and non-creative work in the agency. Creative work appears here as a distributed process. Second, taking references as a starting point helps to makes visible the role played by material devices in the process of qualifying advertising and evaluating the creative concepts in campaign projects.

Using references in the agency

Creative work in an advertising agency is often described by advertisers as related to a series of team meetings where potential creative solutions for a campaign are presented, discussed and reshaped. As one informant put it, a key part of their work consists of meeting and 'throwing up' ideas. This division of labour is also formatted into an agency's building plan (agencies typically have several meeting rooms, some explicitly designed to hold creative meetings). During meetings, time is often spent on the discussion and evaluation of potential creative 'points' (of entry) brought up by the different members of the team. These meetings are often preceded by several other meetings with non-creative members of the agency and clients, in which a general framework of the campaign is discussed, particularly through organization of the brief and discussion of the key insights that define the consumer (Ariztía 2013). In such meetings, different potential paths converge into creative ideas that are clarified and elaborated by the team. Once agreement is produced, conversation moves on to the specifics of the campaign, such as graphics and the media. Producing a campaign is thus a highly distributed process, through which the advertisement emerges:

> We meet to throw up ideas. Then, I come up with the idea that the 'pack', if we can call it that, and the graphic, could be like this, and the draft could be like this one, and the colors this, that and the other. Then we reach a creative agreement and we get going.
>
> (Creative, middle-sized advertising agency)

In creative meetings, references are vital. Meetings, conversations and negotiations about potential creative concepts often take the form of a shared view and assessment of selected references, in turn inspiring advertising campaigns, YouTube videos, images and material from social networks such as memes.[2] More concretely, creative meetings often involve a creative team viewing an advertisement on a computer. In such situations, discussions and the development of new creative concepts are mediated by the very practical process of watching, evaluating and using references for the purposes of qualifying creative paths or 'puntas'.[3]

But from the point of view of references and their role in the process of defining creative concepts, creative meetings are just one specific moment. Before a creative meeting, there is a long process of referencing, in which references that might inspire and shape a specific campaign are sought. References are also key devices for what happens after these creative meetings. They feature in negotiations with planners, account managers and, particularly, clients.

Referencing as a practical activity

Referencing – searching for and collecting visual references for the purpose of isolating and elaborating creative ideas – is perhaps one of the most common activities undertaken by creative professionals (CPs). During my interviews, referencing was typically defined as a practice that occupies most of a CP's day. Referencing occurs on two interrelated levels. First, and more generally, the CP often works on keeping a vast, ongoing collection of references related to advertising, which are used as a repository in which to 'find' new ideas, or to evaluate or refine current ideas. The process of collecting references often continues outside work. It is common for CPs to hold an ongoing conversation online by sending chosen images, videos, phrases, memes, jokes, or any kind of material the CP finds relevant to a working or future project. The practice of referencing also has institutional support. Advertising agencies often have digital tools and/or predefined workflows that help sustain and increase the amount of references in the agency. For example, in one agency, advertising pieces, ideas and/or images were circulated in a weekly newsletter that was prepared by a young CP.

Referencing is also linked to the development and resolution of creative concepts in specific campaigns. This often involves spending several hours looking for references that might help to develop a campaign related to a specific brief. As one creative director explained, the specific process of referencing is more or less as follows: after a new project is assigned, he often asks his team to start referencing – 'feeding' – different aspects of the brief. The team, often comprising two or three creatives, starts searching for references or information that might help inform a creative idea. For some CPs (e.g. art directors) the work of referencing relates mostly to mapping out visual attributes of the campaign, such as finding relevant images of advertising pieces that might help fuel ideas, or pictures that denote a particular atmosphere that might help define the creative idea. Others, such as copywriters, focus more on finding references that help in developing new ideas that define an advertising piece.

Ordering and classifying

Referencing can also be seen as a practical process of classification and order. Here, organizing references involves defining what 'counts' as a key element in advertising (Stark 2009) in order to: (i) organize creative workers and creative trajectories; and (ii) define a standpoint from which creative concepts are qualified and evaluated. In the first case, references are key devices for the framing of advertising work and professional trajectories. One CP explained how he organizes his references in browser bookmarks and the coexistence of different ordering logics. On one hand, he orders references by considering different moments of creative advertising work. His personal order mobilizes a particular version of how to organize creative work in the agency. Collections of references are also critical pieces in how personal working trajectories are organized. This CP keeps his personal collection as something personal, which he relates to as his own trajectory and experience in advertising. At the same time, his references are central in shaping different approaches and 'styles' among CPs, and even between different companies. While some CPs favour one specific type of referencing that might, for example, emphasize the quality of post-production, others might privilege collecting more general creative ideas by looking at sources that are not necessarily related to advertising pieces. As discussed below, this work of collecting is a key device in defining the parameters of good and bad advertising. Later, this CP showed his bookmarks to illustrate our conversation (Figure 3.1). As he told me, they are ordered in a rather chaotic way, which I attribute to the active and ongoing process of collecting. A key ordering principle is the specific aspects and/or moments of creative and artistic design (e.g. image work, logos, retouching, 3D work).

This order coexists with several other ordering principles. References are organized in terms of the different attributes of an advertising campaign (e.g. 'cool', 'fashion', 'chic', 'dark', 'freak', 'unusual'). Furthermore, references are

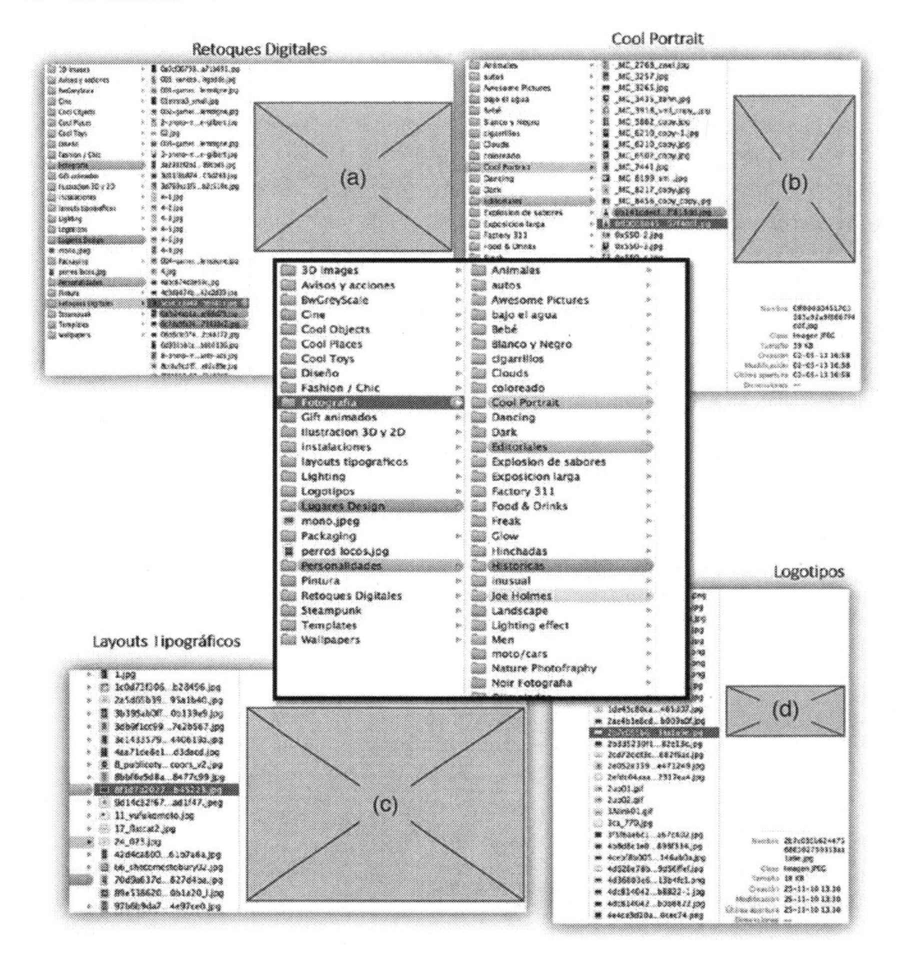

(a) Studio photograph of semi-naked woman with blue eye shadow being splashed with pink liquid against a black background; (b) studio photograph of the actor Christopher Plummer wearing a Tuxedo against a white background; (c) The phrase "GO OUT AND LOVE SOMEONE" written in a 3-dimensional typeface dripping green in colour; (d) The typographical logo 'Artwork' written in a black emboldened sans-serif font.

Figure 3.1 A CP's ordered collection of Internet bookmark references: general categories in the centre; specific categories on the sides

also classified in terms of product or other entities or phenomena (e.g. food, tobacco, cars, natural elements such as sky and cloud).

In the second instance, references are also classified in terms of their proximity with the creative work being undertaken at the time. Notable, here, are the different reference locations, particularly in terms of proximity. At one level, references that come from nearby companies (or from the client's markets) are collected mostly for the purpose of defining a space of competition and differentiation.

Collecting references, at this level, involves looking at different well regarded advertisements, often by pointing to the work of agencies that have a global reputation, or to advertising pieces that have become viral. In several interviews I came across long descriptions of locations in which to look for good references. CPs often collect vast lists of agencies that produce good pieces. In sum, and arguably, the way references are classified in terms of proximity relates to the enactment of different local, regional or global creative contexts (Slater and Ariztía 2009). In the case of references coming from nearby spaces, they work as a point of departure from which differences have to be made. In the case of references coming from contexts that are more distant, they work as a point of departure to develop creative work.

Qualifying and evaluating creative concepts

A second moment in the examination of references concerns unpacking their use in creative teamwork. Here, references can be related to two main interrelated activities: (i) the process of *qualification* of creative concepts, that is, the way in which creative ideas are assembled into a stable formulation, often an outline of a campaign; and (ii) the *evaluation* of creative concepts, that is, the practices and devices through which the worth of concepts is defined. Both qualification (definition) and evaluation (assessment) of a creative concept through the use of references form part of the same process and define ordinary practice in routine creative work (Lamont 2012, Musselin and Paradeise 2005). For purposes of analytical clarity, they are described here as separate moments.

On one hand, the use of references can be described in terms of their role during the process of qualification of creative concepts. After referencing, CPs often choose key references that might help shape and support some creative points of entry that will be discussed in creative meetings. More concretely, references are used to make visible some specific qualities of the points of entry, thus helping to circulate the concept among the team's members. For example, it is possible that one reference is used to show the visual 'tone' of a creative concept and another is used to set the general style of the script, or main message. It is important to note that this is not only related to the visualization of some good or campaign potential qualities, but also contributes to making visible some particular atmospheres.

Furthermore, it is important to note that the role of references in stabilizing the qualities of a creative concept is not reduced to creative meetings. References also play a key role in helping to make creative ideas real, and mobilizing them during encounters and negotiations with clients and non-creative colleagues. Here references are useful as they circulate among different audiences (e.g. they may be presented in different types of meetings), creating awareness of an aspect of the creative concepts and making it stable.

References are particularly relevant in the relationship with clients, as it is difficult for some clients, or people with a less creative background, to 'imagine' how a final campaign will be. During meetings with clients, a creative person will often show references of similar pieces in order to clarify what they are aiming for. In this way, references work as devices that help imagine future paths, as well as allowing the enactment of specific properties of a campaign before the campaign is produced.[4] References, here, can be understood as a particular type of immutable but generative object that helps creative concepts circulate within and outside creative meetings.

While references help to enact specific qualities of creative concepts, it is important to note that, at the same time, creative work involves producing a creative concept that departs radically from the references used. The way in which new creative concepts are constructed, relying on existing references, involves a process of synthesis from which the creative concept is composed. This process of (re)composition, where different references are combined to generate something radically new, is at the centre of creative meetings. All in all, as one CP explained, the work during those meetings often involves making a 'new Frankenstein': in other words, creating something new based on mixing different references. This involves a great deal of negotiation between the participants in meetings. It is possible, for example, that one specific creative concept adopts references coming from other puntas (e.g. music or postproduction effects):

> You always support it with other references that have a lot to do with it. It is very helpful to look for references, to bring printed references that help explain better what you have in mind, because it is difficult to explain how to put it on paper. It is very helpful to bring something, and then say, I imagine it like that, or better with other colours, and then something dynamic happens and someone says, 'I like it like that but I don't like it the way you imagine solving it. What happens if we do it this way?'
>
> (Creative, middle-sized agency)

Thus a key element of how references are manipulated during creative meetings relates to the ability to transpose and dissolve original references into the proposed creative concept. This operation of transposition means creating a new type of creative concept that differs from the references used. The following example shows how this work of recombining references happens. In one case, CPs were working on a campaign for wine. The brief stated that the new wine was made from two different varieties (an assemblage). Based on this entry point, the CP started to look for references related to two things being mixed. The process started when one CP started searching Google for the word 'ensemble'. They also looked at other advertising works related to two things that are mixed. At some point, the creative director found the work of a visual artist whose work consisted of assembling different pictures of people into one face. Once this reference was found and discussed, the idea was developed and framed for the wine. Then other references and ideas were used to produce a final creative concept.

Given the many iterations of creative meetings, it is sometimes difficult (even for the CP) to trace back to the original ideas and references that helped qualify the final piece. It is in this ability to compose something radically new from existing ideas that the originality and quality of creative concepts is at stake. Overall, the worth of a creative concept as an outcome of meetings involves the concept attaining a radical difference from the references used in the process, thus cutting off any explicit connection or element that might link references and the final pieces.

It can be argued, based on this description, that the use of references in studio practices evokes Latour's (1999) notion of 'inscriptions', which can be understood as visual objects that make visible and stable some specific qualities and aspects of creative concepts in various situations. References in advertising, however, differ from scientific inscriptions in important ways. In particular, they account not only for stability, but also for the production of newness. In order to account for the specificities of inscription devices in creative and technical work, scholars have recently identified types of inscription that differ from that in scientific work originally described by Latour.

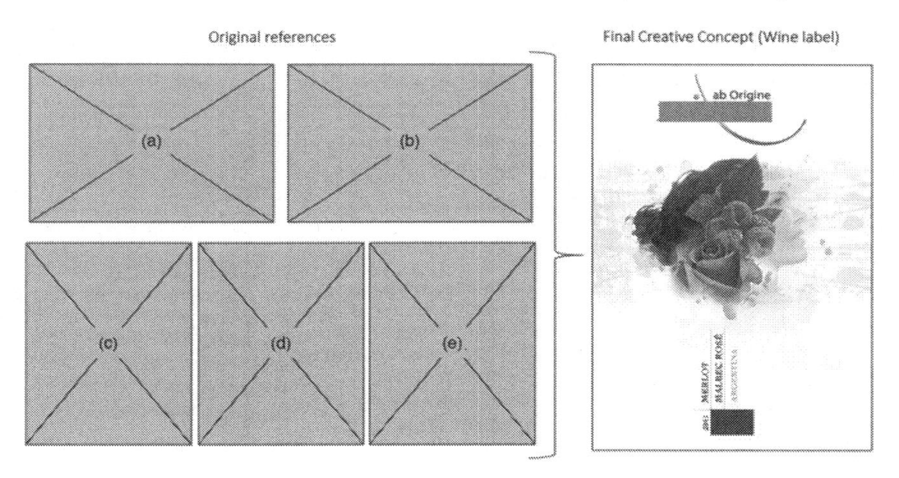

(a) A black and white photograph of a young man and a woman in black clothes looking out to opposite sides of the image blended with a photograph of an urban area industrial on a cloudy day; (b) Two de-saturated colour photographs of Cindy Crawford wearing a parka overcoat blended with one another – one, a close-up portrait, the other, Crawford posing in a landscape; (c) The black and white silhouette of a man into which an urban landscape with a flock of birds has been blended; (d) a black and white portrait of a boy into which a photograph of a forest has been blended; (e) A black and white portrait of a man or woman in a tuxedo, smiling, holding their tie and blended through a pink translucent brush stroke.

Figure 3.2 References used to compose a new creative concept (left) and the outcome (right)

Henderson (1991) employs 'conscription device' to describe the use of drawings in engineering work. *Conscription* devices differ from scientific inscriptions in that their main goal is to organize a process of creation. As Henderson argues: 'conscription devices [...] enlist group participation and are receptacles for knowledge created and adjusted through group interaction aimed toward a common goal' (1991: 456). More recently, Wilkie (2010) uses the notion of 'descriptor' to account for the uses of inscriptions in user-centred design, and design practices more generally. For Wilkie, visual objects in design are not only used as stable representations that can be moved from one process – or setting – to another, but are also central in fostering generative processes during teamwork. *Descriptors*, like concriptors, thus are visual representations that are deeply embedded in processes of creation. Descriptors, however, differ from conscriptors in that their main role is not to produce stability, but to develop a relatively open and flexible programme of action. In other words, descriptors mediate stable properties of users – or other concrete design outputs for that matter – as well as enabling the production of new associations, new capacities and new realities, and can thus participate in the reconfiguring of futures (ibid.: 105).

Based on this, I approach references in advertising as a particular type of descriptor: as visual objects that help in making visible and stable the qualities of the campaign in different situations. Alongside Wilkie and Henderson, I argue that references make visible and stable qualities of creative ideas *and* occasion new 'inventive' possibilities. Understanding reference as descriptors thus involves focusing on the generative capacity of these visual and audio-visual objects in advertising work. Here, a key aspect of references in creative advertising work involves the erasure of the existent connections between original references and the final outcome, thus emphasis is placed on generating the 'radically' new. In scientific practice, however, referencing involves keeping a fluid circulation along the chain of references that are used (Latour 1999, Salinas 2014).

References as a valuation device

References not only play a central role in helping to qualify creative concepts and mobilize them along the advertising pipeline; they are also central pieces in terms of how creative ideas are evaluated throughout the process. Evaluation of creative concepts is not something that happens at the end of the advertising process, but is a central aspect of the mundane work of manufacturing creative ideas. Following recent works on the pragmatics of valuation in the economic world (Muniesa 2011), it can be noted that 'worth' in advertising is not either subjective or objective, but is the result of a practical activity that happens regularly in creative meetings and thereafter, in which valuation devices play a central role. References might be described thus as a particular *valuation device* which participates in the practical process of defining and measuring the worth of a creative concept at different stages of advertising production. First, during the early stages of creative work, references are used as a point of comparison to define the originality and value of a creative concept. As described by Moeran and Christensen (2013), the process of evaluation does not work as a final test, but instead is inscribed in the mundane process of production. This can happen in different ways. On the other hand, creative concepts are constantly confronted with references in order to define their originality and value. The worth of an idea depends on how it is used differently from references. For example, several CPs explained that they often value their colleagues' work by taking as a point of comparison how they depart from and/or relate to well established referents. One specific creative concept can be confronted and assessed many times in terms of other references during a creative process. Often, different ideas and potential creative paths are tested against different sets of references. They might be used to set a point of contrast, but also to mobilize the qualities of a working concept that is being tested:

> Often, if we are not sure about the path to follow, we have, I don't know, three references, three ways of creating the work and we tell ourselves, let's do the exercise with two or three of them, and then when you have a final work with the three references.
>
> And when do you stop?
>
> When you have two end results then you choose which one you like best. 'The one that says John with his hand raised or the other with Peter with 3D animation.' Then you vote and you see it on paper and you decide that it was better in 3D.
>
> (Creative, middle-sized agency)

Festivals and awards, described as tournaments of value by Moeran and Pedersen (2011), are also central spaces from which the worth of a campaign is defined.

On the other hand, references are key devices along the process of negotiating the creative worth of a campaign after the creative work is done. As described above, references are typically mobilized during client meetings to support and show the worthiness of a proposed concept. For example, it is very useful to show clients a reference that might help them to give value to a 'risky' creative concept. Associations with relevant references are often defined as a useful strategy to show the worth of an idea. In other cases, clients suggest and mobilize their own references as a point of comparison from which the worth of an advertising piece is assessed.

Confronting creative work with multiple grammars of worth

While references are key pieces along the process through which the qualities and worth of a creative idea are defined, the place of references as a valuation and qualification device relates only to one of several coexistent grammars of worth existing in advertising that signify the originality and novelty of an idea (Boltanski and Thévenot 2006). Advertising often involves accommodating and moving along other grammars of worth, not described in this chapter. For example, a central place is given to strategic guidelines, as well as the guidelines of the brief. Therefore, while a creative concept can be evaluated as a worthy piece in creative terms (e.g. viewed as innovative in relation to other references), those ideas also have to confront other 'tests' of worth (ibid.). For example, during meetings with clients, campaigns are highly regarded if they are commercially meaningful or maintain a connection with a previously defined and negotiated 'target'. This other test of worth often involves mobilizing other types of market device, such as business models or strategic guidelines, which help define the worth of a given campaign.

Creative professionals' accounts often describe the tensions that arise from their work being evaluated in relation to these different grammars of worth. There is an active coexistence here of multiple principles of valuation throughout the process, such as those described by Stark (2009). It can be noted that, more than an important tension, balancing and moving between the different grammars of worth at stake is a common assumption for CPs (this is why, they say, they are not artists, but advertising professionals). In the end, the final value of a creative concept piece relates to the articulation of several of these principles. The following description of a CP of the worth of a creative concept illustrates how they accommodate different and often contradictory values. In this case, the CP defines the value of a piece as related not only to originality (a mostly creative criterion of worth), but also to its ability to reach consumers' inner 'truth' (Ariztía 2014), that is, its ability to attach with consumers:

> How do you know when a piece is good?
>
> When you say, 'I've got it', it is a truth and I have never seen it before, although it might be similar to other work. I have never seen a piece of advertising for cars from this angle. [...] How can I say this, it is this angle of entry, a different angle never used before and that is valuable.
>
> (Senior creative, middle-sized agency)

This practical accommodation of different grammars of worth is common in advertising work, and it is a tension that somehow defines the logic of advertising work. Considering this, and as argued by others (Ariztía 2013), the final outcome and value of an advertisement cannot be defined in terms of a given set of principles through which the work is confronted. Instead, it is more the result of a practical and open process of inquiry, in which the final value comes from the ability to find a solution that works and is unproblematic for the people involved.

Conclusion

This chapter describes the use of references in creative advertising work. Instead of focusing on the social contexts to explain creativity in advertising by taking references as a point of entry, the focus is on the rather mundane activities that shape creative work in advertising. The chapter explores creative practices in advertising as an open and distributed process. The practice of referencing, as a central creative practice that involves connecting specific work with other external pieces, has been described as a collective process, which is at the base of creative work.

Furthermore, references are described here as key creative devices that help qualify and evaluate creative concepts. They are central pieces in terms of how creative concepts travel within and outside meetings, thus working as a specific type of immutable mobile through which creative qualities are enacted and mobilized at different moments along the process. References are also key to the assembling of creative concepts. I have described the process of synthesis, the generative moment that comes from the use of different references as a key moment of creative work. A central aspect of creative work involves eroding connections between the final product and original references, in contrast to the use of references in scientific work, where an important aspect of referencing relates to maintaining a circulating truth along the chains of reference. Thus it can be argued that referencing in advertising denotes a specific mode of producing truth that differs from the modes of truth of scientific work and from other knowledge practices (Camic et al. 2012). Finally, this article describes how references are key valuation devices through which the worth of a creative concept is assessed. This happens both in daily work and in final meetings, when references are mobilized to state the value of a creative idea and a final campaign.

Notes

1 This chapter draws on research funded by the Chilean National Fund for Scientific and Technological Development (Project 1140078).
2 A meme is a specific picture that passes from person to person by way of social media platforms such as Twitter, WhatsApp or Facebook.
3 'Puntas' (literally 'sharp end' or 'tip') is a word used by my informants to define preliminary creative ideas that might take shape further in the process.
4 It is interesting here to note the similarities with and divergences from other types of device that circulate in commercial spaces. See e.g. Doganova, L. and Eyquem-Renault, M. 2009. What do business models do? *Research Policy*, 38(1), 1559–1570.

References

Ariztía, T. 2013. Unpacking insight: how consumers are qualified by advertising agencies. *Journal of Consumer Culture*, 15(2), 143–162.

Ariztía, T. 2014. Housing markets performing class: middle-class cultures and market professionals in Chile. *Sociological Review*, 62(2), 400–420.

Boltanski, L. and Thévenot, L. 2006. *On Justification: Economies of Worth*. Princeton, NJ: Princeton University Press.

Callon, M., Méadel, C. and Rabeharisoa, V. 2002. The economy of qualities. *Economy and Society*, 31(2), 194–217.

Camic, C., Gross, N. and Lamont, M. 2012. The study of social knowledge in the making. In: Camic, C., Gross, N. and Lamont, M. eds, *Social Knowledge in the Making*. Chicago, IL: University of Chicago Press, pp. 1–40.

Cochoy, F. 2007. A brief theory of the 'captation' of publics: understanding the market with Little Red Riding Hood. *Theory, Culture & Society*, 24(7–8), 203–223.

Doganova, L. and Eyquem-Renault, M. 2009. What do business models do? *Research Policy*, 38(10), 1559–1570.

Dubuisson-Quellier, S. 2010. Product tastes, consumer tastes: the plurality of qualifications in product development and marketing activities. In: Araujo, L., Finch, J. and Kjellberg, H. eds, *Reconnecting Marketing to Markets*. Oxford: Oxford University Press, pp. 74–93.

Grandclément, C. and Gaglio, G. 2011. Convoking the consumer in person: the focus group effect. In: Zwick, D. and Cayla, J. eds, *Inside Marketing: Ideologies, Practices, Devices*. Oxford: Oxford University Press, pp. 87–114.

Henderson, K. 1991. Flexible sketches and inflexible data bases: visual communication, conscription devices, and boundary objects in design engineering. *Science, Technology & Human Values*, 16(4), 448–473.

Lamont, M. 2012. Toward a comparative sociology of valuation and evaluation. *Annual Review of Sociology*, 38(1), 201–221.

Latour, B. 1999. *Pandor's Hope: Essays on the Reality of Science Studies*. Cambridge, MA: Harvard University Press.

Latour, B. and Woolgar, S. 1979. *Laboratory Life: The Social Construction of Scientific Facts*. Beverly Hills, CA: Sage.

Malefyt, T. and Moeran, B. 2003. *Advertising Cultures*. Oxford: Berg.

McFall, L. 2004. *Advertising: A Cultural Economy*. London: Sage.

McFall, L. 2009. Devices and desires: how useful is the 'new' new economic sociology for understanding market attachment? *Sociology Compass*, 3(2), 267–282.

McFall, L. 2014. *Devising Consumption: Cultural Economies of Insurance, Credit and Spending*. London: Routledge.

McLeod, C., O'Donohoe, S. and Townley, B. 2009. The elephant in the room? Class and creative careers in British advertising agencies. *Human Relations*, 62(7), 1011–1039.

Miller, P. and Rose, N. 1997. Mobilising the consumer: assembling the subject of consumption. *Theory, Culture & Society*, 14(1), 1–36.

Moeran, B. 2009. The organization of creativity in Japanese advertising production. *Human Relations*, 62(7), 963–985.

Moeran, B. and Christensen, B. T. 2013. *Exploring Creativity: Evaluative Practices in Innovation, Design, and the Arts*. Cambridge: Cambridge University Press.

Moeran, B. and Pedersen, J. S. 2011. *Negotiating Values in the Creative Industries: Fairs, Festivals and Competitive Events*. Cambridge: Cambridge University Press.

Muniesa, F. 2011. A flank movement in the understanding of valuation. *Sociological Review*, 59(s2), 24–38.

Muniesa, F. and Trébuchet-Breitwiller, A.-S. 2010. Becoming a measuring instrument. *Journal of Cultural Economy*, 3(3), 321–337.

Musselin, C. and Paradeise, C. 2005. Quality: a debate. *Sociologie du Travail*, 47(s1), e89–e123.

Nixon, S. 2003. *Advertising Cultures: Gender, Commerce, Creativity*. London: Sage.

Salinas, F. 2014. Bruno Latour's pragmatic realism: an ontological inquiry. *Global Discourse*, DOI: 10.1080/23269995.2014.992597.

Sklair, L. 2002. *Globalization: Capitalism and its Alternatives*. Oxford: Oxford University Press.

Slater, D. 2011. Between culture and economy: the impossible place of marketing. In: Zwick, D. and Cayla, J. eds, *Inside Marketing: Ideologies, Practices, Devices*. Oxford: Oxford University Press, pp. 23–41.

Slater, D. and Ariztía, T. 2009. Assembling Asturias: scaling devices and cultural leverage. In: Farías, I. and Bender, T. eds, *Urban Assemblages: How Actor–Network Theory Changes Urban Studies*. London: Routledge, pp. 91–108.

Stark, D. 2009. *The Sense of Dissonance: Accounts of Worths in Economic Life*. Princeton, NJ: Princeton University Press.

Wilkie, A. 2010. User assemblages in design: an ethnographic study. PhD thesis, Goldsmiths, University of London.

Zwick, D. and Cayla, J. (2011). Inside marketing: practices, ideologies, devices (intro). In: Zwick, D. and Cayla, J. eds, *Inside Marketing: Practices, Ideologies, Devices*. Oxford: Oxford University Press.

4 From the squid's point of view

Mountable cameras, flexible studios and the perspectivist turn

Emmanuel Grimaud

In his famous thought experiment 'What is it like to be a bat?', Thomas Nagel (1974) argued that subjectivity is irreducible to instrumentation of any kind; it makes no difference whether the perspective is that of a human being or a bat. If I want to know what it is like for a bat to be a bat, 'I am restricted to the resources of my own mind, and those resources are inadequate to the task. I cannot perform it either by imagining additions to my present experience, or by imagining segments gradually subtracted from it, or by imagining some combination of additions, subtractions, and modifications' (Nagel 1974: 435). Thirty years after Nagel's critique, the proliferation of mounted cameras and eye-tracking systems, equipping ever more subjectivities and transforming the world into a vast studio, call for a re-evaluation of this problem. Today 'perspectivism' is *instrumental.* How to evaluate this proliferation of instruments, and does it really carry new perspectives? At Stanford University in 2012, marine biologist William Gilly mounted a camera, the Crittercam, onto a squid. Designed by biologist Greg Marshall, for biologists, the Crittercam enabled Gilly to investigate the life of squids: these carnivores hunt in large, coordinated groups, change colour when approaching other squid to communicate, and are capable of amazing bursts of speed, up to nearly 72 km/h. But 'whose' point of view did the Crittercam represent? That of the biologist who designed it? That of a squid spying on its peers? That of a squid turned biologist? Or the view of a marine biologist playing a squid? 'Mounted perspectivism' designates the attachment of cameras to anything that can hold them, with the aim of getting new points of view on the world, transforming the universe into an enormous studio or a vast playground for video experiments of every kind. A world is captured by a machine which it would be useful to conceive of as a kind of artificial organ that can be attached to many different bodies, but can also be detached. Interchangeability between cameras and the human eye is always only partial. The light and colour sensitivity of the cameras invented so far is different from that of the human eye. And they have not yet been directly connected to any neural network, even if there is good reason to be concerned that this could happen someday. This would mean that the only point of view the Crittercam conveys is its own – that of a machine. But in the case of the squid, is the camera not receptive to other things: its movement, its undulations and its world? In other words, whose point of view does the Crittercam represent? In this chapter, I examine some of the implications of the development of wearable cameras, the problems of point of view that arise from mounting experiments, whether attached to humans and/or non-humans. And I try to address the following issue: does mounted perspectivism constitute a perspective revolution?

Studio studies and perspective problems

Mountable cameras are proliferating, and the rapid development in camera technology calls for a fresh look at the question, 'What is a point of view?'. This is a question that has preoccupied philosophy at least since Leibniz and has recently been the subject of renewed interest in anthropology.[1] To gain a solid understanding of what cinema does to 'perspective', I should begin by noting that in France the term *point de vue* is rarely used on a film set. Rather, it is common to say *prise de vue* (literally 'taking of a view', the French expression for take, shot or shooting in a filming context). A point of view is initially a *prise de vue*, and is later the result of a series of shots that must converge. The notion of *prise de vue* implies a Whiteheadean 'prehensive' model of perspective (Whitehead 1929). Although a *prise de vue* also has a Leibnizian 'conic' aspect, in the sense of a world being folded for and by the camera (Serres 1968, Deleuze 1988), it is always an 'event', a chance, an experiment in prehension that either succeeds or fails, but is something unique and sometimes difficult to repeat. In a classical film studio setup, there are an infinite number of ways to position a camera in an interaction (and engage viewers at the same time), but a number of typical positions are used most of the time: it can be placed next to people, in front of them, in the middle of them, above them (high-angle), below them (low-angle), or it can follow them looking over their shoulder. The distinction usually made between objective and subjective point of view does not stand up very well, even in this division. These points of view are only either closer or more distant, either more enveloping or more partial.

Whenever perspective problems arise, the study of studios can provide insights into the situation, inasmuch as when researchers analyse film sets (e.g. Grimaud 2004, 2007, 2013), they are initially confronted with the task of untangling point-of-view problems. When cameras are said to be more objective, this overlooks the fact that they are often used to infiltrate interactions from the inside, circling them rather than looking at them from above. There is no point of view that is not internal to the configuration in which it resides. Even when looking at things from above, as in Deb Roy's experiment (in which the cognitive scientist filmed 90,000 hours of her child's life by placing fisheye cameras throughout her house), it is really a matter of introducing a device into a space (on its ceiling), and although its perspective might be comprehensive, it is still partial relative to what could potentially be captured. From above, one sees people moving around the house. These movements are captured from a point of view that is only unusual or novel because it is that of a ceiling, removed from the human 'eye-level' perspective. The behaviour of this 'extra' point of view endowed with a specific orientation (the camera) often defines the studio space. The camera introduces a technical bifurcation, and to a certain extent this bifurcation already contains a certain point of view (passive, mechanical), but the person filming is always in an ambiguous position in relation to it, in a paradoxical attachment relationship (it is their duty to occupy it), since their eye and that of the camera are two different things.

When a camera is mounted, the problem of attachment arises. Here, a distinction can be made between three forms of attachment: a camera can be attached to a *site*, an *eye*, or another part of the *body*. The perspective it conveys is qualitatively different in each of these cases. Anyone who has seen a video shot by a surveillance camera is immediately able to recognise how this differs from a film made by a human being, or captured by a camera attached to a part of the body that produces instability and poor framing. An intention is more likely to show through with a camera guided by a human eye or even attached to it (an eye tracker, for example) than with a camera in a dome suspended from a ceiling, capturing a lateral slice of an environment without any discernible intentionality. It offers a point of view devoid of saliencies (or a view plane) in the sense in which one speaks of a point of view in the mountains, for example. The point of view can be occupied or remain unoccupied. But what about the case of the squid on which the camera is mounted? Here again, the camera is not guided by any eye. No squid can take possession of the camera and make it its own. What, then, is the camera's relationship to the squid's point of view? Let us assume that the squid is conceived as an agent of marine biologists who want to study other squid. In that case, the squid's back would not be much different from the ceiling in Deb Roy's experiment. But should it not be perceived as more than that?

These (small and large) perceptual disparities, with all of the problems they engender (such as who is looking? and what is the point of view?), are generated by a 'studioization' of the world that obviously exceeds the narrow frame of a squid's back. Today there is no human practice or field of activity that is not occasionally subjected to the intrusion of cameras enabling viewers to penetrate it, generating perspective problems, even misunderstandings, about the point of view from which the camera is speaking. The task of studio studies is boundless, going well beyond a reconsideration of classic anthropological problems, notably: what is a point of view?

At first glance, mounted cameras continue a long history of cinematographic experimentation at the 'boundaries of the subjective' and can be understood only by looking back. Before its arrival, taking someone's point of view usually meant filming over the person's shoulder. How does one go from an over-the-shoulder perspectivism to a 'mounted' perspectivism? And what are the possibilities and implications of this change? We must look back at the history of point-of-view instrumentation since the eighteenth century to realise that an instrumental solution has never really been found to the question of the subjective point of view. We must also look closely at how point-of-view problems arise in the context of what could be called the 'grand perspectivism' of film sets. We must also speculate, since mounted perspectivism is an intermediate stage on the way to new capturing methods and a more radical form of perspectivism, which the squid's point of view and Crittercams point to.

Machinic perspectivism: the machine that wanted to put itself in the place of others

Let's rewind. What happened to make people stubbornly persist in seeing the world not through eyes (or other sense organs), but over the shoulder? What is this strange form of soft or 'default' perspectivism that survived the whole of the twentieth century and beyond? Lorraine Daston argued that in the eighteenth century, point of view was first a question of moral philosophy before becoming a scientific problem (Daston 1999). This took the form of a search for impartiality or for a 'super point of view', based on analogies with the eye and the mind. Historically, the efforts of the Moderns seemed to lead to an a-perspectivism in which the camera, beginning in the nineteenth century, became the primary means of exploration alongside other capturing and measurement tools. Historically, cameras can be viewed as the endpoint of decades of research and experimentation aiming to find the best means of materializing *from* a point of view, based on the model of the human eye, but outside of humans. However, viewing the camera as the final development in a history that led to an 'escape from perspective' (ibid.) and concluded with an instrumental a-perspectivism is not really accurate: the 'a' takes things a step too far. It is first and foremost a machinic perspectivism, seen from the perspective of a machine.

On a film set, the *prise de vue* space is delimited according to the camera, and putting oneself in the place of a camera is a bit like putting oneself in the place of a disabled person who does not see as well. The film in an analogue camera is only to capture its object able under certain lighting conditions. It is 'exposable' in various ways and does not record what we see, but something quite different. In early twentieth-century film studios, cameras were never alone. They were always surrounded by a certain number of specialized assistants, responsible for cleaning, transporting or dismantling them (attendants), or engaged in simultaneous tasks during shooting. Thus, unlike human eyes, film cameras have always been surrounded and enabled by an administrative collective. In the continuity book maintained by assistants, the camera finds itself endowed with a special kind of agency, independently of all those who support it and make its point of view possible: it is treated as a subject, endowed with a reactive vivacity in moving in relation to actors, sometimes as a lover attracting actors, even a companion (it follows this or that actor). In this context, the main questions become: *How does one put oneself in the place of a camera? And in whose place does the camera put itself?*

Film-set history also includes the problem of the director's point of view, which dominates only in appearance. Those whose performances are supposed to be captured by the camera are reminded of its point of view through orders, position directions, floor markings, and a whole slew of gestures aiming to get actors to do what one wants them to do. The camera requires some minimal mathematical position adjustment, and the filming process is technical and sensitive. Actors have no choice but to trust the director. And the director has to struggle constantly to make his vision understood. On a film set, everyone is asked to move outside themselves in order to take on the film's point of view. Each shot occasions discussions about the right point of view that can only be resolved 'in the name of the camera', 'in the name of the film' or 'in the name of the viewer'. The director's point of view is always within something, a situation or action, something that must unfold and create a world when shooting a fictional film, or something that is waiting to be realized through and beyond the concrete relationships being filmed when shooting a documentary. It is a point of view that will clearly appear only at the end of the shoot, or sometimes it does not appear at all from the inside when the film fails to be connected with a voice, requiring it to be asserted from the outside by other means (through a voiceover), or in the case of a documentary when the images are considered insufficiently evocative.

Over everyone's shoulder

Let's rewind again, since questions concerning a camera's machinic point of view are not new. When 'a-perspective' appears in moral philosophy, it is an (optical and moral) way of putting oneself in the place of others and achieving impartiality. Adam Smith's moral theory of sympathy is interesting in this respect. Full of optical metaphors, it advocates a form of a-perspectivism in which 'imagination' plays a fundamental role: it is thanks to imagination that one is able to *put oneself in the place of others* and therefore hope to achieve impartiality. Here, social life can be compared to a studio that does not yet have a camera; in time, this will crystallize the 'imaginary change' from one situation to another that Smith speaks of – and in which people are sometimes actors and sometimes viewers of their passions and ideas. It is striking that the play of varying positions underpinning empathy – which Smith calls the 'imaginary change of situations' (Smith 2002 [1759]: 21) and Lefebvre 'the ternary agent/object/spectator system' (Lefebvre 2000: 73) – has structured life on film sets as long as film studios have existed. The play of positions on a set would not make much sense without the minimal empathy that Smith speaks of. But this time, however, it comes down to reversing positions literally (not metaphorically).

For the director, it is a matter of putting herself in the place of the actors as well as being a viewer of her film, whilst for the viewers, it is a matter of also being directors of their own screening, and for the actors it is a question of putting themselves in the place of both of them. Consequently, on a film shoot composition is achieved through the points of view of absent people (e.g. audiences), not simply the camera's machinic perspective.

For many directors, taking an audience perspective means putting themselves in the place of another (a disabled person, their own mother, their maid if they have one). Those present take the place of those absent, people take the place of a machine, and the machine then takes the point of view of a person – according to what could be called a principle of serial and inclusive organisation of points of view. The camera takes a point of view, the viewer looks at a screen where a point of view is being taken, and the actors have also their own in the interaction which is being filmed. Each has a point of view that includes the others, but they are all different. The viewer has a point of view on the camera, on the actors, on the world in which the actor is circulating. The actors also keep viewers in mind from the moment filming begins. They can even speak to them, in some cases pretending to look them in the eye, and it is generally preferable that they keep them in mind to at least some minimal extent. The director must put himself in the place of the cameraman, who must put herself in the place of the camera, but the camera is also placed where one wants it to be. Does this mean we can say that the camera is the director's point of view, and the director's point of view is the camera? No, because there is never a strict relationship of equivalence. They are in a relationship of inclusion or comprehension. Each includes the point of view of the other in their/its field of vision and can detach themself/itself from it at any time, later reattaching to it again. Cinema's subjective point of view is not *a point-of-view of* (and I stress this point), it is an inclusion of *he whose point-of-view one wants to take*, one that follows his movement. This 'grand perspectivism' logic of the studios would be incomplete without this other point. One must be aware of the *perceptual gaps.* A viewer might not get the film, might not 'identify' with the director or the actor, but can also leap over the gaps, identifying with the actor without necessarily subscribing to the director's point of view, or share the director's point of view but not that of the actor. A *prise de vue* always implies *going in and out of oneself in order to adopt points of view that are not one's own.*

When a film set formalizes modes of collective organisation, it turns the question of perspective into a concrete, instrumental problem: the a-perspective becomes the machine's point of view, empathy becomes an actor–director–viewer position exchange, and the materialization of someone's perspective amounts to an over-the-shoulder placement. But it also introduces something else I believe is essential for understanding the archaeology of mounted perspectivism. This can be clarified through the following example.

The search for an 'on-board' experience

We are on the film set of Peter Jackson's *King Kong*, during the shooting of an episode which is interesting beyond the fact that it concerns – after the squid – the story of a gorilla. The actress arrives on the set. The technicians have spent many hours rehearsing the camera movements, especially those of the prop the actress is supposed to stand in: a large green mechanical hand. The actress has to position herself in it and struggle, as if she were trapped in King Kong's actual hand. In the special effects studios, the green will be replaced by the texture of a real gorilla hand and the green background will become a jungle. King Kong is supposed to swing from liana to liana, chased by violent and aggressive creatures. An assistant is responsible for goading the actress with a kind of foam-rubber broom. In the scene, King Kong is chased by what looks like prehistoric birds. Between shots, the director mimes what the actress must do. He takes her position and shows her how she should struggle, like a boxer trying to protect herself from punches. He uses a plastic Barbie doll to help the actors understand the scale of the final scene. Another actor, in a black suit, stands high up and outside the frame. He performs the gestures of an overexcited gorilla. He is not King Kong because the actress is in its hands. Rather, he is a second presence, a miniature King Kong geometrically displaced in relation to his real position in the scene, tasked with stimulating a certain emotion in the actress, helping her achieve a state of hysteria. The actress has to look at him during the shot and scream more intensely. Two cameras are used to film the action: one on a track, the other close-up to best capture the actress's face.

In what sense is getting attached to a gorilla different from being mounted on a squid? The operation is technically complex. The director has to take the point of view of the *action*. The delicacy of the operation stems from the fact that one must *put oneself in the place of someone else who is putting himself in the place of yet someone else.* The actress has to put herself in the place of a character who is in a vulnerable and uncomfortable position. Viewers have to be able to put themselves in the place of this character and feel the discomfort of her position. For the director, taking the point of view of the action implies taking the place of the actress who has to place herself in a machine that is taking the point of view of King Kong, which is as if divided in two, propelled outside the frame like an 'active control'. When the scene is filmed, these logistics will of course be invisible, as if smoothed away by the movie screen. The scene will appear as its own fully integrated world. And all of these exchanges of perspective, acts of stimulation and King Kong's double will have disappeared. The camera will be placed in the point of view of the actress or that of King Kong, whose movement it will follow through the liana. This whole apparatus was brought into action precisely because the aim was to provide viewers with an *on-board mounted* experience that carries them into the action with the heroine and King Kong as they move from liana to liana. They are not supposed to see the action from a distance or from above, but rather from inside, circulating through it, while still remaining beside it or nearby. They cannot be King Kong but they can follow him very closely. They cannot be the bird that attacks King Kong but they can get into the action over his shoulder. They cannot get inside the actress's head but through empathy they can project themselves into it and feel what she feels in her body.

Mounted perspectivism and the multiplication of position-exchange experiments

In the search for new perspectives, mountable cameras bring additional *prise de vue* possibilities. It is now possible to film in a 'subjective' mode without being over the shoulder, but instead getting closer to a perspective, as close as possible to the body, closer to the eyes or somewhere else completely. Athletes, amateur divers and scientists are experimenting with all kinds of new points of view by attaching cameras to themselves or to animals that have no idea what it is all about. It seems now possible to take the point of view of an eagle, elephant or squid by equipping it with a mountable camera. And these experiments are proliferating. Not a day goes by without new points of view being attempted in this way. Such experiments of turning the world into one giant video highlight the fact that cinematic points of view are always *next to* something, or slightly offset. A camera on an eagle does not give an eagle's point of view, but the point of view of a machine placed on the back of an eagle, similar to a camera placed on a helicopter. Even a porter in India wearing a mountable camera while carrying a big load transmits more of his locomotion rhythm to the camera, which is sensitive to the swaying of his body. A camera attached to a squid makes it possible to see a few things differently, but it is not a squid's perspective. Rather, it is a point of view *by means of* the squid, *by means of* the eagle, or *by means of* the elephant, and these points of view elude the squid, eagle or elephant.

It is in this sense that mounted perspectivism offers a higher degree of subjectification, but its possibilities should not be overestimated. Is it a simulacra of perspectivism, or yet another kind, a suggestive or incomplete form? By supplying points of view that are always a bit offset and can never be totally superimposed on the individuals, it runs up against exactly the same problem as the 'grand perspectivism' of film sets, that of the studios where, to achieve subjectivity, one has no choice but to place the camera close to people, or use the artifice of a voiceover to make it seem like we are inside someone's head. The novelty lies elsewhere, in the fact that the camera zoomorphizes slightly, that it becomes a bit squid-like, a bit eagle-like or a bit elephant-like when attached to these animals, or because it very simply makes it possible to get a different point of view by positioning the machine near the body. The radically different perception of the squid, eagle or elephant is certainly there, nearby. One senses it in the 'vicinity' of the camera, but it stays out of reach. The captured point of view is still that of the camera, one with no-one behind it. Mounted perspectivism aims for hyper-subjectification: one has to put oneself in people's place and become their perception. But it can only approach this. In terms of subjectification, placing a camera on an eagle or pelican and trying to see things as close as possible to its point of view is not necessarily better than turning the camera around and showing the animal's eyes and beating wings, or even placing the camera on the wings themselves, giving it a wholly extraordinary fluttering movement. When speaking of an eagle's or pelican's point of view, it would be better to specify: it is *in the vicinity* of the eagle or pelican that new points of view are possible – the point of view of their wings, for example. A camera attached to a squid produces a much stronger subjectification effect, since its undulations are transmitted to the camera. This being the case, the definition of a point of view should be less 'ophthalmological' and more corporeal, and one should remember that it is a 'range of affects and abilities, that is at the root of perspectives' (Viveiros de Castro 2014). A camera attached to a squid does not reproduce a squid's vision, but it is sensitive to its style of locomotion and offers a point of view from the top of its flaccid body. And it provides a point of view on other squids as we have never seen them before. This is what inspired William Gilly to say 'A squid is a very flexible platform for a camera' (Science World Report 2013). And from this point of view, not all experiments with mounting cameras on humans or animals have merit. It works well on certain species, and some body parts are more suitable than others (a bird's wing is more interesting than its back). When it works less well, this is essentially because the corporeal signature that makes an animal unique rarely transmits to the camera. This appears as if placed in suspension, incapable of being anything but itself and of 'absorbing' the animal's point of view.

Eye-trackers offer an even greater degree of subjectification since they capture eye movements, but I think it would be another misinterpretation to compare them to the points of view of people. It is interesting to observe how they are obtained. Movements are reconstructed by merging images from a camera placed under the eye with those of a forehead camera worn by the individual (usually attached to eyeglasses). In other words, it is a point of view from the surface of the eye (the movements of the retina are captured by an infrared camera) that is in a sense turned around when this image is merged with that from the mountable camera in order to 'pass for' active looking. But this point of view is not that of the human eye whose movements the eye-tracker analyses. It is a point of view *attached to* an eye. Of course, it provides more insight into the point of view of the person wearing it than would a mountable camera that would only absorb his head movements. Eye-tracking makes it possible to see the very intense eye-pointing activity of a human being in the process of looking, but this does not make an eye-tracker's point of view equivalent to that of the person.

Will a new phase of mounted perspectivism be reached the day we invent a graft, a third eye, that is not just attached to the head, but is also integrated into the individual's neuronal logistics? The upshot of mounted perspectivism is that entities which had no point of view find themselves endowed with one, sometimes giving rise to more or less failed, abortive cinemas. Placing a mountable camera on the end of a cow's muzzle will hardly provide insight into a cow's vision, and not just because its eyes are on the sides of its head. Place a camera on a dog and you get nothing but the oscillations that correspond to its head movements. Using mountable technology in its current state, a canine cinema is still not possible. Praying mantises can be equipped with 3D glasses to get an idea of what they perceive, but praying mantises cannot yet transmit their cinema to us. The intense dream activity of sleeping cats can be studied in a laboratory by experienced neurologists, but cats have not yet been given the means to make their own cinema.

But not all experiments in thus transferring perspectivism into more subjective, mountable forms of cinema have failed – far from it. A cinema by monkeys was attempted (see the Chimpcam Project, Edinburgh).[2] The slightly mad primatologists who attempted this experiment initially ran up against the problem that the monkeys, instead of cooperating enthusiastically, were totally indifferent and even refused, irritated, before receiving many hours of training. The question that obviously arises is: to what extent is their cinema different from ours? Or what does it convey of their world?

Patiently waiting to see what monkeys, bears or other animals do with a camera left in their midst is different from attempting to reproduce animal vision. In the former case, it shows a kind of experimental anthropomorphism by saying that, after all, it might produce something new. In the latter case, a zoomorphosis of perspective is sought in the belief that we might see the world differently. Are the fisheye camera that copies the vision of a fish, and the 360° camera that copies the vision of a fly, not attempts to act 'as if' we were fish or to 'see like' flies? Yes and no. In the history of cameras, the goal has never really been to merge with the point of view of something else, but rather to extend human vision by zoomorphizing it slightly, and never completely. Fisheye cameras copy the convexity of fish vision but never its speed (fish perceive many more images than us, and therefore see fishhooks in slow motion). Flies have 360° vision, but it is in black and white, and is much blurrier and more fragmentary than ours; as far as I know, a fly cinema has never been attempted.

When the BBC ventures among polar bears with an impressive arsenal of cameras (remote-controlled to avoid any human disturbance), the result is interesting: even if we cannot see what is happening in the head of a bear, we can glimpse a little more than usual, and we have never seen the bear-world as close-up as when cameras are left near their bodies, in the 'proximal zone' of their point of view (and not in their point of view itself). At worst, the bears come up to the cameras and whack them with their paws. At best, they let themselves be filmed by these strange, robotized machines serving as the ethnologist's eyes. This results in a peculiar cinema, not a cinema by bears for humans, but a cinema by robots (that humans are hiding behind) in the bears' midst. In some cases the experiment works, when the camera is receptive to what the bears are doing. In other cases it is less successful, as can happen during any film shoot when the important thing is how the camera allows itself to be affected by the subjects it films.

The day bats will make their own films

When Thomas Nagel speaks of the irreducibility of the bat's subjective experience (and of all perspective by extension), he gives no credit to the power of the imagination: 'Even if I could by gradual degrees be transformed into a bat, nothing in my present constitution enables me to imagine what the experiences of such a future stage of myself thus metamorphosed would be like' (Nagel 1974: 439). Nagel does not believe in Smith's notion of 'an imaginary change of situation', or in empathy defined as the *ability to put oneself in another's place*, the foundation of the moral philosophies of the eighteenth century. If we accept Nagel's argument, a mountable camera on a squid is just as little equivalent to the point of view of a squid as a camera attached to a skier's helmet. And this is for the best, since subjectivity cannot be instrumented. Nagel champions a radical, instrument-free perspectivism to better counter the 'aperspectival objectivity' of the sciences inherited from the eighteenth century.

What happened in the twentieth century? Cinema stayed on the surface of beings (including animals and plants) when capturing their point of view. It has never had any choice but to position itself beside or above them. Even Jean Painlevé, who invented submersible cameras and knew how to capture the strangeness of an octopus by filming its eyes, had no choice but to watch for the slightest movement and patiently circle his subject. At best (or at worst), he opened up the sense organs of these animals, dissecting them like a good scientist, offering odd points of view from inside them, but without ever really being able to connect with their point of view or 'rise to' their perception. If one wants to get inside the head of a dog or bat, to momentarily glimpse the mere possibility of taking their point of view of the world, one has to conduct position-exchange experiments as bizarrely instrumented as those of Eduardo Kac, who connected bats to ultrasonic sensors to catch a glimpse of 'what it is like to be a bat' (see Dobrila and Kostic 2000), or even those of William Wegman, an artist who gets dogs to play composition roles and treat them 'as if' they were humans, applying, in an empathetic spirit, all of the classic elements of the golden age of 'studio perspectivism': if one wants to put oneself in a dog's place, this can be suggested through a trick that involves a certain amount of technological 'circuitousness' (Gell 1988).

Cinema has always had a voracious appetite for new tricks. And as the history of cameras shows, it has never stopped generating new hybridizations, 'impure' views that are neither purely human nor purely animal. Although the form that has hitherto dominated has been a cinema made by humans for humans, the role of human/non-human sharing has been underestimated in our understanding of the genesis of cinema. It was in order to capture soap bubbles that Plateau invented emulsion; he was not trying to achieve an 'impartial' point of view, but wanted to use a device to better see and approach an other-than-human as delicate as a soap bubble. It was a desire to understand the movement of horses that motivated Marey to invent chronophotography; he did not invent it because he was looking for an 'objective' recording technique, but because he wanted to get around the limitations of the human eye and make something 'immeasurable' measurable. And it was in order to film molluscs that Jean Painlevé invented the first submersible cameras – not to get way from them but, on the contrary, to get as close as possible and take their point of view. From the very beginning, the tool has been imperfect, far from the sensitivity of the human eye, and has been in need of improvement. It can serve the most naturalistic projects just as it can serve the most animistic objectives, since behind 'exteriority' or 'objectivity' what is really sought is *difference*. Optics are proliferating in every direction, from wide-angle lenses to fisheye lenses, in order to approach the 'perfection' of the human eye or animal vision (the eyes of fish and flies, 360° vision, etc.). Jean Epstein was not wrong when he said of Jean Comandon's first scientific films (*La Croissance des Végétaux*, etc.) 'A new animism has been reborn in the world. Seeing it, we now know that we are surrounded by non-human existences' (Epstein 1974 [1935]: 61). Only a minority of scientific circles considered cameras 'impartial' recording tools. For others – beginning with those who used them – cameras were machines that had their own sensibility, which had to be mastered and 'placed in the service' of another point of view, that of the person filming. And if they provoke so much fascination, this is because they generate point-of-view disparities, generate *another* point of view, before being objective or subjective. So there is another history of cinema to be written, one that is truly 'perspectivist'. Cinema was very early 'cannibalized' by innumerable perspectives, quickly taken in highly experimental directions. But will everything have been said once cameras have been repatriated by non-humans? The history of cinema will only be beginning (again), from an alternative point of view.

To put oneself in the place of a bat, an elephant, a jellyfish (Land 2012) or even a plant, we need other eyes, other senses and therefore other technical means. One is reminded of the nineteenth-century work of Gustav Fechner, the founder of psychophysics, who considered the question of whether or not plants had a soul and concluded, after examining the work of the botanists of his time, that they had one, but that it was radically different from ours (Fechner 1848). Though questionable, Cleve Backster's (1968) experiments on plants in the 1960s contained a genuinely radical perspectivism. More than a century after Fechner's experiments on plant sensitivity, this biologist and former CIA lie-detector specialist advocated the notion of 'primary perception', using a polygraph to demonstrate that plants were extrasensitive to a range of things we do not perceive. The day bats' perception will have no mystery for us, when glasses will be worn to see the world like a dog, fly or praying mantis, then mounted perspectivism will have undergone a new change, towards a form of *radical* perspectivism. This leap might also imply something else: a total abandonment of the 'optical' notion of point of view.

Conclusion

In conclusion, let's return to the philosophical question: How to put oneself in the place of another? Whereas cinema multiplied 'popular experiments' on the subject, philosophical perspectivism never really answers this question.

Either it invokes negotiation or imagination (in moral philosophy), or states its impossibility (as in Nagel's work). But never does it consider the instruments of such an operation – instruments made not with a view to impartiality, but with a view to possibly adopting perspectives and conducting *position-exchange* experiments. From the on-board point of view of the squid to that of the gorilla, into which viewers undergo the extraordinary experience of teleportation, accompanying it in its escape from liana to liana, we can see that it all concerns the same problem. For now, the most accessible means we have found for *putting oneself in someone else's place*, is to *hook onto them*. The King Kong episode shows all of the effort required to make this experience possible. The shot is mastered, miraculously. The camera itself is the hook. Any shot intended for an audience contains mounted perspectivism, but this is revealed as such only from the moment the camera becomes mobile and can carry viewers along in their movement, not only capturing the world from a certain point of view, but carrying the world and the viewers into a shot. In this sense, one can understand why cinema has always oscillated between a soft and ambiguously floating form of perspectivism and a radical form, and why it has never lost hope of being the main instrument for expressing the latter. It continues to aim for this by inventing platforms that are as flexible as possible. Not seeking it would amount to depriving itself of all of its possibilities. Cinema has never really provided a completely satisfying answer to the question, 'What is it like to be a squid?' It has answered another question: 'What is it like to be *on-board* a squid?', allowing some ambiguity to remain about what is transmitted between the squid and the camera attached to it. But faced with the scale of the challenge, neither has it ever wanted to give up, knowing that something can indeed be transmitted, giving rise to this imperfect, hybrid and probably transitory form of mounted perspectivism. When subjectivities are more and more instrumented (or pretend to be), what needs to be evaluated is no more the degree of equivalence between the mounted cam's point of view and the body to which it is attached. It is the quantity of novelty that the mounted device transmits, or in other words, how perceptual differences can make their path through it.

Notes

1 See for instance the recent debates about Eduardo Viveiros de Castro's (2014) 'amerindian perspectivism'.
2 http://chimpcam.com.

References

Backster, C. 1968. Evidence of a primary perception in plant life. *International Journal of Parapsychology*, 10(4), 329–348.

Daston, L. 1999. Objectivity and the escape from perspective. In: Biagioli, M. ed., *The Science Studies Reader*. New York: Routledge, pp. 110–123.

Deleuze, G. 1988. *Le Pli, Leibniz et le Baroque.* Paris: Minuit.

Dobrila, T. and Kostic, A. eds. 2000. *Eduardo Kac: Telepresence, Biotelematics, and Transgenic Art.* Maribor/Slovenia: Kibla.

Epstein, J. 1974 [1935]. *Photographie de l'impondérable.* In: *Ecrits sur le Cinéma Vol. 1: 1921–1947.* Paris: Seghers.

Fechner, G. T. (1848). *Nanna, oder über das Seelenleben der Pflanzen* [*Nanna, or On the Spiritual Life of Plants*]. Moscow: Ripol Classic.

Gell, A. 1988. Technology and magic. *Anthropology Today,* 4(2), 6–9.

Grimaud, E. 2004. *Bollywood Film Studio.* Paris: CNRS Editions.

Grimaud, E. 2007. The film in hand. Modes of coordination and assisted virtuosity in the Bombay film studios. *Qualitative Sociology Review,* 3(3), 59–77.

Grimaud, E. 2013. Pacts of embodiment: a comparative ethnography of filmmakers' gestures. In: Szczepanik, P. and Vonderau, P. eds, *Behind the Screen.* Basingstoke: Palgrave Macmillan, pp. 61–72.

Land, M. 2012. *Animal Eyes.* Oxford: Oxford University Press.

Lefebvre, F. 2000. *La vertu des images. Analogie, proportion et métaphore dans la genèse des sciences sociales au 18ème siècle. Revue de synthèse,* 121(1/2), 45–77.

Nagel, T. 1974. What it is like to be a bat? *Philosophical Review,* LXXXIII, 435–450.

Science World Report. 2013. Hidden camera captures rare moments of what squids see underwater. 29 March. www.scienceworldreport.com/articles/5900/20130329/hidden-camera-captures-rare-moments-what-squids-see-underwater.htm#ixzz3LltgvFfE.

Serres, M. 1968. *Le Système de Leibniz et ses Modèles Mathématiques.* Paris: Presses Universitaires de France.

Smith, A. 2002 [1759]. *The Theory of Moral Sentiments.* Cambridge: Cambridge University Press.

Viveiros de Castro, E. 2014. *Cannibal Metaphysics: Amerindian Perspectivism.* Minneapolis, MN: University of Minnesota Press.

Whitehead, A. N. 1929. *Process and Reality: An Essay in Cosmology.* New York: Macmillan.

Interview 1

5 For a sociology of *maquettes*

An interview with Antoine Hennion

Antoine Hennion and Ignacio Farías

Antoine Hennion: But are there really uses of the word 'studio' outside of the arts? You know, I am just wondering … empirically.

Ignacio Farías: Well, architects, for example, tend to call their workplace the office. They speak of studios to refer to the practice-based workshops at the university. There are quite interesting discussions regarding the tension between the design studio at the university, which is often constructed as a space freed from constraints, and the office … and how architects, when they move from the studio to the office, get confronted with such limitations.

Antoine Hennion: Well, the studio is usually linked to creation. So, empirically you can observe different ways of referring to the studio. For instance, when a kind of device is needed or a dedicated space with devices: an equipped space, dedicated to a kind of production. So perhaps the challenge for ethnographies of studios is to seriously consider what it means to produce things that did not exist. And to do so not by returning to metaphysical issues about creation, but by looking at the spaces, devices and techniques invented to allow invention. In a sense, this quite looks like the STS [Science and Technology Studies] way of dealing with creation, a difficult point: as long as connections come before entities, 'creating' cannot mean producing something new from nobody knows where!

Ignacio Farías: Still we could ask: why the studio? Why should we care about this rather isolated space, when we know from your work and from the work of others that cultural products have long lives and careers, as they go through different mediations and are transformed depending on the networks of people, things, they mobilize each time? So my question is, why the studio? What can we find in the studio that we don't find anywhere else?

Antoine Hennion: To say that things are coordinated and circulate through certain networks doesn't mean that everything is automatically connected. It has to be done. Hence studios! Proofs, trials, tests and so on first have to be made. This is why producers have dedicated special spaces, in both the physical and the organizational sense of the word, involving times, moments and precise people gathering. It is a very good technique, already explored by early STS. The two cases that I have in mind are scientific laboratories, studied by Bruno Latour and Steve Woolgar (1979), and the production of *musique de variétés* – my first paper, in fact (Hennion 1989 [1983]). Artistic directors and producers of popular music really needed the studio, not as a way to 'create' what would then be marketed and sold to a public, but to experiment in a limited, confined space a first loop of production–consumption: it is a way of testing in vitro the first reactions of a real audience, constituted by people in the studio (Hennion 1989 [1983]).

Still, if you have a kind of mechanical or sophisticated organizational view on how work is done, with a clear division between creators, producers, advertisers, the marketing teams and so on, then, I would say, the material organization of co-production is not really a studio. Producers need a studio because things are open, they are not given, they do not belong a priori to one kind of professionals – which implies that a professional can only be a bad spokesperson, even of things he knows better. She needs other eyes, other ears than hers. Studio is a place where realities may be *deployées*, spread out, made present, re-presented – with a hyphen – by diverse professionals. It doesn't mean, either, that their speciality does not count, that it would be only a label. All those people are not just participating in a kind of spontaneous brainstorming session. On the contrary, they do come together with their competencies, expertise, knowledge. But in the studio nobody can apply any fixed knowledge. Instead they engage with their bodies, they negotiate with others, depending on what happens, with the possibility of being surprised, and of commuting roles. So, say, in the music studio I am officially the one who writes the lyrics, but as I am sitting there, listening to the work, taking up the role of the public, or reacting to the music, or blaming the sound. The studio allows changing roles, incarnating, embodying the relationships between different kinds of reality, putting them together. All those components come from outside, brought by the professionals, but to become a song they have to be tested, put into question, mixed, and so on. Technically, this also means all this is not a matter only of ideas and disputes: it heavily relies on material intermediaries, as sketches, drafts, more or less elaborated *maquettes* – anything that can resist, respond and provoke new ideas. Just like laboratories in the case of science (Latour and Woolgar 1979), a studio is a place that makes this possible.

The main experience of the studio, I think, the one we are talking about here, is that it is *situated*, in a very active way. Entering a studio is deciding to situate things: collaborations, producers, drafts of things and *maquettes*. Then, on the basis of that, it can go elsewhere: things resist, it is not that, people react, correct, etc. Saying this is still a common-sense thing. But there is something more here: people have the right to be completely incoherent, precisely because of the presence of things. Let's say that I was defending an idea about the guy who sings in a music studio, or about the presence of particles or waves in a laboratory. But then I see the thing, I listen to the others commenting on it, and it gives me an embodied experience, knowledge and other ideas. And I am not defending my first position any more. I have been put elsewhere, redirected by this *maquette*, which is anything but a closed thing, now it is resisting, it has its own presence, it is not just a producer's will or fantasy … 'Place yourself at the point of view of the thing's *doing*', William James (1909, p. 262) was already asking! This way of materializing the heterogeneity of what is produced by creators is a very important matter. Even in the imaginary of people, this is what a studio is … a guy, a model and a sketch, and it's enough, the sketch of the statue doesn't belong any more to the sculptor. It's about the woman, and the paper and charcoal, or the marble. The presence of the thing makes the sculptor do the sculpture (Souriau 2009 [1956]) … So if we consider this active role that things play and also this precise realization, in the strong sense of the word, of the collaboration among several people, who have different knowledge and experiences, and meet and confront through a thing, through a presence, a present thing, a *maquette*, then maybe we better understand why they come to the studio.

They need a space, they need equipment, they need things that allow, and this is another aspect, *repetition*. If we are in this room and we have an idea, but 'ah, nothing is there, we can't try it'… no, no! You need the media, the computers, the paint: to have all that material and equipment gathered. This is the idea of the studio as a kind of reservoir, an *atelier*. *Atelier* means workshop in French, or the studio in the case of a painter: all those words are very close in this regard, they name a place where you have all the things that you usually need. And if something is missing, you see that it is missing, so you have to get it for the next time: okay, we'll order this and this. This idea of *gathering* is important.

So, one by one, we recollect several important properties of this idea of the studio. And I think the other aspect that is very present in both *Laboratory Life* (Latour and Woolgar 1979) and my *musique de variétés* paper (Hennion 1989 [1983]) is the relationship with the outside. As long as you do everything together, as you are both producing something here and having in mind that it is something for the world market, things are confused. The idea of the studio is something like a performative separation: 'No. The world is outside. Let's first do what we can do here': so instead of an unclear mixture we have both, a studio on one side, and the world outside. But there is nothing in the studio! So we have first to incorporate, to put in what we need, so there is something. We need to consider what things, what relationships have to enter into the studio. And then, once it is there, it is kept from everything, so in a sense we have to re-establish the connection that we had just cut. It is a mediation. My work on mediation is exactly about this (Hennion 2015 [1993]). You don't have the world or the thing like that. You first have to isolate – although not because you believe in purity. Nothing is less pure than what happens there. But all these things have to be tested, proven, etc. So, if there should be a connection, then you have to create it first.

Ignacio Farías: There is a burgeoning of new work focusing on how cultural objects and products move from one site to another, from one time to the next. We seem to have moved from the study of social contexts to the study of how objects circulate, but have somehow missed this precise moment that you are talking about: the moment of realization, in the strong sense, of composition, of creation. Why does the sociology of culture encounter so many difficulties with engaging with this kind of event, a primary moment of creation … ?

Antoine Hennion: [*Long silence*] I am staying silent, because this is a long-running debate in the sociology of culture. How can sociology take creation into account? The trend of sociology is to treat things as signs, to treat them as tokens. If, as a sociologist, you have at your disposal general causes, or grammars of action, then you don't care about how objects are concretely produced. However, neither do we want to return to essentialist conceptions of objectivity. We then need a new mode of analysis, as STS has begun to do for science and technique. Concerning culture, it means forgetting the idea of a 'creation' in favour of an attention to the way things move, gather, produce new configurations, coalesce through resisting connections: i.e. form a new object. It is not a question of creation, it's resistance, it's something coalescent: like a sauce that sets, something *prend*. It's about appearing, and then resisting, being something else, and re-enabling new relationships. So a solution which is always quite good is to look at how people work with things. Still, you can then just consider this as conventions: okay, it's an organization – and you go back to sociology. But instead you can consider gestures, you have the materials, you have spaces, you have the equipment, you have machinery and, of course, bodies. And here, you are much closer to confront with this connected production of things – quite a good way of defining studio work, no?

Technically, I believe the word 'creation' should be put in quotations marks. It's better to treat things that are new in a different way. We are not forced at all, except by the blinding lens of disciplines, to oppose circulation (left to history and sociology) and primary moments (left to aesthetics). Haskell offers an extraordinary example here – the close analysis of Roman statues he has provided, with Penny (Haskell and Penny 1981; see my comment in Hennion 2007a). The great art historians do not care much about theoretical statement. But they study statues in a completely symmetrical way, in the sense of STS showing how the objects emerge exactly in the same way as they analyse how they circulate. It is the same thing: getting broken, forgotten statues out of the earth because the King of France wants to connect with the classical Rome, creating a demand with wealthy people or noble men wanting them in their garden, setting up an international market, displaying them in museums, having whole industries of reproduction, developing a historical knowledge on the antique *ateliers*. Nothing is primary here: is it the object? Come on. The statues change all the time, they are reproduced all the time, at the beginning they are broken, buried pieces. Is it taste, or convention? At first, nobody cares about them. Then they are appreciated for every reason, the less present being their aesthetic value. Haskell and Penny show beautifully, for instance, that the very idea of an original is an outcome of the story: the concept of originality that the increasing importance of the statues has slowly imposed is precisely what will make them fall down from their pedestals in the twentieth century, as pale copies of Greek lost originals. For 500 years they were the *summum* of classical beauty, and in 50 years, they become boring models for students in art schools. Exactly the same argument that makes their success is the one that Haskell uses to explain their failure.

So, you never know which is first: the demand, the circulation, the expectations, the physical objects, or the material work to make them appear. And it's largely studio work. So, where do we go for studying contemporary creation? We can adopt this perfectly tuned *suivi*, this way of following an entangled story with the things, the way we use them, and the changes of the categories through which we like them. Appreciation, pricing and physically producing them is the same story. Nothing like a creation and then a reception: in a kind of circular move, statues and the taste for statues co-produce their own common history, and modify their own frame of evaluation. The beauty of the case is that there is no creation. I mean, we have new objects, many new objects, but they have never been created. That's wonderful. This is a kind of analysis we need to resume the broken web between the sociology of culture and objects.

Ignacio Farías: In *La Passion Musicale* (Hennion 2015 [1993]) you speak of the new history of art as an inspiring discipline because it focuses on all these mediations. What kind of disciplinary traditions do you think might be relevant for approaching the studio?

Antoine Hennion: Well, the history of art is certainly good, but I kind of idealized it, as we often do for other disciplines than ours. I certainly cannot idealize sociology any more! So it was easier to select, in fact, to choose very precise scholars out a lot of history of art. And they are not that rare. Not every discipline has such people as Haskell, Alpers on Rembrandt's studio (1988), or so many others as Baxandall (1972), Marin (1989), Ginzburg (1975), Settis (1978)! And they all did different jobs with incredibly exciting enlightenments.

Another field that has always interested Latour is the anthropology of techniques, all this research focusing on forms of work, gestures, bodies, as did Leroi-Gourhan (1943, 1964) and Simondon (1958) in France. Latour fought with some of these guys, who were anthropologists both in the social sense of the word, but also in a nearly naturalist sense. But in Leroi-Gourhan, for instance, we can find out from prehistory a kind of aesthetic reconception of what it means to deal with things, tools, nature, objects. The sociology of work is also a strong tradition that has focused on working – if not on the work as an outcome of work. The studio is maybe what connects these two meanings of 'work': work as practice and work as product. But anyway, compared to other forms of sociology, in the sociology of work things are present. They are more or less taken for granted, be they fabricated or natural objects, but they are there. When sociologists of work go and see what people in the arts do, and they are clever and witty, as in the case of some studies on cinema production, a real collective may appear, including its materiality. So, either you have your disciplinary lens, and from all the things done in the studio you pick up only the conventions, values, organizational issues, collaborations, and you just see very small, abstracted parts of the game. Or you open your eyes, and this formation really helps you see what's going on there: 'doing things together', as long as you give all their importance to all of the three words in Howard Becker's title (1986) and do not forget things, as usual, then it is a very relevant programme to study studios. And actually such a work may interest studio practitioners: nothing is more reflexive than the studio, they'll wonder how to better organize what they are doing together.

I don't know, maybe cooking might offer an interesting case too: it's just good dishes, but how to do good dishes? The theory of action can be present here. Recipe, for example, is an excellent case to show, with Wittgenstein, that we might always be repeating the same mayonnaise, but we can't apply rules. It is always a little warmer or more humid in the kitchen, or a different flour. And every good cook would say: 'Oh, yes of course, I put a little bit of this ingredient that wasn't in the recipe.' How do I know this! But at the same time, we have recipes. This is not about 'genius'. So looking at this may be very helpful for us, because it is a kind of localized, situated, equipped, bodily experience of what it is to produce things, in which things themselves participate in the acting.

Ignacio Farías: Do you think the notion of craftsmanship can help us to think about what occurs in the studio?

Antoine Hennion: Well, sure, as long as you don't turn craftsmanship into a one single argument. It is a nice idea, as it refers to this closeness of things and this *tour de main* or manual skill that produces a sort of double-sided valorization: the preciosity of things valorizes my knowledge, my *savoir faire*, my know-how; and my craftsmanship valorizes precious things. Apart from this, the notion of craftsmanship is a bad *topos* in art history, because it has been used mainly to draw a one-way long historical progression from artisan to artist, from craftsmanship to art. It is a rather simplistic idea, because at the same time every artist says exactly the opposite: 'I am nothing but a craftsman.' It is not at all a linear story, it looks more like a double-helix one, both defining an autonomous field and overdeveloping specific abilities. And when we enter the studio, we see this still very present dimension, in fact the studio is a kind of reminder of it: a way of getting back to the core of activities, and the core of artistic activity is craftsmanship.

Ignacio Farías: Let me move on to your empirical studies of studios. In your work on the producer of popular music (Hennion 1989), the central issue you discuss is how producers play a central role in bringing the public into the studio, by trying, for example, to convince musicians about what the public is like or would want to hear. Then, in '*Le design industriel, entre création, technique et marché*' together with Sophie Dubuisson (1995), you look mainly at the multiple ways in which designers connect with or mobilize aesthetic criteria or aesthetic values, for example by having a couple of 'crazy' designers in the studio.

Antoine Hennion: Yes. In design, things are a little biased, as you know. You never think of arts without having in mind users and markets too. All sentences are very ambivalent. If one would say I am just making art, he wouldn't be a designer any more. That's why they are always trying to have spokespersons of the users, of the markets, of materials, etc.

Ignacio Farías: Right, but in both studies the main focus was posed on this kind of tension between artistic, aesthetic considerations, on the one hand, and economic, audience, market considerations, on the other. Is this tension, you think, the key thing to study studios?

Antoine Hennion: Yes, I would say so. It's another way of saying the same thing. I think studying studio is something like an anthropology of *maquettes*. And what is a *maquette*? It's precisely a material, technical way of getting rid of such oppositions: here are the constraints, here is the brief on the product, here are the requirements of the users, etc. But how can I connect that? Well, by making them present in a thing that is open and provisional. The *maquette* is an empirical materialization of the plurality of things. So it is very crucial. There are products already in the market. It is not a matter of having ideas in the bathroom, then. The question is rather, how can I produce some kind of fragile doubles of these already existing products and of my ideas, how can I produce things that are precisely between the two, that are filling up the space between them? *Maquettes* do this.

So, another way of saying it: nothing is more misleading than all these dualisms, materiality and idea, ordinary work and creation, imagination and reality. *Maquette* is precisely a way of saying that practically. *Maquette* is half an image made thing, half a thing made image, and it gives life to these images. Then I can be between the two. I am in front of a material thing, which is not really yet the object. Producing this kind of intermediary object, intermediary between, well, between these kinds of layers of virtualities – although virtualities is probably a too strong word – and putting into form, materializing this inequality in the stability of material, that's exactly what people do with *maquettes*. To describe this with words is not an easy task, as you can see, but we are not producing a kind of esoteric analysis either: what is a *maquette* for everybody? It's starting from an idea, having a kind of brief, so it is on the paper with certain properties, making it with a very light material so we can change it, that's it. It's there, but we can change it without having to break everything. It's an intermediary level of stabilization and resistance.

You were searching notions that can feed your studio studies idea. For sure, *maquette* is one: the making of *esquisses* [sketches], models and forms. In French, a *forme* is what you put in shoes to make them (a 'last' in English, I think): you need to draw on materials to make other materials; you need the first form to produce another one. And for all of this we have to invent words, because they are all *between*: forms, objects, images, creative ideas and realizations. All this is about realization. I mean, if we take really seriously the notion of realization – that is, anything but reification, or rei-fication indeed, but taken seriously: the making of things. Trying to see how things give ideas and how ideas are emerging in new things that are *pétries*, kneaded; *sculptées*, formed.

So, indeed, 'studios studies' is a good idea. If we sum up key issues already raised, well, it's not that bad. One is the co-organization of work both as relationship to everything, made possible by gathering diverse professionals, and as separation, centralization, concentration on a precise task they can discuss, negotiate – because it has been isolated and materialized, and they have organized their local confrontation. Another one is the dedication of a space, time, material to that work. It must be at a certain place and can't be everything, so it has to be cut from the world. Then, two other aspects are maybe more central. One concerns the intermediaries, material forms: we really need to launch an anthropology of *maquettes*! And the other is the double sense of 'work', as a work, and as the work to produce the work.

Ignacio Farías: One of the things that can be very problematic, or simply wrong, in many approaches to this, is that the users, markets and publics that are brought into the work process are often seen only as a constraint. This is a very easy game, an Adorno-type of game, where the industrial logic of commoditization and capital accumulation puts the constraints, and high culture is seen as a space of autonomy and freedom.

Antoine Hennion: Yes, this is too simple. People say so, but at the same time, see, the idea of productive constraints, which is a Foucauldian idea, is very strong among professionals. In a sense, it was already the case for Adorno himself. Sure, when he speaks of markets, he is taken by a negative pseudo-marxism (1967), but when he speaks of music, it is exactly like about craftsmanship (1997 [1970]). No, we are not creating anything, there is an idea, there is form, musical forms, and how can we cope with that? Of course, it is in a completely different aesthetics, but when he comes to the core of matter, musical material, he is not that far from the studio. But I think you're right. It's not a problem of the professionals, it's a problem of the theories of the professionals, and stereotyped views of creation, that Adorno's analyses do hold, yes. The notion of marketing, for example, would be much better understood from a 'studio studies' perspective: it means markets have to be done, forged, by forms and *maquettes*. Marketing is *maquetting*! Markets are not abstractions; users and objects have to be put into gear: this is what marketers do. They bring their representatives (human or material) much closer one to the other and, because they're much closer, they see their differences more clearly. That's the game of studio: people working together. Marketers are the studio people of markets, maybe that's why they're seen as the creative part of the corporation.

And it was the same argument in our paper on advertising agencies (Hennion and Méadel 1989), where everyone focuses on the *maquette*. The spokesperson of the public or the user is also a *maquette*. I don't have a public in front of me, I don't have a market in front of me, but I represent them through a person or a body, which enables a discussion about it, so I have a kind of productive constraint there. It's not enough to have a quite beautiful idea, if each time you take the *maquette* it breaks down. So that's a productive constraint: try the same thing, but so that the thing doesn't break in my hand.

Ignacio Farías: You have mentioned a couple of important dimensions to have in mind when approaching the studio: how working together works, craftsmanship, the anthropology of *maquettes*, the space of the studio and so on. Could you tell me something about the differences with regard to these between the music studios and design studios you have studied?

Antoine Hennion: I'm afraid I won't answer, not because the issue is not important; to the contrary, it's so crucial that it needs in-depth enquiries on each case. So I will just support the question. Instead of making a theory of cultural production through using one case after the other, the idea of making studio studies would be precisely to gather them first, to make a studio of studios, and then to see concrete differences, that would be much more relevant than abstract ones, as between music and movies, or design. Yes, this is typically a work to be done. And maybe one criterion of success for a book like this should be whether at the end we get a differentiated, concrete way of understanding studios, with an 's', in their multiplicity – or we have a kind of abstract, general model of a studio, that we could apply to any field – which I would find much less interesting.

Ignacio Farías: But still, at the abstract level, the studio we have been talking about could be described as an *agencement*, in the sense of putting multiple things together that do something, in an active way.

Antoine Hennion: Yes, indeed *agencements* is a notion very connected to the studio.

Ignacio Farías: So, following on from this, an important question is, what role does the notion of *attachment* play in thinking about the studio? How can we use the notions *agencements* and *attachments*, and what kind of 'things' do they bring into play?

Antoine Hennion: One answer to this question is that these approaches, inspired by actor–network theory (ANT), are a way of shifting, of taking in charge the passive/active problem in a different way. But there is a bias here. As we are dealing with questions of production, in the studio, then the words we use are charged with a strongly active polarity: like assemblage, insisting on the heterogeneity of what is assembled; *agencement*, stressing the fact that it has to do with producing something, and something that is required, paid for or expected; or translation, stressing that it has to circulate. All those words refer to an active mode. By contrast, attachments are charged with a more passive polarity, they refer to what makes us be what we are, or do what we do, or like what we like. It does not mean we're just passive, socially determined, as in Bourdieu's theory of taste. It's more a question of *se laisser faire*, let oneself be oneself by realizing what we're attached to: this is passive, and active too. A form of passivity that is nothing but passive – attachment is a kind of activated passivity, an art of actively making oneself be passive (Hennion 2007b, 2010a, 2013). So, looking at music amateurs, for instance, led me to insist on what is already there, in our hearts and souls and in objects: all that resists and makes us realize what we are, or what touches us. It's all about this kind of resistance, a positive resistance. Loving music is a way of making the things that hold us more active, present, eventually transformed. But it implies we actively do something.

In the studio, attachments are all that extremely heterogeneous material, not easy to translate, that the people gathered there bring back into the production process, so that they can eventually be assembled into a work. To answer your question more directly, I think the mistake of critical approaches to culture, like Adorno's, is to take for granted that representing audiences, the demand or markets in the production process means that creators obey or follow them – it's just the opposite! This is what the idea of mediation develops (Hennion 2015 [1993]): making them present in the studio allows new ideas, disobedience, surprise – all that happens in front of a *maquette*. On the contrary, it is when you oppose the public or markets as pure concepts that, in fact, you cannot escape them, even and above all if you take the opposite course to them, and then find no other way out than to defend the absolute autonomy of art or creation: radical criticism is a radical idealism. Reality is nothing but a flat, given thing. To overflow it, one first has to frame it, as in a studio. About markets, this is the precise meaning of the dual concept of attachment–detachment proposed by Callon (1998). We're first in a world full of attachments, so that we have to cut some, produce new ones, etc. No detachment if no attachments! No overwhelming without framing, this is very close to studio work. So, yes, the couple attachment–*agencement* is a good describer (Callon and Caliskan 2005).

Composition is interesting too, to say this, and it is a word used by the actors themselves. It's to com-pose, *poser ensemble*, to gather in order to make something … *pas mal*! To express what would be the output of the studio, it is a good word, if understood this way, with the hyphen: it involves making present the things from which we start, and inventing ways (like *maquettes*, trials and so on), to *realize* them, in the double sense of the word: to understand that they are there, and to make them more real, present in the studio. To compose is indeed to select, to give more importance, to in-form things. It's like going from attachments as a kind of a magma, although it's not a magma at all, because it is full of relations and is very precise, but going from infinite webs of things to a precise realization. So, *agencement* and attachment do not function at all as active versus passive. They are very close to each other. The difference is more like a pass. This passing from attachment to *agencement* would be a good way of describing studio work.

Ignacio Farías: I think this is really important, because a bad interpretation of your work could be: 'he looks at music amateurs and drug users, which are both on the side of consumption'. So, one could conclude that attachment is about consumption and *agencement* about production. This is also a problem I find in the literature, when people approach studios as sites of production that would be completely detached or separated from consumption. So, bringing in this dynamic pass from attachment to *agencement* could …

Antoine Hennion: Well yes, it's funny you see: in my first 1983 paper on *musique de variétés*, when I was not aware of a lot, I already used the expression 'production–consumption' to convey just that idea: it is not first, the production of musical hits and then, consumption. It's a production–consumption from the beginning in the studio. They are listening to it already and it's an enlargement of production–consumption, so the target was exactly what you mention.

Ignacio Farías: And still, even though you were in close contact with Michel Callon and Bruno Latour, you developed your own vocabulary to approach cultural objects. I think one of the major risks of being too much inspired by laboratory studies when studying studios is that you come to the studio with a lot of questions concerning cognition. And, of course, cognitive processes are very important in the studio, and making things appear is a cognitive problem as well. But there seems to be something more in the studio that's not just about cognition and distributed cognition, which is about making things real in a kind of ontological sense. Although Latour would also argue that Pasteur was making microbes real in an ontological way. So this is a difficult issue, but what is the status of cognition in studios?

Antoine Hennion: Well, it's true: labs are not only about cognition. Otherwise you miss a point. Microbes are realized. So, I have no answer for that, apart from taking seriously the idea of making differences appear for each kind of studio. If you have to produce new sales, if you have to produce new mathematical theorems or if you have to produce musical hits, it won't be the same. The differences are very concrete, but it's all about *maquettes*, realization, all the different stuff you gather following what you do. How could we speak of the difference between ways of making things appear (like science or music) without referring to all this precise material in labs or studios? I don't think it's possible. So I wouldn't fight to make them different, because even this fighting could be recognized as a sort of dualism: 'science is about knowledge and art is about creation'. But science is creation too, and art is a knowledge. So let's take theorems as things in the labs, and let's take things as theorems in the studio, in sculpture, movies, photographs, and let us just show how, by diverse means, people in labs and studios compose what they make appear from different materials. There is no more beautiful expression than 'matters matter'. Arts are about making matters matter. The main difference in arts is not about forms and so on, but about materials. Each time you think it as something that belongs to ideas, well, it's the opposite, you try to define a kind of ideal idea of art, be it poetry, painting, music and so on, in spite of their diverse material: it's just nonsense.

Ignacio Farías: So, should we take John Dewey's notion of expression (1985 [1934]), which he develops precisely in connection to the artist and how art is produced, or Souriau's (2009 [1956]) notion of instauration, which is about aesthetic objects, also as models to think about what occurs in the laboratory?

Antoine Hennion: I don't know. At the same time, I do prefer James's wording of *pragmata*, those things 'in their plurality' (1911: 210), in a world 'still in process of making' (ibid.: 226), than Dewey's one: things that 'are what they are experienced as' (Dewey, 1905: 393), a phrase which re-centres the process on human beings. Instead, James writes: 'What really exists is not things made, but things in the making' (1909: 263). He would make a perfect godfather for studio studies! What is beautiful in Souriau is his extreme idea in *l'œuvre à faire* that art is 'for' nothing. Not for a public, of course, but by saying so, he doesn't defend at all the idea of an art for the sake of art. He sees art as a sort of voice given to the work – *l'œuvre tend la main* [the work holds out the hand]. His focus is on this emergence of things, this power of the *œuvre* that is not what we created, but a kind of call to be created. *Œuvre à faire*, to be done, this means precisely that: not that it is 'open' or incomplete, but that the work is an empty, but compelling, obligation addressed to its creator, without providing the creator with any positive answer. That's why Souriau speaks rather of an instauration of things: it's a question of making them be, not of creating them from scratch. It is a suggestive comment on the *Pygmalion* myth, this philosophical tale about a sculpture that escapes her creator and lives her own life. Such an aesthetics does meet our concerns about making things arise: Souriau's *retour à l'œuvre* is one possible format of the presence of things. It is expressive, sure.

Ignacio Farías: Do you think the notion of ex-pression would be more fitting: the idea of squeezing out material forms?

Antoine Hennion: Yes. The double meaning is very appropriate. Etymology can sometimes be misleading, but here, the fact that the same word means both to say what we feel and we didn't know, and to take a piece of earth and press it to make an object appear, is quite incredible. *Ex-primer* … to press a lemon, or say what you are: same thing, same gesture. In both cases, a coming out! In the work of Souriau, there is always this idea that something gets out, like Athena from the sea. This is a conventional theme of what art is about. Art is not about beauty. It is this *retour des choses*, this emergence. Work is a beautiful word, indeed, it expresses this expression.

Of course, any word is misleading too. It's true with expression. It can be used in quite a weak sense, like saying that art is about expressing the sensibility of our times. Okay, yes, but … ! At the same time, all those common-sense expressions always do say the truth, even if in bad ways, even if partially. And if art does not take in charge this 'expression of the sensibility of our times' in one way or another, indeed, it's not doing its job, it's not working. When, in front of a contemporary artwork, people say *c'est n'importe quoi!* ('what a nonsense!') they may be literally right: the French phrase exactly means 'what it is has no importance!' This means that the tie with what art should make, a surprise, an expression of something unknown is broken. It's really a way of saying 'this work doesn't work'. The same when people say 'a child could do that', sophisticated critics read it as a naïve nostalgia for well crafted works, but no, let's listen to them, they mean the connection is not made, it's very different. So, yes, always listen to people who express the truth badly. Well, all this expression stuff is not that easy to connect with what we were saying before, but it is connectable, I think.

Ignacio Farías: One last topic: politics. We have been talking about the 'realization' of things, and not just in the case of the arts, but also in design and architecture, where what is at stake is a cosmopolitics, an ontological politics about the real. So how could we approach the issue of the political in connection to studios? Is it a new form or a new site for political action?

Antoine Hennion: I think this is too general. It would be interesting to look at cases that look like a studio but formally are in the political game, like when raw people try to get new ideas before elections or, more interestingly, when little assemblies gather because a local issue arises, performing the shift from representative to participatory democracy. And to look at these forms as getting closer to the studio work because, as in studios, there people know less about the stakes and know less about the answers, and the list of actors and issues is open, in a very Deweyian approach (Dewey 1927). Why not consider this as a kind of political studio? This doesn't answer your grand question, it just introduces the studio as a tool to analyse something that exists in politics.

Another side of the question is what we would see in the studio as being politics, that is officially nothing political. Even if somehow emphatic, I would say that as a studio is a way of making a new world, it does politics. I think it's true. That's the main idea. There is no way now to address politics, or cosmopolitics, without first filling back the world we are talking about with things. In that sense, even if we didn't talk about politics from the beginning, we did, as we have only talked about concrete ways of giving back its importance to the massive presence of objects, in a very open way: ties, networks, connection, assemblage. Probably the case is quite general: now we can only speak of politics when we don't use the word. Because if you take politics as a specialty, then to compose a world, it can't be done. If you name it politics, in the traditional sense, you have already cut it from too many things. And this is precisely what lay people are concerned about. They say politicians … why 'ticians'? Because if they only do politics, they don't make politics any more. It is common sense and it is true. If you are fighting about the post of deputy, then … come on. Are there some debated issues? Okay, that is politics. But often politicians are not debating any more … Sure, there is another way of doing politics, a Deweyan one: collecting things, making issues arise, assembling assemblies and getting people concerned. This reminds us of studios: it's a way of both bringing the world back to us, and creating small enclosures with precise devices, procedures … Maybe participatory democracy is inventing the studios of our common will. It exists, everyone is now sensitive for the environment. From all these new ways of composing a world with things, and things with a world, we are more and more aware of the co-production of cosmopolitics. But probably we see it better if we forget about politics. It would be a return towards pure politics, or the autonomy of a profession: maybe we kill politics if we name it.

Ignacio Farías: There is also another aspect to this. If you look at discourses of contemporary art, it's not just that everything is very political, critical. And this political claim is also interestingly connected with the idea of a post-studio, which is also connected with a relational aesthetics. So, we are left with the studio as a very romanticized space, and we put art in society, and we do things and transform the social …

Antoine Hennion: Well, this is a bit of normative, but from what we say, it is a mistake. To think that, then, the artist can just be in the world, like that, where everything is there, without needing to perform all the work to make concerns arise, as in a studio. Some contemporary artists also fight against materiality, which is very paradoxical. No matter? Are you sure? This idea that digital things are not material … So, we are producing nothing. 'Nothing.' You sure? 'Nothing' is the ideal of art? It often looks like an idealistic fight against a very poor definition of materiality. It is also a concern about social sciences, if we want them to be considering their objects more respectfully. The way economy and sociology consider art as a non-object raises crude aesthetic and political questions. Is it that art is an activity whose products themselves would not matter? Is the art market a market where objects are arbitrary? Do art amateurs constitute a network of actors interested only in sharing codes? Economists' and sociologists' relentless effort to not address art's value makes them reduce it to an expensive speculation or to a gratuitous social game. I would suggest rather that, by making it a public problem and the result of an enquiry, a pragmatist approach may help address the complicated issue of both evaluating and valuing contemporary art. Reciprocally, this leads to another sort of social and political critique of art which demands that it confronts its responsibility: how does it empower people, give form to emerging identities, and express critical issues? Is art making other worlds possible? But it's another issue, let me just refer to my article on Jeff Koons (Hennion forhtcoming, 2010b).

Ignacio Farías: Yes. This is another mistake because it assumes that the studio was an isolated place, which is wrong. And the other mistake is to say 'we are not in a studio'. But studios are being enacted in whichever sites works are being done. So, when you are an artist and you are intervening in streets, for example, in a way you are also transforming that street into a studio.

Antoine Hennion: Yes, right. And it leads to the more naïve comprehension of what is a public. It's the contrary of Dewey's understanding of it. Instead of having concerned people, it is the *passant*, the passer-by: 'Come on and see!'. So the artist puts himself in a beggar's posture: 'Please, be interested in me'. Then instead of *inter-esting* concerned people by raising novel issues, they have to provoke passers-by to arouse their interest. It looks like something is wrong there!

This interview was conducted in Berlin in July 2011

References

Adorno, T. W. 1967. *Prisms.* London: Neville Spearman.

Adorno, T. W. 1997 [1970]. *Aesthetic Theory.* Minneapolis, MN: University of Minnesota Press.

Alpers, S. 1988. *Rembrandt's Enterprise: The Studio and the Market.* Chicago, IL: University of Chicago Press.

Baxandall, M. 1972. *Painting and Experience in Fifteenth Century Italy.* Oxford: Oxford University Press.

Becker, H. S. 1986. *Doing Things Together.* Evanston, IL: Northwestern University Press.

Callon, M. 1998. An essay on framing and overflowing: economic externalities revisited by sociology. In: Callon, M. ed., *The Laws of the Markets.* Oxford: Blackwell, pp. 244–269.

Callon, M. and Caliskan, K. 2005. *New and Old Directions in the Anthropology of Markets.* Unpublished paper. Wenner-Gren Foundation for Anthropological Research, New York.

Dewey, J. 1905. The postulate of immediate empiricism. *Journal of Philosophy, Psychology and Scientific Methods,* 2(15), 393–399.

Dewey, J. 1927. *The Public and Its Problems.* New York: Holt.

Dewey, J. 1985 [1934]. *Art as Experience.* New York: G. P. Putnam.

Ginzburg, C. 1985. *The Enigma of Piero.* London: Verso.

Haskell, F. and Penny, N. 1981. *Taste and the Antique. The Lure of Classical Sculpture. 1500–1900.* New Haven, CT, London: Yale University Press.

Hennion, A. 1989 [1983]. An intermediary between production and consumption: the producer of popular music. *Science, Technology and human Values* 14(4), 400–424. [French original: *Une sociologie de l'intermédiaire is broken: le cas du directeur artistique de variétés. Sociologie du Travail* 4(83), 459–474.]

Hennion, A. 2007a. Rewriting history from the losers' point of view: French grand opera and modernity. In: Johnson, V., Ertman, T. and Fulcher, J. eds, *Opera and Society,* Cambridge: Cambridge University Press, pp. 330–350.

Hennion, A. 2007b. Those things that hold us together: taste and sociology. *Cultural Sociology,* 1(1), 97–114.

Hennion, A. 2010a. Vous avez dit attachement… ?. In: Akrich, M. et al. eds, *Débordements, élanges en l'honneur de Michel Callon.* Paris: Presses de l'École des Mines, pp. 179–190.

Hennion, A. 2010b. L'art contemporain est-il politique? Création, marché, public. In: Popelard, M.-H. ed., *Art, Éducation, Politique.* Paris: Sandre Actes, pp. 15–32.

Hennion, A. 2013. D'une sociologie de la médiation à une pragmatique des attachements. *SociologieS* [online], 13 June. http://sociologies.revues.org/4353.

Hennion, A. 2015 [1993]. *The Passion for Music.* Farnham: Ashgate.

Hennion, A. Forthcoming. A Plea For Responsible Art. Politics, the market, creation. In: Alexander, V.D., Häyrynen, S., Sevänen, E. eds, *Art and the Challenge of Markets.*

Hennion, A. and Dubuisson, S. 1995. Le design industriel, entre création, technique et marché. *Sociologie de l'Art,* 8, 9–30.

Hennion, A. and Méadel, C. 1989. The artisans of desire: the mediation of advertising between product and consumer. *Sociological Theory,* 7(2), 191–209.

James, W. 1909. *A Pluralistic Universe.* New York: Longmans, Green & Co.

James, W. 1911. *The Meaning of Truth.* New York: Longmans, Green & Co.

Latour, B. and Woolgar, S. 1979. *Laboratory Life: The Social Construction of Scientific Facts.* Beverly Hills, CA, London: Sage.

Leroi-Gourhan, A. 1943. *L'Homme et la Matière.* Paris: Albin Michel.

Leroi-Gourhan, A. 1964. *Le Geste et la Parole.* Paris: Albin Michel.

Marin, L. 1989. *Opacité de la Peinture.* Paris: Usher.

Settis, S. 1978. *La Tempesta Interpretata. Giorgione, i Committenti il Soggetto.* Turin: Einaudi.

Simondon, G. 1958. *Du Mode d'Existence des Objets Techniques.* Paris: Aubier.

Souriau, É. 2009 [1956]. *Du mode d'existence de l'œuvre à faire.* In: Souriau, E. ed., *Les Différents Modes d'Existence*, prés Stengers, I. and Latour, B.. Paris: PUF, pp. 195–217.

Part 2
Topologies

6 Theorizing studio space

Spheres and atmospheres in a video game design studio

James Ash

Introduction

Writing in the first part of his *Spheres* trilogy, Peter Sloterdijk (2011) argues that human existence and dwelling be rethought through the concept of spheres. For Sloterdijk, spheres are forms of shelter that humans generate in order to protect themselves from the openness of the world (Elden and Mendieta 2009, Elden 2013). Spheres are both material architectural forms of inhabitation, such as buildings, and more ephemeral constructions, such as psychological states used to protect oneself from mental harm (Castro Nogueira 2009). Spheres can be understood both as individual bubbles in which humans find themselves, and as shared spaces that allow and enable contact to be possible between beings. For example, a campfire could be considered to generate a sphere in the sense that it provides a focal point for people to gather round, opening a space for conversation and shared warmth, and in doing so separating the campers from the cold and darkness of the woods where the campfire was located. In this sense, the spatial extension of spheres is limited by their capacity for transferring matter or energy between beings. In Sloterdijk's (2011: 13) words: 'the limits of my capacity for transference are the limits of my world'. At the same time, every act of transference is itself the creation or re-enforcement of a sphere and an associated interior in which activity can take place: 'every act of solidarity is an act of sphere formation, that is to say the creation of an interior' (Sloterdijk 2011: 12).

This chapter develops Sloterdijk's account of spheres to theorize the 'spaces' of studio processes. Specifically, it argues that studio space should be understood not as geometric containers in which action takes place, but instead as a series of co-existent spheres and atmospheres that shape the possibilities for action of those who work in studio settings. As I argue throughout the chapter, non-human and technical objects, in concert with human bodies, are key to the construction of spheres and atmospheres. As such, space itself can be theorized as the gaps or spaces between objects, which work to construct a particular sphere and atmosphere of activity.

To make these claims, the chapter examines an ethnographic case study of a video game design studio, which I observed creating a first-person shooting game for Xbox 360, PlayStation 3 and PC. Throughout this case study I show that the many objects utilized in creation of the game help to constitute a multiplicity of spheres and atmospheres of the studio.[1]

To make the argument about the studio as sphere, the chapter is organized into two parts. In the first, I theorize the notion of space in relation to accounts of work and productivity in studios, and argue that space can be understood as sets of spheres which all have their own atmosphere that, in turn, shape the potential for work to occur. In the second part I explicitly develop the concept of 'atmosphere' in relation to the video game studio and show how the various technical objects that make up the studio environment create multiple spheres and atmospheres. In conclusion, the chapter points to how the concepts of spheres and atmospheres contribute to broader understandings of studio spaces.

Spheres, space and atmospheres

When imagining a studio space, we may consider its physical structure, its size and shape, or the objects that exist within that space such as desks, chairs, computers and whiteboards. Work in what might tentatively be called studio studies (after this book) is beginning to recognize the importance of space to how activities unfold within studios. This work has been keen to argue against a purely geometric view of space as a container for action, instead positing a relational view of space. For example, ethnomethodological accounts of studio space argue that 'instead of treating "space" and "place" as "already there" when interaction begins and statically encompassing it as it unfolds, it is proposed that these phenomena are accomplished, maintained and dynamically shaped in and for a particular interaction …' (Broth 2009: 1998).

As Mackenzie (2006) argues, the objects that mediate interactions in studios have important repercussions for the types of space and knowledge generated. In *Cutting Code*, Mackenzie describes the development of a software program at a British company, Knowledge Management Systems (KMS). Tasks associated with the project were assigned to paper cards with different colours and numerical values, which indicated the type and relative difficulty of a task that needed to be completed. The movement of the cards around the studio space at KMS was significant: 'cards were strewn on tables singly and in packs; they were pinned to the memo board in rows and sometimes in envelopes. People walked to the memo board, put cards on and took them off. Individual cards were scattered between workstations … The production, distribution and consumption of these cards threaded through much of the work of the Universal team' (ibid. 2006: 148). For Mackenzie, the movement of the cards and their associated tasks highlighted a contestation of agency:

> whenever code or programming becomes an object of attention as such, agency is contested. Here, the contest was played out between different doctrines for the control of software production. These cards literally

> moved control of the project away from the hands and eyes of the managers.
>
> (ibid.: 148)

Space and agency within a studio are inherently linked. As Mackenzie suggests, the space of KMS was actively produced through the relations between various objects and actors. In turn, this relational account of studio space points to the ways in which any form of knowledge produced within a studio does not simply emerge from individual human bodies or brains, but is co-produced with a range of objects, which in turn produces the space of the studio as a particular location in which particular activities take place (Farías 2015).

While these accounts of studio space are certainly interesting, they also have some limitations. First, they tend to underplay the emotional or affective aspects of labour. In Mackenzie's case, although issues of emotion and affect are raised in relation to KMS, they seem incidental to the type of knowledge and space that is created. Second, when emotion or affect is discussed in relation to studio space, it is often considered a uniquely human phenomenon. That is to say, affects or emotions are implicitly posited as a product or relation between different bio-culturally located human bodies. Here affects and emotions are considered in very human terms as anger, frustration, despondency etc. In doing so, the affective capacities of the non-human are ignored. Instead, non-human objects become considered as background props or tools that have agency only when utilized through human practices.

Against this, and following Yaneva (2009), I want to argue that the affective capacities of non-human objects are absolutely fundamental to how a studio space is produced, and that affect also shapes the potentials for new knowledges and objects to be generated. Affect is not, then, an additive or emergent effect of a relation between human bodies, but is one of the basic components that enables the possibilities and limitations of a space to appear through non-human objects as well. To make this claim, I use the work of Sloterdijk and Anderson to consider studio spaces as constituted through multiple spheres, each with their own atmospheres.

Drawing upon the work of Bohme (1993) and McCormack (2008), Anderson (2009) has developed the concept of atmosphere to discuss the ways in which spaces are loaded with particular feelings that do not seem to originate from any one person or object (Adey et al. 2013, Wetherell 2013). He defines atmosphere as: 'perpetually forming and deforming, appearing and disappearing, as bodies enter into relation with one another. They are never finished, static or at rest' (Anderson 2009: 79). What is crucial to Anderson's account is the notion that:

> On the one hand, atmospheres require completion by the subjects that 'apprehend' them. They belong to the perceiving subject. On the other

> hand, atmospheres 'emanate' from the ensemble of elements that make up the aesthetic object.
>
> (ibid.)

For Anderson, atmospheres are ambiguous and 'emanate from but exceed the assembling of bodies' (ibid.: 80). The concept of atmosphere arguably emerges from a meteorological metaphor of gaseousness. As Anderson suggests, the etymology of atmosphere is based on two roots: 'atmos to indicate a tendency for qualities of feeling to fill spaces like a gas, and sphere to indicate a particular form of spatial organization based on the circle' (ibid.).

Sloterdijk's (2011) notion of spheres offers a linked but alternative concept of atmosphere for thinking about the space of the studio. For Anderson, an atmosphere is an open assemblage of elements that change when new elements enter or leave the scene (also see Paulos et al. 2007, Bille 2014, Edensor 2014, Healy 2014, Shaw 2014). For Sloterdijk, atmospheres emerge within spheres and are specific to those spheres. Elements of objects that might affect the atmosphere of a sphere cannot simply leave or enter freely without that sphere breaking down, precisely because the sphere acts to both bound and separate the atmosphere from a broader world or environment. Sloterdijk (2009) offers a useful summary of this argument in the following quote:

> being means someone (1) being together with someone else (2) and with something else (3) in something (4). This formula describes the minimum complexity you need to construct in order to arrive at an appropriate concept of world.
>
> (ibid.)

In the language developed here, (4) is a sphere while (3) and (2) shape an atmosphere. As such, an atmosphere in Sloterdijk's sense is always bound and linked to a set of non-human objects, and is not reducible to a particular human's affective or emotional state of being (on non-human atmospheres see Ash 2013b, Sørensen 2014).

While there are some similarities between Sloterdijk's account of spheres and Anderson's concept of atmospheres, there are also important differences. There is not space to explore these differences in detail here, but my main point is that Anderson's account of atmosphere emphasizes non-human forms of affect as key to atmospheres, whereas Sloterdijk considers affect to be only one possible aspect or component of an atmosphere. Anderson's concept of atmospheres is a useful way of focusing on the relationship between spheres and atmospheres as a question of affect. Developing aspects of Anderson and Sloterdijk's account, we can define atmospheres as the affects, forces and affordances contained and brought into being by the specific objects that make up a sphere, which in turn create the appearance of objects as being discrete and spatially differentiated from one another. In other words, spheres and space are intimately linked. Rather than a container in which objects are situated, space can be understood as emergent from the relations and non-relations (Harrison 2007) between objects, which in turn constitute a specific sphere. Objects, spheres and atmospheres are therefore linked to one another in processes of co-emergence.

As I will unpack in the following section, in video game studios, objects are always creating spheres, so the constant (re)arranging of objects alters studio spheres by shifting their boundaries and limits. Altering the boundary and limits of a sphere in turn alters the atmosphere associated with that sphere, which in turn alters or reconstitutes the space of the sphere (understood as the relations and non-relations between objects). In other words, studio space is constructed as objects, tools and technologies are arranged and rearranged. More formally put, studio spaces can be understood as the atmospheres that emanate from objects that are intentionally and unintentionally assembled by both humans and non-humans. Expanding on the concept of atmosphere as a set of affects that are localized to particular spheres, we can consider how studio atmospheres shape the potential for action and work to take place. Turning to the concrete example of a video game design studio, Angle Games, we can identify a number of objects that help generate both a sphere of activity and an atmosphere that shapes the conditions of possibility of that sphere.

Spheres and atmospheres of the studio

Large-scale contemporary video game design is a complex process that often consists of hundreds of individual staff members working on different aspects of a game. These staff are generally split into teams, such as an art team, a programming team, a testing team and so on. This is a common practice in video game design, and the rationale for a team-based approach is that it follows the largely modular nature of games production. For example, artists produce objects and artefacts that make up the game world, which are then organized and arranged by the game or level designers. Each team has a set of specialist skills and uses particular forms of specialist hardware and software, and this is a key reason why staff are organized into distinct teams.

At Angle Games, these teams were split across several buildings on a small, campus-style industrial development. Each building was designed around an open-plan setting and consisted of a variety of objects, such as tables, chairs, computers, specialist console development kits and so on. My own involvement with the game came late in the development cycle. In return for access to the studio, I agreed to work as an external quality assurance (QA) tester. External QA testers were usually friends of the developers who were brought in towards the end of the project to allow the designers to check that the game was playable and enjoyable by people who had not been involved in the project from the beginning. These sessions took place in three-hour slots during the evening, between once and twice a week, over a two-month period.

In this section I want to reflect on my experiences and observations during this testing period, and concentrate on three objects in Angle Games: the studio's development servers, audio headphones and screens. I focus on these three objects to show how they each generated a particular sphere (and thus space), which in turn enabled the production of an atmosphere that shaped the game being made by the studio. The key point here is that atmospheres, through the mediation and arrangement of objects, can overflow physical, conventional or assumed boundaries between different types of space. As I discuss in the following vignettes, these boundaries might include the distinction between the digital space of the game on screen and the extended space of the monitor on which the game was played, or the networked space of the server which allowed information to travel between different screens and the server as a physical object.

Servers

Staff at Angle Games needed to be using the same version of the game as everyone else. This was made possible by a networked computing environment where a series of central servers contained the current 'build' of the game. At any one moment, the game was in a state of flux and under modification by various staff. Aspects of the game, such as character animations or rules regarding bullet physics, were constantly tweaked on a daily or even hourly basis. The central servers allowed appropriate staff to access the current build to ensure that their work would fit into the existing changes that had been made.

It would be tempting to think of the servers in the offices of Angle Games as a central hub around which the space of the studio was organized. To be sure, other objects and bodies needed to be arranged in a particular way to connect to the server. For example, to access the server, developers required a PC, a screen and networking cables, as well as the correct operating system and software to access the files on the server. However, thinking spherically about the server as an object suggests that the server is not located 'in' a space, nor does it organize other objects in the space that surrounds it. Rather, the server creates multiple spheres and atmospheres between particular pieces of equipment to which it connects and the people who use that equipment.

An example that clarifies this point is the way the server was used as part of the multiplayer testing for the game. As the game was not finished, the game could be played via builds that were contained on the server, to which individual workstations could connect. In the multiplayer component, players form teams and play on specially designed maps to fight against one another in real time. The multiplayer component supported up to 12 players and so needed to be stress-tested with the maximum number of players. This would mean people from different departments outside the internal QA testing team would have to join in. On one occasion, designers and programmers in one office played against the internal QA team, who were situated in another office. This moment was one example among many others I observed, both through testing and in interviews with staff, where it became apparent that there were significant differences of opinion between the design team and the internal QA team about what the game should be and how it should work. In this empirical instance, these differences were partly amplified by the spheres the server created. As I reflect in my research diary:

> We were using voice communications for the first time today and the external testing team and the designers were in the same room, playing against the internal QA team. People from design were making jokes about the internal QA, which they heard and commented on as snide remarks. In particular, design were goading the internal QA, repeatedly asking them if they liked the bunker level, which we were all currently playing on. This was in response to earlier feedback from the internal QA, which suggested that the bunker level be dropped from the multiplayer playlist because the design did not work in a particular online mode. Testers from the internal QA team responded to this by making personal jokes about how bad the designers were at actually playing the game. There was definitely some disconnect between the two groups, both in terms of physical location (being housed in different buildings) but also in terms of communication. As the game designers had told me on other occasions, they thought QA couldn't understand the publisher limitations and ideal of the design, while QA had very strong ideas about what features of levels should 'obviously' be dropped they were no good from a design perspective.
>
> (Research diary: 16/08/07)

Although the servers allowed the game to be distributed and updated in real time, this form of distribution was also central to creating an antagonistic atmosphere between the internal QA and design teams. In this example, the server created a sphere that was particular to the 12 individuals testing the online component of the game. Here the sphere was constructed via two main sources. First, the sphere was constructed from the game level that existed as digital data on the server and expressed as a shared space through each player's screen, which allowed players to engage in battle with one another. Second, the sphere was constructed from the voice communication between players, which travelled through the server. The sphere of play was therefore constituted by a number of relations and non-relations between objects and bodies. For example, the voice communication allowed players to relate to one another and provided a sense of proximity. However, the game environment (experienced through the objects of the screen and workstation) allowed the players' avatars to move around separately and created a sense of distance and distinction between players, while remaining a shared location where contact was possible (for instance, through shooting at one another).

The specific sphere of the multiplayer match, as enabled by the server and workstations created an atmosphere of disconnection and annoyance between members of the internal QA and design teams. Perhaps the main reason was that, within the atmosphere of the match, the internal QA team felt able to speak their minds in ways that they couldn't in face-to-face meetings with the designers. The spheres created through the relations and non-relations between objects cultivated emotionally charged atmospheres that were localized to that sphere. What is important is that the sphere and atmosphere of the multiplayer match was specific to the 12 bodies, servers and other associated objects that allowed those bodies to communicate with one another. As the multiplayer testing was going on, there were many other staff working on other issues with the game, accessing the servers and performing tasks, which in turn created other spheres and atmospheres of activity and affect. As this example makes clear, studios that use computers and software are not a single site or space, but a variety of overlapping spheres and atmospheres that coexist alongside one another and are localized to the relations between particular objects, such as computers and servers and the bodies that engage with those objects. In relation to studying studios more broadly, we could consider the types of objects in the studio, which may or may not create overlapping spheres in a way similar to the servers at Angle Games.

Headphones

Another notable object that created a sphere and shaped an atmosphere in the studio was headphones. Headphones were seemingly simple but quite significant objects in the studio, especially during the testing sessions I participated in. The testing booths at Angle Games used PC monitors to display the game, which did not have inbuilt speakers. In order to hear the in-game sounds, the player required headphones to be plugged into the monitor. Headphones produced spheres by connecting the player to the audio environment of the game, which itself was constructed from a series of objects, such as weapons, buildings and vehicles within the game, and the software and hardware needed to play the game. These spheres created an atmosphere in at least two senses. First, the headphones and the soundscape they communicated to the player helped create an affective relation with the narrative, story and events in the game. Hearing weapon sounds, or enemies shouting in-game, helped to create a sense of immersion in the gameworld. Second, the headphones also enabled a sense of affective detachment from what was going on in the broader studio space of Angle Games. In this sense, wearing headphones could be considered as creating a small sphere and atmosphere within the sphere and atmosphere created between the tester and the booth they were sitting in.

However, on several occasions during the testing sessions, there were no headphones available for the play testers. This had a range of consequences for the outcomes of the test. In one test I was playing a level that required stealth. If the enemy spots the player, they sound an alarm that causes enemy reinforcements to arrive and attack them. As I reflect in my research diary:

> There was no sound on the tests today and at the last testing session this had a big impact on the experience. Me and David couldn't hear if the alarms had been sounded by the enemies or any of the audio cues to hear the position of the enemies ... There were audio adaptors for speakers, but the team weren't that interested in having the sound, even though it was mentioned that the lack of sound was an impediment to the gameplay.
>
> (Research diary: 13/08/07)

In another example, while testing a level set in an oil tanker, the lack of sound caused other problems. When steam pipes lining the walls of the ship were shot, they emitted steam that could hurt the character. However, without the sound effect of whooshing gas, I died a number of times without realizing that the gas was present in the level or could cause damage.

Both these examples point to how the presence of objects created both a sphere and an associated emotional atmosphere for the staff and testers at Angle Games. Without the headphones, there was a palpable sense of annoyance on the part of the developers when the testers didn't respond to the environments of the game as they wanted them to. Furthermore, without headphones, immersion in the atmosphere of the game was also made difficult because testers could hear other employees chat and engage in tasks that distracted them from the game. Objects, spheres and atmospheres are therefore intimately linked to one another. The distribution of objects creates a sphere of spatial proximity and distance based on the relations and non-relations between objects, which in turn generates a palpable atmosphere that shapes the kind of work that gets done in the studio. In the case of the game audio, without headphones players could not relate to or experience the in-game sound, which created a fundamental non-relation between player and game and generated a negative atmosphere that was specific to that sphere.

Screens

A third and final example can be used to examine the different kinds of sphere and atmosphere that emerge from the relations between objects and humans in the studio. Specifically, we can examine how the placement of particular screens created an important sphere and atmosphere that ended up contributing to the change of a key mechanic in the game. On my first trip to Angle Games, I was asked to play a demo of the opening level, which was the first thing players would experience if they bought the game. While there were screens and development kits throughout the office, I was asked to play on a very large monitor in a cleared area in the middle of the office. As I played the opening level, I recalled the following in my research diary:

> The first thing I played was the intro of the first level and its associated tutorial (which introduced the player to the basic mechanisms of the game). The tutorial was not at all obvious to me, even though Brian had mentioned Seb had been working on it. It wasn't clear how the two player mechanic worked … the navigation marker was also unclear and I quickly got lost in what was supposed to be an easy opening section … Kevin picked up on this and thought it was interesting. As I played, a group of five people gathered behind me. They were very eager to watch 'fresh eyes' play something they had been working so hard on.
>
> (Research diary: 09/08/07)

The location of the large television screen and its distance from the surrounding desks created a sphere that allowed the group of developers to gather together and focus on watching me play the game for the first time. This sphere, constituted by the particular relations and non-relations between objects, such as the distance between the desks that allowed more than one person to stand, and the size of the screen that allowed more than one person to watch, created an anxious and slightly tense atmosphere as the developers looked on, hoping I could make my way through the tutorial without too many problems. When it became apparent that I was having problems, the five developers became more anxious. We could argue that the co-presence of bodies in the same sphere created a more anxious atmosphere than if only a single developer was watching. As Kevin realized the problems I was encountering would need to be fixed, his quiet mutterings had a contagious effect on other developers who came to see what was going on. This atmosphere was not shaped simply by the fresh eyes of a newcomer (although that certainly contributed to the production of this atmosphere). Rather, it was the arrangement of objects and the size of the screen that created a sphere in where people could gather to watch a newcomer play the game, which co-contributed to the production of the anxious atmosphere. In other words, the space created by the opening between objects (such as desks and chairs) allowed the developers to gather and stand together, which in turn amplified the collective emotional and affective response they had to the situation. After this event, both the opening tutorial section and the navigation marker were redesigned for the final release of the game. While it is impossible to know whether this event in particular was central to the decision to rework these systems, this sphere certainly created an atmosphere in which multiple designers at the studio recognized that something needed to change.

Across the three vignettes in this section, I have gestured towards a few of the spheres that emerged from the (non-)relations between objects and humans at Angle Games and how these spheres generated atmospheres. In turn, I have suggested that these atmospheres have tangible effects on the emotional and affective sensibilities of those working within them. However, it is important to state that the atmosphere of Angle Games (or any studio) was not a single thing that enveloped the entire studio. Rather, Angle Games was a site of multiple spheres that were appearing and shifting at any moment as objects were moved, added or modified at the studio. In this case, spheres and atmospheres are multiple phenomena that emerge from the localized (non-)relations between objects and undergo more or less continual change. With this in mind, the objects examined in this section are only a small number of the objects that constituted the multiple spheres and atmospheres of Angle Games. However, while modest, it is hoped that these three vignettes provide some openings for beginning to think productively about studio spaces as atmospheric.

Conclusion: spatial atmospherics

This chapter develops the concept of spheres to think about the production of particular atmospheres within video game studio spaces, and the effects of these atmospheres on the quality of products that are produced. An account of studio space as multiple spheres with particular atmospheres has a number of implications for studio studies more generally. First, the concept of atmosphere troubles simple accounts of work, when work is understood as the instrumental undertaking of an activity by a human being for some end goal. From a spherical perspective, work is also about creating and maintaining multiple spheres and atmospheres in which the right kinds of activity can take place. Furthermore, work is thoroughly distributed across a set of non-human entities, all of which inhibit and enable the cultivation of appropriate atmospheres within a studio. Second, the issue of intentionality and authorship is also radically called into question. A spherical account highlights the difficulty in pinpointing the location or origin of a particular idea or catalyst that is central to the success of a product (either technically or commercially) within a particular individual human body or object. Perhaps it is better to say that it is the spheres and atmospheres themselves (that exceed any individual body or object) that are equally responsible for a moment of artistic inspiration, or the innovation that leads to the development of a particular feature of a product or artwork in a studio space.

More generally, the chapter develops Sloterdijk's notion of the sphere to think about space as multiple, fragmented and localized to the relations and non-relations between particular objects. This has been achieved through linking Sloterdijk's account of spheres to Anderson's notion of atmospheres. Creating this link has allowed me to discuss both the affective relations between non-human objects and the emotional qualities created through encounters between human and non-human things in productive ways. This notion of spheres and atmospheres complicates an account of the studio as a single place or site. Rather, any studio is a continuously shifting set of spheres and atmospheres within which localized struggles and encounters take place between a variety of objects and bodies, many of which do not appear to the humans who supposedly wield authority in these studios. While I have used the concepts of spheres and atmospheres to talk about video game design studios in particular, these concepts also have important implications for thinking about studios more broadly. These implications are twofold.

First, the notions of sphere and atmosphere allow us to theorize action as occurring between different spaces that are often considered to be discrete or distinct from one another. For example, the sphere and atmosphere of a space are not just determined by physical extension. Objects that appear on screens, or sounds pumped through headphones, can contribute to broader atmospheres in ways that cut across distinctions between the digital space of the game or software or screen and the physical space of the studio in which these objects are located. The key strength of the concepts of sphere and atmosphere developed here is that they allow us to cut across distinctions that may seem to limit the affective capacities of objects to particular zones or areas. Rather than thinking in terms of type of object or type of space, we can instead classify spaces through the types of sphere and atmosphere they create.

Second, the concepts of sphere and atmosphere emphasize the multiple nature of space. Spaces are not one, but many. Spaces, defined as sets of relations and non-relations opened up within a particular sphere of objects, can overlap and co-exist without necessarily appearing to the human beings present within a particular situation. This understanding of space complicates how we might investigate a seemingly obvious or normal situation or space. Rather than as a single scene apprehended by a human body, any one set of objects can open up multiple spheres and atmospheres, depending on how a human body might encounter these objects or how these objects might encounter one another.

A notion of studio space as multiple may help explain why it is so difficult to create coherent and successful products and artwork within studios. Speculating beyond the particular examples developed in this chapter, success seems to be a matter of calibrating the multiple spheres and atmospheres that emerge in a studio in an attempt to cultivate some kind of shared atmosphere. Unfortunately, if we take seriously a non-relational account of space, then spheres and atmospheres cannot ever be fully shared because they are specific to the relations between particular objects. If one attempts to alter the relations between the objects that make up a sphere, then one ultimately changes the atmosphere, and therefore the creative or productive potential that atmosphere may contain. Studio studies is an important new field of inquiry, and it is hoped that the concepts and examples developed in this chapter begin to offer some ways of thinking about how products emerge from, while also being potentially suffocated by, the multiple spheres and atmospheres that make up studios.

Note

1 On video game design ethnography see Ash (2010), and on video game design more broadly see Ash (2012, Ash 2013a).

References

Adey, P., Brayer, L., Masson, D., Murphy, P., Simpson, P. and Tixier, N. 2013. *Pour votre tranquillité*: ambiance, atmosphere, and surveillance. *Geoforum*, 49(1), 299–309.

Anderson, B. 2009. Affective atmospheres. *Emotion, Space and Society*, 2(2), 77–81.

Ash, J. 2010. Architectures of affect: anticipating and manipulating the event in processes of videogame design and testing. *Environment and Planning D: Society & Space*, 28(4), 653–671.

Ash, J. 2012. Attention, videogames and the retentional economies of affective amplification. *Theory, Culture & Society*, 29(6), 3–26.

Ash, J. 2013a. Technologies of captivation videogames and the attunement of affect. *Body & Society*, 19(1), 27–51

Ash, J. 2013b. Rethinking affective atmospheres: technology, perturbation and space times of the non-human. *Geoforum*, 49(1), 20–28.

Bille, M. 2014. Lighting up cosy atmospheres in Denmark. *Emotion, Space and Society*, DOI: 10.1016/j.emospa.2013.12.008.

Bohme, G. 1993. Atmosphere as a fundamental concept of a new aesthetics. *Thesis Eleven*, 36(1), 113–126.

Broth, M. 2009. Seeing through screens, hearing through speakers: managing distant studio space in television control room interaction. *Journal of Pragmatics*, 41(10), 1998–2016.

Castro Nogueira, L. 2009. Bubbles, globes, wrappings, and *plektopoi*: minimal notes to rethink metaphysics from the standpoint of the social sciences. *Environment and Planning D: Society and Space*, 27(1), 87–104.

Edensor, T. 2014. Producing atmospheres at the match: fan cultures, commercialisation and mood management in English football. *Emotion, Space and Society*, DOI: 10.1016/j.emospa.2013.12.010.

Elden, S. 2013. *Sloterdijk Now*. London: Wiley.

Elden, S. and Mendieta, E. 2009. Being-with as making worlds: the 'second coming of Peter Sloterdijk'. *Environment and Planning D: Society & Space*, 27(1), 1–11.

Farías, I. 2015. Epistemic dissonance: reconfiguring valuation in architectural practice. In: Berthoin Antal, A., Hutter, M. and Stark, D. eds, *Moments of Valuation. Exploring Sites of Dissonance*. Oxford: Oxford University Press, pp. 271–289.

Harrison: 2007. 'How shall I say it … ?' Relating the nonrelational. *Environment and Planning A*, 39(3), 590–608.

Healy, S. 2014. Atmospheres of consumption: shopping as involuntary vulnerability. *Emotion, Space and Society*, 10(1), 35–43.

Mackenzie, A. 2006. *Cutting Code: Software and Sociality*. New York: Peter Lang.

McCormack, D. P. 2008. Engineering affective atmospheres on the moving geographies of the 1897 Andrée expedition. *Cultural Geographies*, 15(4), 413–430.

Paulos, E., Honicky, R. J. and Goodman, E. 2007. Sensing atmosphere. In: ACM Conference on Embedded Networked Sensor Systems (SenSys 2007), Sydney.

Shaw, R. 2014. Beyond night-time economy: affective atmospheres of the urban night. *Geoforum*, 51(1), 87–95.

Sloterdijk, P. 2009. Talking to myself and the poetics of space. *Harvard Design Magazine*, 30.

Sloterdijk, P. 2011. *Bubbles: Microspherology*. Los Angeles, CA: Semiotexte/Smart Art.

Sørensen, T. F. 2014. More than a feeling: towards an archaeology of atmosphere. *Emotion, Space and Society*, DOI: 10.1016/j.emospa.2013.12.009.

Wetherell, M. 2013. Feeling rules, atmospheres and affective practice: some reflections on the analysis of emotional episodes. In: Maxwell, C. and Aggleton, P. eds, *Privilege, Agency and Affect: Understanding the Production and Effects of Action*, London: Palgrave, pp. 221–240.

Yaneva, A. 2009. *The Making of a Building: A Pragmatist Approach to Architecture.* Oxford: Peter Lang.

7 Inter- to intracorporeality

The haptic hotshop heat of a glassblowing studio

Erin O'Connor

Glassblowers regularly describe their work as a dance, as have novelists, tourists and social scientists (D'Annunzio 1991, Palmer Schwind 1984, Martineau 1852). A collaborative art, glassblowing has been practised by teams from the early Roman Empire, through the Venetian Renaissance, into pre-industrial nineteenth-century factories and contemporary glassblowing studios (Klein and Lloyd 1984, Polak 1975). The politics of these formations has been analysed by cultural theorists as well as those of labour history, but in these historical, socio-political and socio-economic accounts of teamwork, the site itself, namely the glassblowing atelier, is often the silent backdrop against which the drama of larger social forces plays out (Armstrong 2008, Wallach Scott 1974, Scoville 1948, Davis 1949).

By mobilizing all of the players of studio glassblowing – the tools, hot glass, equipment, the breath, colour, heat and techniques – in an analysis of teamwork, this chapter, which draws from four years of ethnographic research at New York Glass, in which I became a glassblower, reveals the inter- and intracorporeality of studio glassblowing. In the context of an analysis of the role of shops, including workshops, the shop labour system in the factory and the hotshop in the development of studio glassblowing, this analysis shifts understandings of artistic practice away from subjective careers or expressions of institutions or markets toward that of embodiment and materialities as embedded in intercorporeality (Becker 1982). In addition, this chapter conceptualizes intracorporeality by showing how heat and vitrification (the process of becoming glass) are shared and embodied across the multiple bodies of the hotshop. Thus the chapter contributes to an understanding of how inter- and intracorporeality generate studio life to ethnographies of the formation of community and meaning through, with and from the crafting body in relation to the material world (Crawford 2009, Marchand 2009, 2001, Herzfeld 2003, Harper 1987).

Revealing the 'shop' of the 'studio'

A roar and heady scent of heat filled my senses as the elevator opened. I had arrived at New York Glass, a public-access glassblowing studio, and the site of my research on embodied knowledge in craft. Luminous orange brilliance caught my attention as undulating molten glass, turned by glassblowers working between hip-height barrels filled with fire, arced through space at the pipes' ends, trailing orange comet tails. While my grandfather had made neon-glass signs, I had never seen him work glass, let alone glassblowing like this – free-style, molten, blown, collaborative.

A receptionist waved me into her area, separated by a glass partition from the glassblowers – all male – at their furnaces. I explained that I had an appointment with the Educational Director and turned to watch the glassblowers at work as she phoned him. Noting my interest, she suggested that I 'wait out there'. 'Sign in first Although', she called, pushing a clipboard toward me. On the sheet, three categories were listed across a table: 'date', 'name' and 'destination'. Date: easy – 9/14. Name: easy – Erin O'Connor. Destination: confusing – was I not already at the glassblowing studio? 'What should I write for my destination?' I asked. Slightly annoyed, she replied: 'Hotshop'. I dutifully wrote H-O-T-S-H-O-P and asked, 'Hotshop?' 'Yeah', she smiled, pointing through the glass partition, 'That place in there where it is hot.' Returning the smile sheepishly, I turned to enter. Crossing the threshold, the heat enveloped me, as had the roar and scent.

The glassblowers laboured in teams, wiping sweat from their brows, as tools steamed and sizzled. Unlike those workers in industrial glass factories, who were viewed by nineteenth-century bourgeoisie tourists, these glassblowers were self-proclaimed artists and strove to distinguish themselves from their proletariat predecessors in part by the setting of their practice (see Armstrong 2008, Drexler-Lynn 2004: 14). Mid-twentieth-century American artists moved hot glass out of industrialized factories into studios, a place in which the artists perceived themselves to have complete control of the creative process, giving rise to American studio glassblowing (Labino 1968: 117). Hot glass was the last form of glasswork to enter artists' studios, following 'warm' and 'cold' glass methodologies in the early twentieth century, such as stained glass, enamelling and etching (Drexler-Lynn 2004: 35–40). The artists using warm and cold methodologies are regarded as 'proto-studio' glass artists, however, since they did not melt or blow glass: in its origins, 'studio glassblowing' was synonymous with hot glass (ibid.: 14).

Although the nomenclature of the origins of studio glassblowing uses 'studio' to distinguish glassblowing by singular artists, in practice early studio glassblowing was often done collectively in workshops. The first institutionally supported gathering of artists working in glass, held in Toledo, Ohio in 1962, was called The Toledo Workshop. Similarly, in 1971 a 'No Deposit, Lots of Returns Glass Etc. Workshop' was advertised to attract students to rustic glassblowing facilities built by artists in the woodlands of the American Pacific-Northwest, and became known as the Peanut Farm Glass Workshop (Oldknow 1996: 33, 74). This site was officially named the Pilchuck Workshop in 1973 before taking its current name, Pilchuck Glass School, the global hub of contemporary studio glassblowing (ibid.: 127). Four years later, as the use of hot glass by artists burgeoned, New York Glass was founded as an experimental workshop.

The practical history of the emergence of American studio glassblowing is situated to a great extent outside of any given studio, distributed between and among collaborating individuals, as well as more or less sufficient tools, equipment, materials and, importantly, the American factory. The Toledo workshops, for example, happened on the grounds of a glass museum neighboring a glass factory, where factory workers demonstrated techniques, and industry provided glass in the form of marbles to melt, while the Pilchuck workshops used roughly built equipment, materials donated from glass companies and the working knowledge that had been achieved in the Toledo workshops with factory workers – situations far from a 'studio' idealized as a place where an individual controls production and creativity is unmediated (Oldknow 1996: 59). Although the challenge to factory monopolization of hot glass was in intent launched from the studio, in practice it emerged from workshops, where authority, as noted by Richard Sennett in *The Craftsman*, has historically been challenged (2008: 54). While the workshops were sites of experimentation that challenged both American and European glassmaking conventions, they also were early gestures toward the multi-bodied collaboration with which hot glass, difficult to work alone, 'asks' to be worked.

As workshops proliferated and more people began to blow glass, 'studio' functioned less as a noun than as adjective, as described by Harvey Littleton, the 'putative founder of the glass movement': 'studio and glass were used in the earliest proposals [for grants] as two separate nouns, not as an adjective modifying a noun' (Drexler-Lynn 2004: 14). At the same time, 'hotshop' rather than 'studio' was used to designate the area in which hot glass was blown. It is unclear when hotshop came into usage, as American studio glassblower Fritz Dreisbach explains: '[Hotshop] is one of those words [in the 70s] that we were just using, but who used it first, or where, I can't remember'. Likely passed down from the American factory tradition, as no counterpart for the word 'shop' exists in the Swedish or German glassmaking traditions from which American studio glassblowers also drew working knowledge, hotshop not only captures the intent of the artists, namely to explore glass as a hot medium, but also articulates the collective dynamic with which hot glass became a studio practice via workshops.[1]

While the 'shop' of hotshop does not refer to the American proto-industrial form of the division of labour known as the 'shop system', which diminished the autonomy of glassblowers and subjected glassblowers to the principles of rationalized production, as a vestige of factory culture it gestures toward collective practice and thereby the significance of collaboration, a division of labour (Scoville 1948: 22). The shift of the use of studio from a place of glassblowing to a manner of glassblowing emerged as collaboration became the prominent method of blowing glass. Thus the direct access to the molten medium sought by the artists widely became achieved via studio teamwork, instead of by an individual in a studio.

Glassblowers inhabit sets of relations choreographed as teamwork – an entanglement of heat, roaring furnaces, techniques, sizzling and steaming tools, equipment, working properties, bodily capabilities and others – rather than a 'studio' per se. Through analysing teamwork in the hotshop – what glassblowers refer as the 'choreography of production' of the 'dance' of glassblowing – I will unpack how glassblowing bodies interact and relate, demonstrating not only the intercorporeal, but also the intracorporeal meanings of blowing glass, thereby theorizing 'studio' as a metabolic dynamic of interrelation, inhabitation and intrachange.

Teamwork: the choreography of production

In 1854, the American glass manufacturer Deming Jarves was struck by an unknown seventeenth-century writer's description of teamwork:

> The work passes through three hands. First, the gentlemen apprentices gather the glass and prepare the same. It is then handed to the second gentlemen, who are more advanced in the art. Then the master gentleman takes it, and makes it perfect by blowing it.
>
> (Jarves 1968 [1854]: 27)

In this description, Jarves wrote, '[e]very glass-maker will perceive … that the same system prevails at the present time' (ibid.). Four hundred years following the unknown writer's observation, when I landed my first assistant job on a glassblowing team, it was led, much as both he and Jarves described, by a head glassblower, Oren, and teamed by two assistants in addition to myself. What these writers failed to note, but surely had noticed, was the extent to which any one of these persons – master or assistant – practises in relation with the glass itself, the heat, the tools, the equipment and each other.

Although teams could be upwards of seven or more people, teams at New York Glass are typically, like centuries of pre-industrial teams, of two or three people, and are led by a 'gaffer', which broadly means 'boss' (Polak 1975: 21). Gaffers shape the glass while seated in a workbench, direct assistants, and are regarded as the centre of the game. As a twentieth-century glass manual notes, gaffers 'call the shots' and 'their wishes should be obeyed and carried out to the best of [the team member's abilities]' (Schmid 1997: 60). Unlike the gentlemen of the unknown writer's and Jarves' descriptions, who were likely maestros, gaffers at New York Glass are not necessarily masters of their art, since in the studio context, which places hot glass in the hands of amateurs, the gaffing experience is available to all.

Oren was known in the studio for 'blowing big' and needed an extra hand to assist with the production of his signature incalmo vases. Incalmo refers to a technique in which two or more blown glass elements are fused and, in Oren's case, involved joining two bowl-like vessels, each with multiple layers of colour. Since two vessels were simultaneously needed, so too were two glory holes (re-heating furnaces), two benches, and at least two assistants, so that neither bench would be without an assistant at any given time. His work, in keeping with his character, was a big production.

On the day of work, I arrived early and found Oren in the hotshop, setting up both workstations: bench, table for tools, bucket of water for the wooden blocks and paddles, dry bucket and drop pan – all before the glory hole – and a pot of water by the furnace. Oren laid out his tools, including a blowtorch and air hose and I, after putting pipes into the warming rack, searched for fans – although morning, it was midsummer and the studio was already hot and muggy. When Paul, my beginning glassblowing instructor, who had recommended me to Oren, and Zach, a production glassblower and artist, arrived, the team was complete and we ran through the day's game plan. In addition to our main jobs, Paul, Zach and I were expected to blow, assist with the handwork of gaffing, maintain the equipment, and otherwise to tell good stories and jokes.

Blowing an incalmo vessel

Paul was hired as the first assistant to start the bubbles for Oren to gaff. To make an incalmo vase, we needed to 'gather', 'block' or 'marver', and 'tool', i.e. shape, the glass with a variety of hand tools in a bench – steps that are needed to blow any vessel. To gather, Paul heated the end of a 'blowpipe', a hollow pipe under five feet long, as he intended to blow a bubble, and approached the furnace. I slid the furnace door aside releasing the roar of the fire and a fiery bath of heat, and he extended the pipe over the sill of the opening, lowering its tip into the molten glass. Having played on the ability of glass to grip itself (viscosity), glass mounted on the pipe's heated end as Paul rotated quickly enough to ensure the glass remained hot, but slowly enough so that it coiled around, rather than spun off, the pipe. Paul withdrew the large gather needed to start an incalmo vase and carried the molten orb to the workbench to block.

Blocking uses a tool by the same name – a block – which, made of fruitwood, typically cherry, looks like a roughly hewn ladle. Sitting in the bench, crafted from forged steel and wood, Paul rolled the pipe back and forth over the arms, which extended outwards just beyond arm's length from above the bench seat, with his left hand, while using his right hand to cup the gather with a large block that shaped the glass. He embodied and extended himself through the block – 'We pour ourselves out into [tools] and assimilate them as parts of our own existence' (Polanyi 1962: 59) – insofar as he felt the glass not at the point where his hand held the block, but rather at the block's end. He cupped the gather with the block as would a palm, its wet wood changing the opaque molten red gather into a clear, eggplant-shaped orb. Having 'skinned' the molten glass, i.e. cooled the outermost layer, and set the shape, he then 'popped the bubble' – gave a quick puff into the blowpipe and then covered the hole of the mouthpiece with his thumb to prevent the air from escaping.

Lowering the capped end of the pipe and raising the now-translucent orb before his eyes, he watched the air 'push out' into the centre of the hot glass, carving the cavity that would become the interior of the vessel. As Paul prepared this bubble, Oren did the same for the second bubble and I alternately opened the furnace door, which I had learned to lift slightly as I slid it open so as to avoid a 'catch', and handed them blocks.

Meanwhile, Zach prepared the colour – orange, white, blue, brick, crimson. The preparation of colour involves yet another furnace called a 'garage', where 'chunks of colour' from a colour rod (imagine three- to five-inch pieces cut from a solid, foot-long, inch-and-a-half-thick bar of coloured glass) are warmed. First, he gathered from the furnace to make a 'collar' with which to 'pick up the colour' and, turning to the marver, a hip-height steel table once made of marble in the Italian tradition, marvered – rolled the glass back and forth over the surface.

Zach swayed back and forth as his left palm undulated in waves and his right hand rotated the pipe and buoyed the malleable hot glass against the cold steel of the marver, propelling it back and forth. His light touch not only minimized the loss of heat – steel steals – but also ensured the gather did not become lopsided. While the viscosity of hot glass allows it to be gathered, its malleability allows it to take on innumerable forms. With the cool steel, Zach marvered the glass into a flattish, mushroom cap-like collar and picked up the colour, which meant touching the warmed collar to the warmed colour chunk in the garage so that they tacked together, and took it to the glory hole to heat.

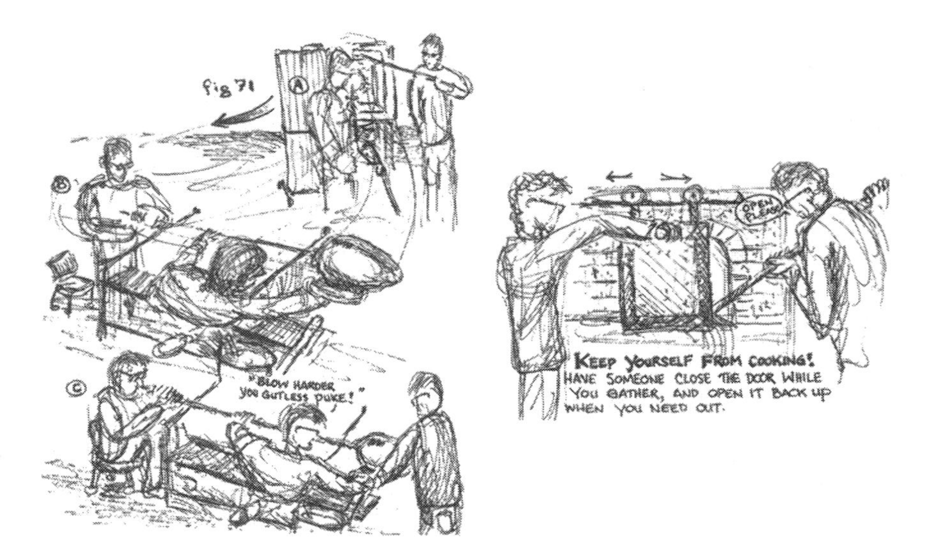

Figure 7.1 Gathering, heating at the glory hole and shaping at the bench
Source: Drawing © Ed Schmid

Paul called out, 'Blow!' and I squatted to the level of the pipe's mouthpiece, extended over the left arm of the bench, and blew whilst watching the cavity, popped by Paul, expand. He rolled the pipe back and forth over the bench's arms as I blew, and sculpted the glass with a folded wet newspaper (one of the many hand-tools kept atop the table adjacent to the bench) that lined the palm of his right hand, sending up streams of steam and smoke. When the bubble lost its hot glow – colour is seen, felt and smelled as temperature in glass-blowing – he yanked the pipe from my mouth and returned to the glory hole for heat.

After Paul had shaped the bubble and Zach the colour drop, they met back at the main bench before the larger glory hole, where Zach dropped the colour onto the bubble, like an extra-viscous glob of honey falling from a spoon, which Paul then marvered. With each chilling pass on the steel marver, the red-hot drop smeared over the clear bubble, turning blue. Colour, achieved by mineral additives – in this case cobalt – becomes molten orange-red when heated, but regains its mineral colour when chilled. Paul gathered clear glass over the colour overlay, and Zach prepared and dropped more colour onto the ever-growing bubble until enough clear and coloured glass had been layered – blue, brick and orange – and the bubbles had been blown to the size deemed suitable by Oren. Large, like watermelons, the bubbles had exceeded the aperture in the centre of the glory hole, formed by a half-moon shape opening at the inside edge of each door, such that I had begun to 'work the doors' – my official job for the day.

Typically the least skilled person of the team, such as myself, is given the job of working the doors of the glory hole. To open and close the doors, which are too hot to touch with bare hands, I lassoed a steel loop at the end of a long pipe over a peg welded atop the inside corners of the steel frames of the doors, and pulled to open and pushed to close. Working the doors of the glory hole, fired to 2300°F (1260°C), is gruelling as one stands just to the side of the barrel-furnace of fire with only the glory hole doors and the cotton of one's clothes for protection. For large pieces like Oren's, that require large glory holes and for the doors to be constantly opened and closed, it is especially gruelling. As I worked the doors, Paul blew and Oren finished shaping the bubble against the burning ash of the soaked newspaper, while the sweet smell of honey wafted from the touch of hot steel tools against the block of beeswax atop the tool table. With the two largest glory holes in the hotshop ablaze, we were thick in heat, swirling, arcing, and turning between and amongst each other, the hot glass, tools and equipment: the hotshop had become downright swampy.

Only an hour into making the vessel, however, the dance had only just begun. With the bubbles 'blown up' (the first stage of blowing a vessel), we moved onto the second stage of vessel making – 'opening up' the bubbles, making them into deep, bowl-like vases. Once the bowls were achieved, the defining moment of making an incalmo piece had arrived: fusing. Oren, seated, called out from the bench to both Paul and Zach as they heated the bowls, 'Ready?' Both nodded and immediately brought the pipes with the warmed bowls at their ends to Oren's bench, setting one down on the bench arms, which Oren took hold of and began to rotate, while 'serving' the other right of the bench. Oren, who had donned a heat-resistant metallic sleeve and was blowtorching the bowl of the pipe resting on the bench arms, asked me to 'shield' him, that is, hold wooden paddles between his forearm and the radiant heat of the vessel. Setting the torch down, he grabbed the 'served' pipe with the tweezers held in his right hand and drew it toward the first bowl, each bowl constantly rotating. Ruddy-faced and sweating profusely, he grimaced and winced as he leaned over both bowls, the rims of which now almost touched. I could see the waves of heat around the bubbles, blurring space, felt my own skin crinkle, and struggled to inhale the burning air as I shielded him. With a concise pull, Oren touched the rim of the rotating served bowl to that of the one rotating on the bench arms – an eternal kiss from which neither could withdraw. The two bowls, now fused, had yet again become one bubble and they 'cracked off' the serving pipe.

I dropped the paddle onto the bench and ran to the glory hole to throw open the doors for the fused bubble, and continued to lasso the pegs, opening and closing, as they shaped and opened the bubble, flattening it into a wide, hollow disc that required that I leave the doors fully opened as they heated. Having never worked on a team, the intricate work between two benches was dizzying, as I noted in my field notes that night – the sounds, scents, sensations, and the total inhabitation by, within and of heat. When Zach finally carried the finished vessel to the kiln, where it would anneal overnight, the relief of all team members was palpable. We attempted to blow three incalmo vessels that day, but at the culmination of the second piece, the vessel popped off the pipe and two hours of labour smashed into a thousand shards of glass across the cement floor.

From intercorporeality to intracorporeality

In 1824, Caroline Harrison toured Brooklyn Flint Glass Works and noted in a letter to her husband that 'every man seems to have his part to perform – they work into each other's hands as it were' (Palmer Schwind 1984: 181). For the philosopher Maurice Merleau-Ponty, the glassblowers 'are like organs of one single intercorporeality', in which each person completes the other (1964: 168). As Nick, a glassblower just out of college, who forsook an engineering career to pursue glassblowing, described:

> The dance of it – it really is a full body thing. The team aspect of it – I love working in a team … I love it when you're working with a person enough so that they are doing exactly what you think they should do. … But when there is a disconnect there, I think I get pretty frustrated. It's one of those things where you wish that you could be that other person

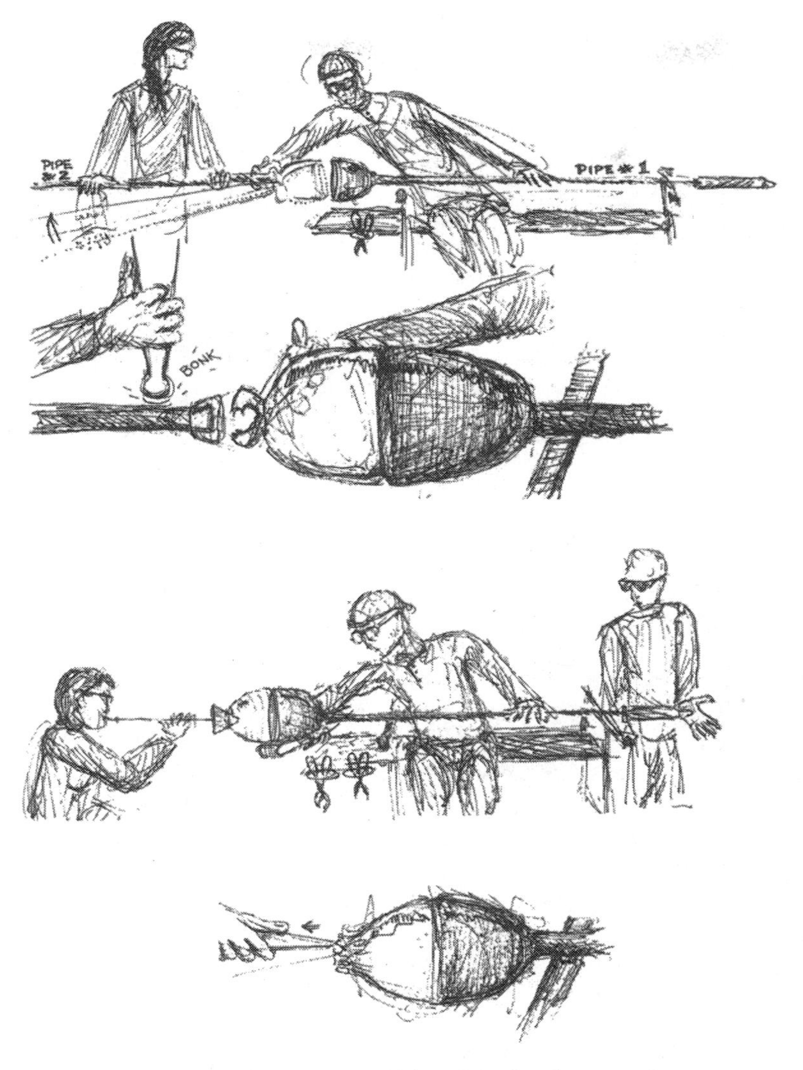

Figure 7.2 Fusing and opening up the bubbles of the incalmo vessel
Source: Drawing © Ed Schmid

> too. … When I'm assisting someone, I'm trying to think what they're going to do next so that I can help them.
>
> (Interview, July 15, 2005)

While the gaffer is perceived to be the one calling the shots, teamwork is in practice reliant upon the ability of every team member to anticipate needs, as noted by *Advanced Glassworking Techniques*, a twentieth-century glass manual: '[a] well-honed team understands what each member is doing, and what they are about to do' (Schmid 1997: 60). In Oren's case, we had run through the 'game plan' at the beginning of the day and were assigned positions in relation to the techniques required for blowing the incalmo vessels. To understand what each team member is about to do, that is to anticipate, knowledge beyond that of the techniques associated with the assigned position or the game plan is required, however.

A proficient choreography of production requires that the team members inhabit and extend themselves through each other's bodies *in unison*, true to the meaning of 'choreography'. I needed to serve the block as Paul reached for it, as Paul needed to take the colour as Zach dropped it, and Oren needed to slide the bubble into the glory hole as I opened its doors. For anthropologist Thomas Csordas, such corporeal interstices of interaction, wherein persons experience themselves as extended in relation to and interaction with each other, constitutes intercorporeal meaning (2008). Being body and experiencing bodily meaning happens at the interstices of interaction. Thus the gaffer's directives and the organization of work according to the production needs of the object become meaningful only in practice.

In this sense, the style of the choreography of production, that is how the glassblowers interact, shapes the emergence of the object. Thus while Oren looked for technical causes to explain the last-minute crash of the finished incalmo vase, Sarkis, the most accomplished glassblower at New York Glass, who had witnessed the failed incalmo, referred to his standing critique of the 'out-of-control' working style of Oren's regular team: 'He doesn't make them focus enough so that when the moment comes to actually focus, it is difficult and mistakes are made and pieces are fucked up. A lot of the tempo and synchronicity of the team comes from the mode of communication, actually (field notes, 30 March 2005). By lack of focus, Sarkis meant that the team was not attuned to the material, as he believed that the achievement of proficiency lies in the glassblower's ability to 'follow the glass'.

Without knowledge of the heat required to blow an incalmo, I did not always anticipate when the doors of the glory hole needed to be opened, leading Oren to regularly bark, 'Open!'. For the same reason, I opened too slowly once and the vessel touched the glory hole door, taking with it a chunk of plaster-cement, which Oren then had to cut out, as he did the unwanted bubbles with which the glass, which studio technicians had forged, was blemished. In addition, the largest glory hole's heat, controlled by studio technicians, had been unsteady – at first too cold, then too hot – while the air hose did not work initially and the propane tank of the blowtorch ran out, such that the malleability of the glass was inconsistent. Sometimes, banter took precedent over tending to the glass and antics, such as Paul's ability to literally slap a fresh gather of glass from the furnace barehanded, plugged extra steps, like rounding out the slap mark, into the production process. The team gave weight to social communication and camaraderie – verbal directives and jokes – rather than corporeal communication that conversed in a shared material sensibility. From Sarkis' perspective, this sloppy material attunement translated into sloppy teamwork and losses such as the failed incalmo vessel.

Glassblowers not only interrelate with each other, but also must, if they are to work proficiently, become 'intimate', as Sarkis explained, with the hot glass (O'Connor 2007). Craftwork, as described by Parolin and Mattozzi, is an 'interaction [by craftsmen] with other bodies', that is material bodies (2014: 10). In the hotshop, the hot glass extended itself toward us – needing to be turned, heated, cooled, opened, etc. – as often, if not more so, than the hand of a teammate, gesturing toward the 'matterly constitution of culture' (O'Connor 2007). The 'corporeal' of 'intercorporeality' is inclusive not only of other persons, but also of matter, understood not just as hot glass, but also tools and equipment, in addition to forces, notably gravity and centrifugal force in glassblowing, in which matter is. Thus intercorporeality is not only interactions and interstitial meanings among glassblowers, but also those of hot glass, tools and equipment through and within forces; non-human materials and forces are constitutive players. Thus blowing the incalmo vessel is less an expression and realization of Oren's intentionality than an intercorporeal adaptation within and among an emergent constellation of bodies in flux, heeding and following each other toward the incalmo vessel: tools as waxed tools, waterlogged tools, smoking tools, fire-torching hoses, air-cooling hoses; equipment as open doors, closed doors, full tank, empty tank, hot kiln ready for annealing; bodies as blocking, sweating, turning, blowing, rotating, sitting, squatting, burning; hot glass as dripping, shattering, expanding, imploding. The dance of glassblowing – that intercorporeality – is emergent from a materially attuned choreography.

At the heart of these interrelated corpuses is the heat – furnace heat, glory hole heat, molten glass heat, hot tools, hot skin, hot air, hot roar, hot colour. While the team left two finished incalmo vases in the kiln to cool, glassblowers take home, more often than objects, the heat itself. As the philosopher Gaston Bachelard noted, 'Heat penetrates' (1964: 40). Nowhere was this more obvious than in my field notes from that evening:

> When I left the studio, I felt unsteady and weak. I was utterly exhausted. Although I drank my 1.5 liter bottle five or six times during the course of the day, I still felt thirsty. Could barely stand for the bus. Could barely stand on the bus. Held onto the handle on the back of one of the seats, just wishing that someone would stand up. I wanted to announce, 'I'm tired. I've just been blowing glass all day. I've been standing in front of a glory hole that is over 2000 degrees Fahrenheit. My feet are tired. My mind is absent. Can you please get the fuck up for someone who has worked and is tired and needs the rest, for someone who would appreciate it so much?' … I closed my eyes at one point, holding tight, and swaying with the rhythms of the bus. From the bus, I dragged myself up the stairs to the apartment, opened the door, came in, dropped my bag,

> and immediately started to take off my clothes. ... I literally peeled off my pants and underwear, stuck together with the salt and dampness of my gum-arabic sweat. I could hardly manage, losing my balance as I stepped on the bottom of one pant leg to leverage the other leg out. I peeled off my T-shirt and unclasped my bra – it remained just as firmly in place as when it was clasped. Glued. I wedged my fingertips between my flesh and its cotton and pulled it outward and off. Everything was damp or outright wet; the back of my blue T-shirt patterned by cascading white salt deposits.
>
> ... I had been sweating for over seven hours solid ... I wanted to fall into bed, but went for the shower. The running water elicited an uncommon moan – the physical exhaustion. I could feel the water loosing the crusted salt of all the sweat, could literally feel the weighted crystals rolling off. My hands were so dirty that I didn't even want to wash my hair with them. I soaped up my scrub brush and scrubbed them for a long while and let the water run over me for an even longer time. I washed my hair twice. Out of the shower, I brushed my teeth – my mouth scummed-over with soot – slowly foaming up the anise paste with warm water. I came back into my bedroom, pulled back the covers off of the bed and collapsed. That's when the thunder started ripping outside and I felt so at home, and exhausted, and worked, and in my body – drawn in, or downwards, into the bed, by my own fatigue.
>
> (Field notes, 27 April 2005)

Contemplating 'thermal delight' in 1923, W. H. Auden wrote of a 'great financier and millionaire who, when his day's business was done, would shut himself up in a room scared from intrusion, where, throwing off his clothes, he would lie naked on a rug before a huge fire and soak himself in the heat for an hour or so', claiming it to be 'his chief happiness in life' (Classen 2005: 81). Unlike the millionaire who basked in heat only to fulfilment, I had been penetrated by heat beyond what my body could assimilate. I had been so hot, and sweated so profusely, that my body had become viscous like the hot glass, tacking to itself, to my clothes, gathering every dust fleck into ridges carved across my skin by currents of sweat; I had been so imbued by heat that I had begun to vitrify, that is to become 'glassy' and myself produced crystals – crystals large enough to be felt falling from my body under the shower's waterfall.[2] With this vitreous metabolism came an intimacy with hot glass that I had not yet known: with intercorporeality was intracorporeality. The glassy state was shared via heat's penetration and inhabitation.

Despite this intracorporeality, which, building on the concept of 'intra-action', demonstrates the dynamic symbiosis and simultaneity of becoming glassblower and becoming glass via 'hot relations', it was not an inferno of relations that I wrote of leaving in my field notes, but rather a 'studio', which rings, so cool against 'hotshop' (Barad 2003: 815). Why? Through writing of leaving the studio, I withdrew my body from the inter- and intracorporeal penetration of the working bodies of the glassblowing team into a private relation with the heat, like the millionaire before his fire. No longer extended through tools touching other bodies, themselves extended and variant, no longer breathing the mixed sweat of our team and those teams whose sweat had long oiled the communal benches and wetted the porous cement floor, no longer feeling the heat of the fires or of the amorous attention that blowing glass kindles, bodies rubbing like two sticks sparked by friction, I could, ensconced in the solitude of contemplation, imagine my 'self', perhaps as had those very artists, who brought hot glass into the 'studio', as a distinct, intentional subject. To recognize the studio as a set of hot processes and the inter- and intracorporeal nature of glassblowing may have been to lose that sense of intentionality, prized so dearly within a cultural imaginary fuelled by individualism.

Conclusion

Situating the 'hotshop' within the 'studio', where the artist is perceived to be in total control of the creative process, is not a neutral act. When the hotshop is perceived as within the studio, the interdependent, collaborative and sentient practice of glassblowing is subjected to an idea of a place, in which the artist's intentionality and capacity for 'creativity' governs. As Hattie, a contemporary glass artist explained: 'What I do in the shop is one thing, but what I do in the studio is another. They are in dialogue, but they're different. As I gain knowledge about the material [in the hotshop], it becomes more evident how I want to use the material.' For Hattie, this back-and-forth between shop and studio was mutually definitive, yet the studio had the final word: 'After five or six years, I'm finally actually making the work that uses the hotshop in a way that I like.' When the 'shop' is 'used' by the 'studio', inter- and intracorporeality, those dynamic processes marked by the interrelation of material and bodies from which meaning arises, are circumscribed. Thus what occurs in the hotshop can be subjected to the scrutiny of a self, perceived as autonomous and driven by conscious decisions. The studio–hotshop dyad enacts a social order in which the perception of the artist's intentionality can reign, mirroring an unwarranted dichotomy between mind and body.

While the studio is a set of practices and processes, the nomenclature of 'studio' in many artistic communities, including glassblowing, preserves and perpetuates the idea of individual intentionality, allowing the artist to 'author' her work. Thus the practical reality of inter- and intracorporeality in being and becoming a glassblower and teamwork did not undo Oren's reputation within the studio as a big mouth, who liked to blow big, or the gossip that he could not control his team. In the hotshop–studio dyad, the haptic space of making is circumscribed by the studio, imagined as independent of the hotshop processes constitutive of it. Over the embodied experience of dynamic materialities, like heat and colour, it was Oren's position as gaffer, perceived as the subjective interstice between form and matter, which was assigned meaning in studio life. Despite this exercise of stratification based on notions of subjective intentionality and artistic 'work', everyone who had put in a full day of the hotshop left thirsty, often adjourning to the tavern around the corner: everyone embodied and carried the heat.

Acknowledgements

I would like to thank the glassblowers at New York Glass and beyond, including Ed Schmid and Suzanne Peck, who continually support my research. In addition, I owe my pursuit of the concept of intercorporeality and thereafter intracorporeality in this chapter to discussions with participants in the Studio Studies Author Conference – many thanks.

Notes

1 Swedes refer to the area as the *Hytta,* meaning foundry, while Germans call it the *Hütte*, meaning little hut or cottage, as a contemporary glass artist explained to me via informal correspondence.
2 The science of this analogy is not exact: 'Substances in the glassy state or vitreous condition, as distinguished from substances that are crystalline, do not have the internal structure characteristic of crystals; this is, the atoms have only a random arrangement and not the regular lattices which become manifest in crystals' (Scholes 1975: 2).

References

Armstrong, I. 2008. *Victorian Glassworlds: Glass Culture and the Imagination 1830–1880*. Oxford: Oxford University Press.
Bachelard, G. 1964. *The Psychoanalysis of Fire*. Boston, MA: Beacon Press.
Barad, K. 2003. Posthumanist performativity: toward an understanding of how matter comes to matter. *Signs: Journal of Women in Culture and Society*, 28(3), 801–831.
Becker, H. 1982. *Art Worlds*. Berkeley, CA: University of California Press.
Classen, C. 2005. *The Book of Touch*. Oxford: Berg.
Crawford, M. 2009. *Shopclass as Soulcraft: An Inquiry into the Value of Work*. New York: Penguin.
Csordas, T. J. 2008. Intersubjectivity and intercorporeality. *Subjectivity*, 22, 110–121.
D'Annunzio, G. 1991. *The Flame*. New York: Marsilio.
Davis: 1949. *The Development of the Glass Industry*. Cambridge, MA: Harvard University Press.
Drexler-Lynn, M. 2004. *American Studio Glass: 1960–1990*. New York and Manchester: Hudson Hills Press.
Harper, D.A. 1987. *Working Knowledge: Skill and Community in a Small Shop*. Chicago, IL: University of Chicago Press.
Herzfeld, M. 2003. *The Body Impolitic: Artisans and Artifice in the Global Hierarchy of Value*. Chicago, IL: University of Chicago Press.
Jarves, D. 1968 [1865]. *Reminiscences of Glass-Making*. Great Neck, NY: Beatrice C. Weinstock.
Klein, D. and Lloyd, W. 1984. *The History of Glass*. London: Orbis.

Labino, D. 1968. *Visual Art in Glass*. Dubuque, IA: William C. Brown.
Marchand, T. 2001. *Minaret Building and Apprenticeship in Yemen*. Richmond: Curzon.
Marchand, T. 2009. *The Masons of Djenne*. Bloomington, IN: Indiana University Press.
Martineau, H. 1852. Birmingham glass works. *Household Words*, 5(105), 32–38.
Merleau-Ponty, M. 1964. *Signs*. Evanston, IL: Northwestern University Press.
O'Connor, E. 2007. Hot glass: the calorific imagination of glassblowing. In: Calhoun, C. and Sennett, R. eds, *Practicing Culture (Taking Culture Seriously)*. London: Routledge, pp. 57–81.
Oldknow, T. 1996. *Pilchuck: A Glass School*. Seattle, WA: University of Washington Press.
Palmer Schwind, A. 1984. The glassmakers of Early America. In: Quimby, I. M. G. ed., *The Craftsman in Early America*. London, New York: W. W. Norton & Co., pp. 158–189.
Parolin, L. L. and Mattozzi, A. 2014. Reprint of 'Sensitive translations: sensitive dimension and knowledge within two craftsmen's workplaces'. *Scandinavian Journal of Management*. http://dx.doi.org/10.1016/j.scaman.2013.12.004.
Polak, A. 1975. *Glass: Its Traditions and its Makers*. New York: Putnam.
Polanyi, M. 1962. *Personal Knowledge: Towards a Post-Critical Philosophy*. Chicago, IL: University of Chicago Press.
Schmid, E. 1997. *Advanced Glassworking Techniques*. Bellingham, WA: Glass Mountain Press.
Scholes, S. 1975. *Modern Glass Practice*. Boston, MA: Cahners Books.
Scoville, W. 1948. *Revolution in Glassmaking: Entrepreneurship and Technological Change in the American Industry*. Cambridge, MA: Harvard University Press.
Sennett, R. 2008. *The Craftsman*. New Haven, CT: Yale University Press.
Wallach Scott, J. 1974. *The Glassworkers of Carmaux: French Craftsmen and Political Action in a Nineteenth-Century City*. Cambridge, MA: Harvard University Press.

8 Architecture in the wild

The studio overflowed

Sophie Houdart

Tokyo. The ninth floor of a building that has seen better days. We are at Kengo Kuma and Associates' office. I have come here to understand the nature of the operation that characterizes the various stages of the architect's work, and more globally to grasp the operations at work in contemporary design. Kuma, an architect of the nowadays well established generation, who is known nationally and internationally, has agreed to let me spend time in his studio.

Entering the architectural studio and seeing how things go was inspired by the whole enterprise of science studies that brought to the table the possibility of comparing several sites of production by looking at its 'trajectories': 'Why should we be concerned with the nitty-gritty of laboratory practices?', asked physician Peter Galison and art historian Caroline Jones. 'Because the architecture, social structure, and cultural sitting of laboratories matters; it matters to the character of the science produced, it matters to the shifting definition of what counts as experimentation and who counts as an experimenter' (Galison and Jones 2001: 205). To 'go and see' the architectural studio (Callon 1996) relied as well on the basic assumption that what takes place on sites such as laboratories or studios counts for what is produced. Consequently, over the eight months of my visit in Kuma's office, I worked with the hypothesis that, if it were more than merely a way with words, if something were recognizable in 'Kuma's architecture', then it should be possible to see it at work in the studio, in the routine. I also suggested the hypothesis that the materiality upheld by Kuma and his 'sense of space' have something to do with the materiality as it circulated in the studio (wood, polystyrene, paint, glue, pixels) – in other words, that what the architect was working with was part of his architecture, or, to put it differently, that the architecture he creates is related to the media and space of its conception.

At various points during my study, however, I had to extend the meaning and length of what should be considered as 'the space of conception'. First sign of this extension: I often found it hard to know where I was or to find room for myself in the studio, both because of the space itself and its intrinsic crowdedness and because of the singularity of my position as an observer. Kuma's office was on two floors, the fourth and the ninth. On both floors, the work spaces, the shelving units designed to separate them and even the floor were heaped with documents and materials of all sorts. A corridor narrowed off by an impressive set of bookshelves made the ninth floor something of a maze, while down on the fourth floor the models for various projects were piled high, forming tottering edifices that threatened to topple over.

This spatial configuration accentuated my feeling that the process I was observing was a fragmented one – or more accurately, a distributed one (Cuff 1991, Hutchins 1995). No-one, from Kuma to the young architects around him, seems to hold all the cards. Kuma, although supervising the process, has trouble describing all the details when he visits the clients and represents the practice and the project – the architects cannot make a single decision without Kuma's approval, and then there are also the students who make the models, in the dark as to what materials are being used and where the project is located. The students do not interact with Kuma – the architects go between one level (explaining details to the students so that they can create the models) and the other (discussing the same details with Kuma, noting down suggested modifications) – and back again; the architects come back downstairs to tell the students of Kuma's suggested modifications. This all seemed to me slightly complicated for everyone concerned – and from my point of view, it also creates the problem of knowing where things are actually taking place. Looking at architects or trainers constantly moving from one

Figure 8.1. Models forming tottering edifices in the studio
Source: © the author

floor to another, I soon realized there was something going on here that defied anyone to remain static. There were frantic moves of people, of materials, of models, of drawings or data, that made architectural objects seem to move along the way – that made them seem to move as long as I decide to move with them, letting them guide me in and out the walls of the studio (Latour and Yaneva 2008, Yaneva 2009a). But how far from the studio should one consider following these moves?

Visits to sites or meetings with clients or engineers are constitutive of architects' routine. It has already been shown how public confrontations of architectural projects at large are more than presentations: they are part of the design process per se, and can be seen as 'complex networks [that] extend and prolong the work of the architects' (Yaneva 2009a: 162). They often constitute critical moments to observe in making negotiations between interest groups about what should figure in the project, what should be taken care of, what should be modified. Concentrating on the 'heterogeneous engineering' (Law 1987) required to get a building completed, works devoted to architectural practices mostly focus on what happens within the studio. To put it straightforwardly, one could say that a first set of statements has been made to externalize the moment of conception outside the head of the architect–creator (e.g. Cuff 1991). A second set of statements shows the heuristic benefit of following trajectories of models or drawings 'in the office environment as they move from one material arrangement to another' (Yaneva 2009b: 64). I have described at length elsewhere architectural practices as they take place within the studio (Houdart 2009). In this chapter, I aim to go through some of my ethnographic data once again to tackle more precisely what circulates not only within the studio, but also out of it. Mimicking the reflexion developed by historical or social studies of science regarding field sciences, and notably the relationships between outdoor spaces and laboratories, I will interrogate the peculiar work of architectural objects as they come in and out of the studio to eventually make clear that the studio is constantly overflowed by heterogeneous things. I will therefore complicate the common idea that:

> Architects do not build buildings, they make drawings and models; at least that is what most do most of the time in most contemporary practices. Because of this, the open space of the physical world is really not the framework for creative work in architecture; substituting for it, or serving as its site, is the surface of a drawing a map, survey, or plan whether executed graphically or digitally. The 'space' of the drawing is assumed to be like that of the environment, sky-like or unbounded.
>
> (Leatherbarrow 2002: 25)

Without opposing this general statement, I will show that 'the open space of the physical world' and the relations stated in the field, with people as well as with elements, objects or atmospheres, stretch the space of conception.

I will start by briefly describing what serves as the basic pathway for Kuma to reflexively construct, without leaving the studio, the relationships between his architecture and its environment. Then I move on to a detailed narrative of two visits on site, taking place with an interval of a few weeks, for one of the projects for which I followed the design process. As I tried laboriously to catch up with all the steps that supposedly inform the project, the assumption that something of the project may originate in the wild was put to test.

What does the garden do to the studio?

The model to which Kuma's own architectural practice refers is very elaborate. One of Kuma's *leitmotifs* is to 'erase' architecture, or to make it 'invisible', to fragment or 'particlize' it. For supporting such an ambition, Kuma invokes the Japanese logic of the place that considers as a continuous whole 'the environment and the object, the subject and the object, the time and the world' (Kuma 1997: 9), but also Gilles Deleuze's concept of the elasticity of materials, for instance:

> By particlising materials, they become ingredients awaiting action by the architect. They are not a result of action, but rather ingredients for action. [...] Where Deleuze uses elasticity to illustrate this argument, I use particles.
>
> (Kuma 2000: 86)

How does Kuma enact his proposal? It is one thing to yearn for buildings as transient as rainbows, it is another to have them effectively built in the outside world. How does Kuma get a building to disappear? How does he 'particlize' materials, but yet have buildings standing up? How could the studio be the place of such transmutation? According to Kuma himself, the operation originates not within the studio but outside it, along a slight but very significant change of what architectural competencies should be. Having a building disappear is first a relationship with its environment, and here Kuma opposes the standpoint of the planner and the standpoint of the gardener:

> The planner stands 'outside' the landscape and visually manipulates it. In gardening, on the other hand, no privileged position from which a 'planner' observes and manipulates the scenery exists. The 'gardener' is always inside the garden
>
> (Kuma 1997: 8)

and therefore can never reduce the strength of local circumstances. Such statements don't really need the studio to exist. They need computers and software, sheets of paper and editors. These are architectural concepts that define, at most, a line of action (acting in such a way as to have a discrete building) or a line of recognition (the possibility of recognizing Kuma's architectural patterns among international contemporary architectures). But the pragmatic value of the gardener's standpoint on the architect's one in settling a building into an environment can only be fully understood by grasping their 'decisive go-between' (Latour 1999: 40). As Latour puts it: 'One never travels directly from objects to worlds, from the referent to the sign, but always through a risky intermediary pathway' (ibid.).

So, as Kuma invites me to do, let's move closer to one particular project and risk ourselves on the pathway that would connect, in a way still to be defined, the world out there and the object to be designed. When we negotiated my presence as a cultural anthropologist in his studio, Kuma suggested that, instead of observing the day-to-day running of the studio, as I introduced my own project, I should follow a project or two; I should not observe the studio itself, but an architectural project – what to Kuma seemed the most relevant unit in order to understand what he was up to. I made my choice, on Kuma's suggestion, to follow one of the studio's latest projects: a building to house the workshop – yet another studio – of a famous Japanese glassblower, Makoto Nishikawa, on the southern tip of Honshu Island. The project was only just getting under way and I would be able to follow it as it unfolded from the very beginning.

I am lucky. A visit to the site is soon organized and I take it as an opportunity to confront the philosophical horizon of Kuma's architecture on site and landscape with surveying practices in the making. A few weeks later, I am on my way to Yamaguchi to accompany Kuma and his assistant on this project, Makoto. The three of us meet up at the airport. Kuma, his hands in his pockets, has only his diary and mobile phone as luggage. Makoto carries an A3-sized portfolio. I am as lightly equipped as they are, bringing with me the basic tools to document the day. With regard to my own theoretical kit, I have in mind at this very moment the pedologists studied by Bruno Latour (1999). I can't help myself in expecting Kuma or Makoto to roll up their sleeves, as the pedologists in the Amazonian forest did, in order to handle the territory and eventually know something about it. I expect them to point fingers on plans in place of actual sites, or format soil specimens. 'For the world to become knowable, it must become a laboratory', argues Latour (ibid.: 43). Laboratories being sites to produce certainty, scientists have no better option than to stabilize and reduce, as much as they can, the forest into workable items. Latour's pedologists illustrate the complexity of detaching knowledge from the place it relates to, a land, its peculiarities, its instabilities but also its flavours. This detachment process itself has a long history in science, of which the Prussian traveller Alexander von Humboldt's expeditions are probably one of the best examples. Michael Dettelbach explains how precise measurement instruments were the only way, for Humboldt, to 'analyze the total impression made by Nature on our organs [...] Only the application of sensitive instruments, with determinable limits of error, could render nature's lawfulness sensible' (Dettelbach 1999: 480). But from what I already learned about Kuma by reading his books, I guess that, contrary to Humboldt or contemporaneous pedologists who have to stand artificially outside the landscape to know about it, Kuma wouldn't choose to occupy the same position. Choosing to proceed as a gardener, as he invokes, he shouldn't want to map the site, to objectify it. So how is he going to proceed to learn something from his visit? How is he going to manage to bring back to the studio something that he can work with? What can Kuma and his colleagues not gain or reach without moving out of the studio? Without making this move? What is there outside that architects cannot project or foresee within the space of the studio?

When we arrive at our destination, a man who is to be our driver for the day is waiting for us. I know nothing of the day's programme, and let myself go with the flow. We reach a wasteland, which looks out over the sea. On the right side of the plot there is a building that appears to be a somewhat refined prefabricated building; it is Makoto's glassblowing studio awaiting revision by Kuma. We get out of the car, and before entering the prefabricated building, Kuma and Makoto walk across the plot to the concrete fortifications marking its boundaries and separating it from the beach below. Makoto unrolls the tape measure he has been carrying in his pocket and the two men exchange a few words. The sequence doesn't last more than a minute. If this holds for measurement, it obviously doesn't look for exactitude, but rather consists of a mere equipped estimation of a certain depth to be inscribed into the building to come.

Turning our back to the wall, we enter the building by the huge French windows facing the sea, which open directly into the studio. We are welcomed by the artist Nishikawa Makoto, who soon begins to show us around, pointing out the different furnaces which he designed himself; this one functions at a certain temperature, and this one at another; this one is for this use, and this one for another… We look over the different equipment in the first room (the hot room), then in the second (the cold room). Kuma interrupts Nishikawa's explanations, verifies a term (the name of the furnace), and signals to Makoto to take notes on the different names. Makoto gets out his notebook and writes that he will need a list of the various pieces of equipment.

All of a sudden our visit is interrupted by a tidal wave of men in grey suits and tight ties, invading the studio with their incongruous presence. Kuma, Makoto and I stand back and observe, amused, these self-assured men who have taken over the studio. Their social standing obviously justifies the artist's abandoning us for a moment to undertake a new lightning tour of the workshop. Kuma is introduced briefly, evidently not the keystone of the conversation. What is at stake here takes place on a local level – and Kuma is from elsewhere. Then, as rapidly as they appeared, they disappear, leaving our host to continue his guided tour where he had left off. As soon as the tour has finished, our driver, anxious to stick to the agenda, hurries us to the exit, cutting short our visit to the boutique adjoining the studio.

We stop at a restaurant a few hundred metres further on. I recognize it as one of Kuma's completed buildings. Recognizing the architect, the chef and his team greet us effusively. We are invited into a reserved room upstairs.

Figure 8.2. The glassblower explaining his studio
Source: © the author.

Makoto, Kuma and I take our seats, looking out over the beach where surfers are getting ready to take to the waves… I enthuse, without having to make an effort, about the restaurant, the magnificent view, the building's light with its glass partitions. Opposite us sit the restaurant owner, our driver and timekeeper, and the artist Nishikawa. As the dishes arrive one after the other, the artist explains the conditions when working with glass. The cold during the winter in a badly insulated locale, the heat during the summer, the intense heat (the temperature in the 'hot room' can reach 50°C); the problems opening the hot room because of the wind and the fragility of the material, and the fact that the glass should not be exposed to direct sunlight. From the conversation, it arises that the crucial factors when working with glass are the air and ventilation: 'it's a real problem', the artist says once again. The meal draws to a close, and we resume our hectic schedule. We return to the car, leaving Nishikawa at the restaurant. It's the second time I bid him goodbye today. As we drive, Kuma, obviously impressed, discusses Nishikawa's merits, both as a glassblower and as a teacher; the artist has an enlightened vision of education, and the age range of his pupils stretches from the very young to the very old.

We reach the Town Hall. Polite greetings are exchanged each time we pass in front of a counter. We are led to an office with large leather chairs, and Kuma, Makoto and I take our places on one side of an immense glass table.

The men from the Town Hall – the same ones who turned up at the glass factory before lunch – sit down opposite us. The circle is completed by a man, older than the others, who arrives after everyone else, and around whom everyone is bustling, placing him at the centre. Somewhat naively, I am expecting the negotiations for the project to take place there and then, and I take the opening conversation to be the usual exchange of courtesies, a gentle introduction before getting to the heart of the problem. Kuma starts the conversation by talking about Nishikawa, saying that he really is unrivalled in Japan, and that his work can be found as far afield as Tokyo. As though repeating a well learned lesson, Kuma talks about Nishikawa's teaching, open to everyone – even children can blow glass. He even teaches five-year-olds, imagine – it's amazing; and mainly women. We then enthuse about the proposed site for the glass factory and also about the county of Yamaguchi in general. Kuma asks if the surfers on the beach are a new phenomenon in the region – he hadn't seen any when the restaurant was being built. It's the latest craze, and the windy climate is ideal. Kuma says he feels that, with such a wonderful view, one is sure to blow glass differently. He then moves on to talk about the culture of glass in Europe, especially at weddings. Kuma also boasts of Nishikawa's presence at the biennial festival in Venice, the event that brings together artists from all over the world, he explains. Nishikawa even built his own furnaces! It's 100% handmade… I'm still waiting for the crux of the matter to be addressed, but the conversation appears to be almost over, as though extinguishing itself with the reason for a French ethnologist's presence in Japan. The officials precede us, leaving the room as we bid our farewells. Our driver takes over, showing us out. We leave Makoto in the Town Hall, in the Public Works Department. On the way back, I tell Kuma how daunting I found the group of men. Here it is not like in Tokyo, he explains, in Tokyo it is far more 'administrative', here it is 'like a family', and courtesy visits are expected. Meetings between Kuma and local authorities can only take place, I understand much later, in a polite mode, and by contrast without content, or rather without any content other than the social exchange itself.

We stop once again at the glassblowing studio. We have a little time before our return flight to Tokyo, and Nishikawa suggests that Kuma try his hand at glassblowing. The lesson begins; everyone is laughing and rather excited. Nishikawa, who addresses Kuma in the habitual respectful terms, humbly explains the different steps and asks Kuma to begin by drawing the glass he wants to make. The architect removes his jacket. In the shop, Kuma is given a paper and pencil and he sketches a few lines, like a champagne flute, and everyone admires the master's sketch. Kuma is then told what to do, amidst the crackles and flashes.

Kuma's glass almost completed, Nishikawa tells him how talented he is and congratulates him for his first attempt as we admire the finished glass; Nishikawa puts it in the furnace and we quickly gather up our belongings and jackets and leave the effusive crowd. We rush to catch the plane, and sleep for the entire journey.

Figure 8.3. Skills exchange: from the artist to the architect
Source: © the author.

So this is what it means to go out of the studio, feel the site and work with the place – an architect and a glassblower sharing their different talents and, above all, getting along without saying too much to design a new object. It involves photographs of the site itself (or rather one of its boundaries) as well as of Kuma rolling up his sleeves, not to survey the site, as I expected, but to perform his creativity on a material he is not used to. It's about strengthening ties with a 'family' which has the power of life and death over the project. It's about the names of furnaces and techniques, the edifying properties of glass, and the constraints which have to be worked with rather than endured – heat, light and air. Kuma gains experience of the atmosphere by himself. He got the feeling of the absence of breeze while opening the oven; the almost suffocating atmosphere of the inner space, for which the atmosphere of the outdoor space is not of much help on this summer day. All these experiences don't count for nothing. They have to be taken into consideration in order to comprehend what was at work on such a day. There was nothing grandiloquent about this visit to the site, just the activation of a disparate group of connections between humans as well as between humans and non-humans, more or less close, that will all be part of the definitive work in one way or another.

Architecture in a box

Some weeks after the first visit, we're setting off once again for Yamaguchi to present a model that Makoto is carrying with him in a large box. During the interlude between the two visits, long sequences took place within the studio that gave the impression that the project was progressing along a more-or-less stable trajectory. On the fourth floor, at the 'model table', I have been observing two interns, Asako and Yuzuru, in turns, working on constructing models for the Glass Factory. I was struck to realize that to do this, the interns did not need to 'know' Yamaguchi's beaches; they did not even need to figure out what it is to blow glass. Plans designed by Makoto played their role perfectly. Apart from the 'accidental or circumstantial [horizon] tacitly known by virtue of the typical negotiations and relationships of a people and a region' (Leatherbarrow 2002: 10) that characterized the visit on site, plans convoked 'situation' rather than 'position' that allowed interns to build models without being preoccupied by the features of the site itself. This is why, back in Tokyo, I could not locate Yamaguchi's beaches, the heat of the glassblower's studio or the Japanese summer all mixed together. On the model table in the studio, all these aspects ended up next to a Japanese countryside known for its abundant snowfall, or to a dense urban area. Here projects cross each other and converge together to draw something that gains, project after project, a particular texture – what eventually becomes the 'signature' of the architect or his style. In contrast to the architectural site, the studio appears as a place where the logic is one of reduction and accumulation. Year after year, project after project, there are motifs that prove to work, and all of their versions count. For the Glass Factory project, louvres became, during the interlude between the two visits, one of the major pieces of the design, as they were already for other projects. At the time of the study, louvre motifs pervaded Kuma's architecture to the point that, half ironically and half in the hope of minimizing the time and effort devoted to each project, printed louvre motifs were systematically archived in what looked like a shoebox: 'Recycling Louvres!' says the box.

Sticking to the Glass Factory project, I observed Asako and Yuzuru regularly picking them up in the box whenever they needed to integrate or superimpose the motif onto a model. Something is clearly gained in the process of archiving louvres (Arellano-Lechuga 2012) that allows those who are building models to work on the basis of a shared knowledge. But the experiences of heat or meeting with the 'family' of local politicians over there didn't seem to be part of it.

Kuma does not come on the second visit. When I meet up with Makoto at the airport, he is smiling broadly and very excited, telling me that yesterday evening, 'the volume was completely altered'. He and Kuma had started to look over the design as a whole together in the late afternoon, and Asako stayed to work on the new model and plans all night. Kuma suddenly decided that the louvres should cover the entire height of the façade. This decision changed everything, the height of the walls and the overall volume. Makoto went back to the office this morning to fetch the model and had to take a taxi

Figure 8.4. Architecture in a shoebox: 'Recycling Louvres!'
Source: © the author.

to the airport, hurrying the driver along so as not to miss the flight. Quite an adventure. The same man picks us up at the airport and takes us first to the site. The engine is still running while Makoto photographs the empty plot from the concrete fortifications, to the right and left, approaching the seafront and positioning himself in the middle of the wasteland.

It takes even less time for Makoto to take the photographs than it took him to unroll his tape measure in the previous sequence. Acting as a surveyor, Makoto is collecting a view rather than a topographic plot. This view, obstructed by a wall, is hardly a horizon. But the wall is precisely the thing that matters here because it is what architects will have to work with once back in the studio. Makoto will catch the plane that evening with this new 'data' to add to that already covering the floor of the office: among other things, this photograph which, no sooner back in the office, Makoto will download then share with the graphic designer, Hiroaki, for the conception of the perspective drawings. On another workstation, the digitalized images will await their transformation. Hiroaki will 'turn over' the image showing the band of concrete separating the wasteland and the fortifications, in such a way as to show it as though we could see the scene from the sea (which is also the position from which we look at the 'perspective').

The visit does not end with the wall, however. We dine at the same restaurant we visited during the first trip. After our dessert, our driver asks Makoto

Figure 8.5. Sampling the site
Source: © the author.

if he could see the new documents. We set up the model on one of the chairs, made of black laces and itself designed by Kuma and Associates. On site, the model has the light behind it from the bay window with the sea beyond. We all take photos, although it is hard to render the details because of the light, which is so bright at this time of day. The impromptu photo session draws to a close, and the model is put back into its cardboard box.

We return to the car and drive to the Public Works Department in the Town Hall. Makoto and I wait for several men from the 'family' and engineers to take their seats opposite us. The model is placed in the middle of the table. Gradually, the subject is introduced: one of the men asks Makoto if they are planning to design a building in the same vein as the restaurant. No, not really, although the louvres are a point in common, Kuma uses them a lot, but here, the important thing is ventilation: the louvres become 'jalousies' which open (using his hand, his fingers closed, Makoto mimics the movement of the slats). Makoto situates the model we have in front of us with regard to the sea and the wall on the right-hand side of the table, which blocks the view of the current building on the right and the block of buildings to the left. Makoto begins his presentation, excusing Kuma's absence in a very conventional manner and explaining modestly that he will be representing him today. Three major themes have influenced the design of the initial plans: (i) to be able to see the sea from the hall, so as to have a view from inside the building;

Figure 8.6. The studio on site
Source: © the author.

(ii) taking very seriously the problem of ventilation because of the presence of the hot shop; and (iii) giving visual access from the hall to the activities in the various rooms. Makoto has handed everyone a set of documents stapled together. He begins his comments with a perspective rendering which shows the building from the seafront side. In order to give an idea of the general layout of the building, he comes back to the model, tracing imaginary circles on the roof, which indicate the highest part, the factory; the lowest part with the classroom; and the hall in the centre. With the flat of his hand, Makoto strokes and points out the slope of the roof, the axis on which the building is orientated. Moving on from the model to the perspective drawing, Makoto then emphasizes the main graphic element – the louvres which are jalousies. 'When we were talking with the artist', Makoto explains, 'it came to light that the ventilation was really the most important factor. The idea was, literally, to take the sea air and make it the main source of ventilation, regulated by the system of the slatted blinds.' Still talking of the façade facing the sea, Makoto draws our attention to the horizontal louvres, and then to the vertical concrete overhangs: one of the conditions was also to 'cut out direct sunlight' which is not good when working with glass. 'And with the jalousies, one could still have a view of the sea from inside', insists Makoto. For a moment, louvres seem the perfect architectural objects to resolve local problems: they show their functional strength in supporting the specific environment required by a glassblower's studio.

However, if this reduction can operate at ease within the studio, it has to be confronted on site by a whole range of considerations that Makoto could not anticipate. Stepping forward in the plan of the interior, Makoto demonstrates that from the hall, 'we can see everything': both rooms and the sea. He points out the terrace, which can be reached from both wings and the hall, to make the most of the view. But there's a problem: someone is concerned that it will be too easy to get into the building via the sea-facing side:

CLIENT 1: In the summer a lot of young people come here. They'll come from the beach thinking they've found a good spot to shelter!
MAKOTO: But it would be a pity to close off this area …
CLIENT 1: They might accept a graffiti culture in America, but here we really don't want that sort of thing!
CLIENT 2: What about metal shutters?
MAKOTO: That wouldn't really fit in well with the rest of the design …
CLIENT 2: Or railings?
CLIENT 1: Well, this is going to be a problem … it is the conclusion reached.

The hint is quite clear – the problem will not be solved straight away, and the question will have to be seriously reconsidered. Obviously, Kuma and Makoto will have to start again and study 'the' question once more, and offer new alternatives. But on the way, the question itself has diffracted: it doesn't just concern the problem of ventilation inside the glassblower's studio any more, but extends to the people and habits of this particular place. 'In creative architectural work', notes Leatherbarrow, 'sites are not the framework for design, they do not provide rule and pattern; sites are revealed through design and construction, which is to say articulated. To some degree this is always a rearticulation' (Leatherbarrow 2002: 57).

So what has been achieved during this second visit? What has been conveyed? What has changed? Makoto has returned with far more information – the first time, he was equipped only with his notebook; now he comes with a model of the Glass Factory which he can confront (come face to face with) in several ways; by photographing it in the restaurant, and in doing so giving it a setting, its own setting, with the blue of the sky which will soon be its own, the sea stretching before it, as it will do shortly; by placing it in the middle of the table, at the centre of the discussions, discussions which will involve it a little more in the concerns of the place, the sea winds and the young people on the beach. Makoto arrived here today richer in information, and leaves richer still. All these things (such as properties, aspects and conditions) are expected to be distorted. The sun and the wind do not act as physical constraints; they are things that the architects can work with. This sun, this wind, these heats are the elements that eventually make these louvres different from others.

Concluding remarks

It now seems a long time ago, and so very antiquated, that studios could be described as 'sites of purely individual contemplation and creation, closer to its monkish and medieval sources in the Latin studium, for zealous learning, than to the bustling scriptorium or guild workshop' (Galison and Jones 1999: 510). The time is past when 'assistants, wives, and the entire outside world were figured as inhabitants of a periphery that bears no functional relationship to the laboratory/studio domain' (ibid: 510). How many people have I encountered who, in some way or another, have contributed to making this project happen? How many moves from one place to another? How many slight transformations and 'displacements' (Latour 1999: 39)? The studio no longer appears as a self-contained and self-constrained space, but rather as a distributed site from where to proceed with conception work which could be redefined essentially as a 'composition' work (Descola 2014).

The in-depth description mode I have adopted in this chapter to render these moves has been purposely intensified in order to neutralize the temptation to read in these many moves a simple input/output scheme. Taking the studio from one of its outsides – the visit on site – is a way to accentuate the idea that the architectural studio is 'a mosaic field built up situation by situation' (Leatherbarrow 2002: 19), rather than a controlled room from which to project the world to come. Going back and forth between two studios, that of the architect and that of the glassblower who delegated the architect (by the way of local administration) to redesign his place, I had first to extend my perspective in order to understand how specifications for a creative space moved to another one, and how these moves operated to give the building-to-come its specific colour and texture. But specifications that would count for the Glass Factory project don't limit themselves to the technical constraints required by glassblowing. If the garden does something to the studio, this is by softening the appreciation of objective measures, or by making denser the knowledge of a place acquired in the process of building. Obviously, places cannot be considered as givens, and one couldn't reasonably expect the space of conception outside the studio to be more stable than the space of conception within the studio. Sites are all but the stable framework on which architects or designers can rely to erect proper objects. They are co-constructed during the many trials that occur both in the wild and in the studio. The logic of accumulation and reduction that seems to prevail within the studio is put to test in the wild; but the test is a two-sided coin: There is accumulation there too (Kuma having learned to know the people and places over time and projects, for instance), and there is reduction too (remember the model being put on a chair with the sea in the background), which require to be accounted for if one wants to comprehend what is at stake in architectural practices.

Acknowledgements

I am grateful to Ignacio Farías and Alex Wilkie for their patience and support in editing this manuscript. Many thanks to Lucy Lyall-Grant for part of the translation.

References

Arellano-Lechuga, L. 2012. Archives, memory of architectural creation? In: Zavatta, S. ed., *Architecture and Time*. Besançon: Les Presses du Réel, pp. 227–235.

Callon, M. 1996. Le travail de la conception en architecture. *Les Cahiers de la Recherche Architecturale*, 37, 25–35.

Cuff, D. 1991. *Architecture: The Story of Practice*. Cambridge, MA and London: MIT Press.

Descola, P. 2014. *La composition des mondes. Entretiens avec Pierre Charbonnier*. Paris: Flammarion.

Dettelbach, M. 1999. The face of nature: precise measurement, mapping, and sensibility in the work of Alexander von Humboldt. *Studies in History and Philosophy of Biological and Biomedical Sciences*, 30(4): 473–504.

Galison, P. and Jones, C. 1999. Factory, laboratory, studio: dispersing sites of production. In: Galison, P. and Thompson, E. eds, *The Architecture of Science*. Cambridge, MA and London: MIT Press, pp. 497–540.

Galison, P. and Jones, C. 2001. Trajectories of production: laboratories/factories/studios. In: Obrist, H. U. ed., *Laboratorium*. Germany: Dumont, Antwerpen Open, Roomade, pp. 205–210.

Houdart, S. 2007. *La cour des miracles. Ethnologie d'un laboratoire japonais.* Paris: CNRS Editions.
Houdart, S. 2008. Importing, cutting–pasting social spheres: computer designers' participation on an architectural project. *Science Studies* (special issue: Understanding Architecture, Accounting Society), 1, 47–63.
Houdart, S. and Minato, C. 2009. *Kuma Kengo. An Unconventional Monograph.* Paris: Donner Lieu.
Hutchins, E. 1995. *Cognition in the Wild.* Cambridge, MA and London: MIT Press.
Kuma, K. 1997. Digital gardening. *Space Design: Monthly Journal of Art and Architecture*, 398, 6–132.
Kuma, K. 2000. *Han obujekuto. Kenchiku wo tokashi, kudaku (Anti-Object. Or How to Dissolve or Fragment Architecture)*. Tokyo: Chûo Seihan.
Latour, B. 1999. *Pandora's Hope. Essays on the Reality of Science Studies.* Cambridge, MA: Harvard University Press.
Latour, B. and Yaneva, A. 2008. 'Give me a gun and I will make all buildings move': an ANT's view of architecture. In: Geiser, R. ed., *Explorations in Architecture: Teaching, Design, Research.* Basel: Birkhäuser, pp. 80–89.
Law, J. 1987. Technology and heterogeneous engineering. In: Bijker, W. et al. eds, *The Social Construction of Technology.* Cambridge, MA: MIT Press.
Leatherbarrow, D. 2002. *Uncommon Ground. Architecture, Technology, and Topography.* Cambridge, MA, London: MIT Press.
Yaneva, A. 2009a. *The Making of a Building. A Pragmatist Approach to Architecture.* Oxford, Bern, Berlin, Bruxelles, Frankfurt am Main, New York, Wien: Peter Lang.
Yaneva, A. 2009b. *Made by the Office for Metropolitan Architecture: An Ethnography of Design.* Rotterdam: 010 Publishers.

Interview 2

9 Temporalities, aesthetics and the studio

An interview with Georgina Born

Georgina Born and Alex Wilkie

Alex Wilkie: Your foundational study of the Institute de Recherche et Coordination Acoustique/Musique (IRCAM) in Paris (Born 1995), where the 'studio' hosts the production of high modernist and experimental electronic music, seems to have played an instrumental part in your approach?

Georgina Born: With my ethnography of IRCAM I arrived in this high modernist computer music institution in 1984 having never been in an environment of electronic music – except for Henry Cow, the avant-garde rock group I played in – and having never touched a computer before. I realised that for this study it was necessary to invent an analysis of mediation as a methodology that could cope with music's profuse mediations. This involved the idea that musical sound always comes to us both embodied in and transformed by its numerous simultaneous mediations: discursive, social, technological, visual, spatial, temporal and so on. The discursive was particularly interesting at IRCAM because the production and inscription of knowledge via computers was central to the place, so I had to understand the status of this production. I quickly realized the radically arbitrary nature of the relationship between all this discursive production and sound, informed by the semiotic anthropology of Steven Feld (Feld and Fox 1994). It's interesting how little this is grasped by musicology in as much as discursivity can't be understood as having any necessary or natural relationship to musical sound.

So my work on IRCAM resonates with the premise of studio studies, since the site of music production there, the 'studio', is a very extended one. The studios inside IRCAM were in fact engaged in the production of software and hardware as much as the making of music. I took all of this as the 'site' of creativity, in a strongly distributed sense; and it led me not only to do the first ethnography of the materiality and the distributed labour of software production (Born 1996, 1997), but also provocatively to analyse the entire hierarchical institutional division of labour within which music was being produced – from the top echelons of scientific and artistic management, through engineers and composers, to secretaries and cleaners, i.e. the whole spectrum of contributions – as amounting to the social mediation of IRCAM music. This came from an anthropological sensibility, and I commend it: the Latourian conception of the 'social' as network, now often uncritically adopted, can blind us to the enduring forms within which cultural production proceeds, such as extended social hierarchies.

Alex Wilkie: What I find interesting about your work is that it acts as a corrective to thinking about the studio as a vessel or container of artistic and so-called 'creative' practices. In your account, the studio is always situated in some kind of institutional arrangement …

Georgina Born: … or, I'd say, in relation to other scales, wider arenas. I studied two major institutions, IRCAM (Born 1995) and the BBC (Born 2005b), and my work on art–science also engages with the University of California, Irvine (Born and Barry 2010). The key question here is: what's the relevant unit of analysis at such scales? For our research at Irvine it was important to take the university into account: our enquiry into the Arts, Computation and Engineering master's programme there focused on interdisciplinarity, and this had been the premise of UC Irvine since its inception. So with our art–science ethnography, the university necessarily enters the analysis, but so does the University of California system-wide Digital Arts Research Network. And ditto for my work on IRCAM and the BBC because they, like most major cultural institutions, have policies and management credos that condition how 'creativity' proceeds in the 'studio'. It's standard anthropological method to take such policies or discursive forms and hold them up against practices and actualities, so as to analyse both their influence and the drift and disparities that become apparent.

For the past four years I've been working with a team of ethnographers on a project, 'MusDig', studying music and digitization in six countries.[1] Most of these studies are multi-sited, and music circulates amongst various settings. What's striking here is that what we call 'digital art musics', the inheritors of earlier computer and electronic art musics, is a differential and a plural category, and one that is defined around the question of the institution. Much of this musical practice occurs within academia, and the boundary between this and outside, non-academic practices is highly charged and marked. One of the themes of our work concerns the transformation of this very boundary, noting how many artists who've emerged outside the academic scene are busily trying to accrue the authority to enter the academy and influence academic music. So this is a key era of transition in which the relationship between academic and non-academic musics is being reconfigured as we watch. In Montreal, for example, Patrick Valiquet, one of the researchers, is looking at practices both inside and outside the universities, and charting the changing relationship between those scenes.

In contrast, our research on digital popular musics in Kenya and Argentina, two other sites in the MusDig project, is very different. In both countries, we're looking at tiny studio and bedroom operations, or at small labels and production houses, where there's no larger institutional identity. The economy of such outfits and how they survive is varied. Some survive simply by a very rapid throughput of production. So one inventive production house in Nairobi, Still Alive Records, is run by a producer called Tim Boikwa who charges for his expertise and studio time by the hour, serving queues of people down the block who all consider themselves to be 'artists'. In a typical day he will have a dozen people through, lay down a track for them, produce it, arrange it, and turn them out with a burned CD. This is how his studio economy operates: it's immediate, non-collaborative labour, and very rapid throughput.

Across Nairobi, in the production house Ketebul Music, they are trying to create would-be Kenyan equivalents to Youssou N'Dour or Salif Keïta so as to enter world music markets. This is supported by a huge range of transnational charities and corporations: the Ford Foundation, Goethe Institut, Alliance Francaise, Total Oil, BP as well as EU development funds. All this development and charity money is coming in because they are doing a kind of music that is understood to have potential civil society effects. So to understand the Ketebul 'studio' and what it's doing aesthetically, right down to particular gestures at the mixing desk, we need to understand the ethos of production – and that's in part to do with funding policies supporting their work. The studio is enmeshed in a particular development paradigm in which the idea of the 'creative economy' has become highly influential. Evidentially, we can follow the mediations: how the creative economy paradigm entered development, such that aid comes in the guise of support for cultural production – and, prominently, music. Ketebul, a production house built around a senior figure in Kenyan popular music, is seen as a prime conduit for bringing this vision, at once a musical and a political vision, into being. The audience that's envisaged in this setup is a new national Kenyan middle class that, it's imagined, will be assembled by particular sounds that are inflected by a range of Kenyan ethnic musics. This is, then, a hugely important cultural political project, the aim of which is nothing less than to assist in overcoming the ethnic divisions still rife in Kenya, and to do this by combined aesthetic-and-social projections (Born 2011a).

Allowing the wider arenas, the institutions and/or political economy, into the analysis makes it possible, then, to follow how they enter into the minutiae of creative practices – into the studio. In Ketebul, this happens through a preference for certain kinds of sounds, production techniques and uses of the digital audio workstation, all of which are oriented to the imagination of a certain trans- or post-ethnic sound, which it is believed will, in turn, produce a new audience – a Kenyan national middle class.

Alex Wilkie: So, such studio distributions operate to elicit new publics through post-ethnic sounds, and this is mediated through concatenations of intermediaries including specific gestures, tones, technologies as well as institutional and economic arrangements. In that context, could you describe how you became interested in the mediations of music? Your work relates to Antoine Hennion's, but differs in many distinctive ways.

Georgina Born: I had a version of my own mediation theory from the early 1990s. But I returned to mediation through a reading of Alfred Gell's *Art and Agency* (1998) when I wrote 'On musical mediation' (Born 2005a), asking:

what would happen if we took Gell's approach to music? It suggested two starting points. First, Gell addresses the way objects in their circulation are both embedded in, and engender, social relations. His is a Durkheimian account of the social, but I've developed a distinctive account of music's multiple social mediations (Born 2011b). Second, there's a temporal aspect to the circulation of art objects, and this is often neglected. So what interested me was to develop an analysis of the socialities and the temporalities engendered by the object's circulation; and then to take these ideas to music and consider the ways in which music, as a form, demands a specific theory of mediation.

In this sense my work comes close to Antoine Hennion's, yet differs. I extended Gell's work to think about music's social and temporal mediations. But what was still missing was any account of how such mediations relate to music's plural ontologies – by which I refer to how human actors understand what music is, how it is lived and experienced. In 'On musical mediation' I contrast two prominent historical ontologies of music. The first is the romantic ontology of the musical work, anatomized by Lydia Goehr (1992), where an essentialized conception of the work ideal goes along with the absolute denial or absenting of almost all of music's material and social mediations. This contrasts with a huge body of work from cultural studies and popular music studies since the 1970s on black musics – jazz, hip-hop and dub reggae, for instance – in which music's material and social mediations are to the fore in terms of how music is experienced. Here, the materiality of the vinyl record, the beat box or the drum machine, along with social relations of race and class, figure powerfully in what music is. This is not only about mediation, but about ontology: together the two musics evidence radically different ontologies.

It became obvious to me, further, that this way of approaching music was in tension with a Latourian stance, where the world is addressed through an *a priori* ontology. In my paper on Gabriel Tarde's social theory (Born 2010a), I make the point that we should distinguish between the ontology of the analyst and the ontology of our actors. We shouldn't confuse the two, nor should we project our own ontology onto those we study. I turned to Lisa Blackman's work, which I admire greatly, to point to the risk in psychosocial thought of projecting analytical ontologies that occlude the ontologies of those we study. It's a similar problem with Latour: beyond the dualism of moderns and non-moderns, he's not really interested in the ontology of the actors, which, as anthropology shows, is a rich and complex matter. My own method in the ethnography of distributed objects is to analyse the multiple mediations as an assemblage or constellation, and then move to the actors' ontology (Born 2013); what is interesting with this step is how certain mediations become prominent ontologically while, as I suggested above, others disappear or are absented.

Alex Wilkie: I'm also struck by the temporalities of the studio, something that seems especially relevant to musical practices and modes of production. A feature of the Nairobi studios, you mentioned before, is the tempo at which they produce musical output, via the coordination of all sorts of studio temporalities?

Georgina Born: Yes: at Still Alive studio, as I said, the tempo of production is incessant. It's a very rapid throughput of would-be artists, and the owner–producer Tim Boikwa sells his services hourly, producing a recording, a CD, that they walk away with. He lays down guitar, keyboard and rhythm tracks, which he processes, mixes, quantizes and de-quantizes. He's a master, hence the studio's reputation for rapidity.

My work on digital art music also brings home just how radically significant time is in the economy of the music studio. I focused on universities in the UK and Europe, to see how the academic scene had changed in the 30 years since my IRCAM research. Things are extraordinarily different in some ways. In terms of time, one of the composers I encountered in my fieldwork at the Sonic Arts Research Centre (SARC), Queen's University Belfast exemplified a totally different studio temporality, the opposite of Still Alive's. This acoustic composer, trained in the post-serialist tradition, used digital studio processes but employed PhD students to do the programming. In an interview, the composer described the production of a recent piece involving a solo instrumentalist learning a complex score, with digital manipulations. The piece required the virtuoso soloist to learn a 12-page score at roughly one day of rehearsal to absorb one page. The composer had no source of funding, so he himself paid the soloist to learn the score. That's 12 days of work for a top instrumentalist, several thousand pounds. The piece had already been in planning and preparation for four years; so four years of 'creative imagination' had been devoted to this work. The composer hired a PhD student to do the programming and a lot of the realization in the studio, including recording – another few thousand pounds. This culminated in a couple of local performances. Our dialogue ended with the composer sharing his despair because the temporal horizons of this kind of creative process are untenable. He felt he couldn't sustain the ethos and the belief in the necessity of his own compositional practice, given its temporal arc and economic basis, as it eventuates in a very limited set of performances and a tiny audience. I bring this up to touch upon other ways in which time mediates the studio, and the studio itself mediates variable kinds of time. Of course, somewhere in the middle is where much music production happens.

Alex Wilkie: And the fact that software and software practices engender their own temporalities, both in production and execution, must connect to your work on IRCAM and digital art musics as well?

Georgina Born: At IRCAM I observed software development as a relatively undisciplined R&D process. In the book, I describe how software was constantly and recursively being developed, collaboratively, in minor ways. There didn't seem to be any kind of larger management. There were phases of work and then a point of stabilization would be reached where the software could be distributed internally and tested out by others; then it would enter back into flux. Musicians would enter into the collaboration with programmers and scientists, working intensively together, forming what I called the 'musicians group vanguard'. Together, they would test the latest version: the musician would voice problems and criticisms, the programmers would make changes. This seemed to be a productive 'studio' dynamic; and yet IRCAM was widely known never to produce a working software program. So this dynamic also caused controversy and dissent: scientific management criticized it, while software developers staunchly defended this collaborative tinkering. There was a utopian cast to the undisciplined R&D processes, but whether they resulted in software that could be distributed and used externally was unclear. So, while I saw this collaborative and recursive process as the most creative kernel within IRCAM's studios, the irony was that it didn't result in particularly powerful software development, nor in notably great music.

As I began to read about artificial intelligence (AI), I saw that the dynamics around software R&D that I'd observed at IRCAM were more pervasive in AI research. The recursive tinkering was considered to be an 'experimental' method of programming, without telos, and it was opposed to more disciplined, instrumental, ends-oriented forms of programming. Perhaps this speaks to two general types of 'design', which are more or less ends-oriented.

Alex Wilkie: What you've outlined also raises the epistemic status of studios. My studies of design research in universities – and maybe this is also evident in your work on music and art–science studios – shows that designers routinely and explicitly invoke the term 'lab' to designate the epistemic conditions in which work is conducted. It's actually very rare that you find an academic research group that uses the term 'studio'.

Georgina Born: That's right. One of the themes from my IRCAM study, which something like Culture Lab at Newcastle University also exemplifies, is the intrinsically interdisciplinary nature of these projects that operate at the interface of music/sound, the arts, and the sciences and engineering, and, as you say, the epistemic authority and legitimation that accrue from these apparent links to science. What is extraordinary from the field I'm looking at now – broadly, music technology – is how varied are these forms of interdisciplinarity. While many centres attempt to span music and science and technology, recently I've been looking at the Centre for Digital Music at Queen Mary, University of London. It's set within a School of Electronic Engineering and Computer Science, one of the most engineering-focused groups in the UK; but there's no music department. It's basically a grant machine, very close to commercial music technology research, and they undertake many hybrid projects with commerce. Recently they 'discovered' ethnography as a tool for user research – an instrumental use of ethnography, just as it's evolved in design. So, there's a strong purely engineering culture in music, whether in the lab or the studio. But I would say that in places like Culture Lab, it's a metaphorical use of 'Lab' expressing a different, artistically experimental set of commitments. Where we've gone in MusDig, 'studio' is the vernacular term for these workplaces, but of course this also remediates the earlier 'recording studio' usage.

Alex Wilkie: Your work has also taken you to television studios, which I'm sure are very different from music studios. Does this throw a different light on our premise for the book – the studio as distributed and as process?

Georgina Born: The production processes I studied at the BBC were distributed across many sites. I spent most of my time in pre-production, in rooms with groups working creatively and editorially on scripts, or putting the funding packages together. This makes me think that the notion of the distributed nature of creativity needs to be extended not only temporally, but spatially. So there isn't one 'site', but numerous sites all involved in types of collaborative labour, often themselves hierarchized, that eventuate in the TV programme. In my BBC ethnography (Born 2005b) there really was no boundary to the corporate processes, or trajectories, that together converged on, and resulted in, production – from the revolutionary reform of accounting techniques, which closely prefigured what's happened since across Britain's universities, to the explosion of audience research and marketing. All of these trajectories participate in the assemblage, the distributed event, that produces BBC television output.

Alex Wilkie: Indeed, that is something that we want to capture with the notion of distribution, alongside the symmetries and asymmetries we try to emphasise between human and non-human distributions. As I've explored in my PhD (Wilkie 2010) and Chapter 2 in this book (with Mike Michael), design studios can be understood as centres of synthesis that exist in relation to other productive sites and centres of expertise, including other studios, labs, manufacturing facilities and so on. So we have various registers of distribution operating simultaneously. Thus, rather than a Hegelian synthesis of antithetical opposites, we are here thinking and working through the synthesis and becoming of concrete and practical multiplicities.

Georgina Born: Yes, I agree. But to give another view: TV and film are clearly different in this regard from music. The music studio, like the conventional artist's studio, seems still to be a centre of a kind of alchemical material practice where certain decisions are taken in real-time using faders and knobs, applying filters and reverb, and hearing the results back as close to real-time as possible. So in the music studio, as in the real-time application of paint and its immediate results, there's something alchemical in the way materials act that remains powerful and important.

But throughout my work – on IRCAM, the BBC, through to my post-Bourdieuian stance on cultural production – I've insisted that we can't understand this alchemy of real-time practice in the studio without understanding the genealogies that inform it (Born 2010b: 16, 25, 27).[2] Every creative practice that I've encountered is relational in time: constituted in relation to other, prior practices. This requires deciphering the genealogy of current practices, whether of movements, groups, individuals or materials. The relationship is complex; in my work on art–science, for instance, I encountered artists who claimed that when they work, at a certain point, they have to bracket out the historical influences bearing on their work, or they could not act. However, in saying they bracket these influences, they acknowledge their reality. Another talked about 'firstism', or 'genre-hunting': looking for the next thing, in light of the past. I've been reading a thesis by Luke Skrebowski (2009), an art historian, on post-conceptual art. He makes a reading of conceptual art's several genealogies: what they 'protend' or hold out for the present, and how differently they're being remixed in art of the present. What I find missing in Bourdieuian and Latourian work is any understanding of this temporal situatedness, which is absolutely not to be deterministic or to foreclose what any individual or collective can do. But it is to say that it isn't *ex nihilo*: it doesn't begin from nowhere.

Alex Wilkie: You present a powerful critique of Bourdieu (Born 2010b), which chimes with my reading of Donald Schön, whose booklet on pedagogical practices in architectural design studios (1984) fails to account for the emergence of new design practices. The master teaches the student, the student mimics the master, and so pedagogical practices are reduced to imitation. How new practices emerge, however, remains a mystery, as in social practice theory generally. This connects, if I understand you correctly, with your interest in histories of the present.

Georgina Born: Yes, but it's also a critique of the lack of attention to time in actor–network theory. In my contribution to the book *The Social After Gabriel Tarde* (Born 2010a), I develop a Tardean approach to time. I argue that you can't have a Tardean account of imitation, repetition or circulation without noticing their temporal dimensions. When we come to any genre of practice, especially artistic and musical practices, the temporal dimensions are striking; yet this aspect is absent in almost all sociology of art. Bourdieu gestures at the specificity of certain historical moments and genres in the *Rules of Art* (1996); but this doesn't enter his theory. In my work I've used the anthropology of time, which has been saying for years that we have to understand time as multiple, to address multiple temporalities in cultural production. In Alain Pottage's (2001) reading of Latour, the idea of the network entails the assemblage itself producing time and space; yet despite Latour's debt to Tarde, time is not something that he's developed – hence the gap between his reading of Tarde and mine. Latour's stance is to forbid any notion of a 'transcendant' time or space, so the focus is strictly on the constitution of space and time by the assemblage. In contrast, in my current work on digital musics, but going back to my work on IRCAM, in addition to the obvious way that time is constituted in practice, in the studio, there are other very material ways in which time is being produced through the mutual modulation of multiple temporalities.

Let me expand on this through an example. For 20 years there have been two dominant software paradigms in digital music production. The first consists of the digital audio workstations (DAWs) exemplified by Ableton Live, Pro Tools, REAPER and so on. These commercial software packages favour the temporal paradigm of sequencing, along with sampling and looping – skeuomorphic digital inheritances of analogue techniques that are represented in the horizontal, left-to-right flow of time across the screen. The second paradigm consists of programming environments for interactive music and multimedia art. These allow the synthesis, processing and analysis of sound and image in real-time, and usually come in one of two forms: text-based languages such as SuperCollider, and graphical programming languages such as Max. These real-time environments model time in a completely different way, making it difficult to concatenate events in an ongoing sequence or flow. Instead, they favour interactive, performance-oriented work focused on the 'now'. Max is by far the leading product in this paradigm; it was written at IRCAM in the late 1980s, and commercialized by Cycling '74. For two decades these two approaches have been pretty stable; each embodies a particular paradigm at once of human–computer interface and of musical–temporal imagination.

However, Max and Ableton Live have been converging: from the release of Live 8, in 2009, Live software has offered an optional add-on, Max for Live, which integrates the two paradigms, allowing you to use Max as a plug-in editor for Live effects. Meanwhile, recent updates to Max, such as Max 7, have begun to emulate the look and feel of Live in order to integrate the two architectures more firmly and make the crossover more appealing to Live users. So the materiality, the design and visual style of the two environments, is transforming, making them more integrated and arguably bringing Live users – a huge market – to Max; and some commentators interpret these developments as auguring an eventual corporate merger. In other words, here software materialities are evolving, along with the musical temporalities immanent in them, in parallel with the time of the evolving relationship of the two companies. These simultaneous temporal layers bear, then, directly on practical musical 'temporalizations' in the studio, requiring us to be interested in long-term corporate arcs and mutating technical paradigms as they inhere in dominant software packages.

So back to Latour: it isn't enough to analyse what I've depicted just now as he would – as a dimension of the space–time produced by the studio itself as a hybrid assemblage. We have to be interested in the larger temporal arcs, and the conditions, that mediate enactments in the studio, just as we also need to acknowledge how the musico-temporal practices of the studio – that is, making music – in turn mediate those wider corporate strategies. This is a bidirectional model of mutual mediation. In theoretical terms, I combine several sources in this stance. One is the work of the anthropologist Chris Pinney, who works on Indian visual cultures, particularly the history and ethnography of vernacular Indian photography. Pinney (1997) has been a vocal advocate of the analysis of multiple temporalities, with reference to Kracauer and others, and resists the reduction of the time produced by the object – the photograph – to wider political times. Instead, he argues that the photograph, the art object, is itself engaged in the production of time, while being committed also to the analysis of genealogies and genres. This is great to work with.

Another source for my thinking about time is William Connolly's *A World of Becoming* (2011), where he develops process theory in interesting ways. Connolly speaks of multiple trajectories – biological, cosmological, material and social – in theorizing process and event. His view is that the way these trajectories interact produces many potential outcomes, that together they produce emergence through the synergies enlivened by their 'pluripotentialities'. I've developed similar ideas by extending Gell's reading of Husserl, especially Husserl's notions of 'protention' and 'retention' by which he conceives of the co-production in the present of both futures and pasts. In this account, any object, any musical event, any result of a studio practice itself entails or engenders potentialities or futures: what could occur next. This is to think time in terms of both the genealogies that subtend current practices, and the opening out of new possibilities. I think this accords with your post-humanist idea of the studio as irreducible to the subjects that gather there. But it also throws light on traditional humanist problems; for example, I've had to address recently the question of what the 'event' of John Cage is, through not only what 'goes into' Cage, but the protentions – or pluripotentialities – that he has enlivened in music and art since at least the late 1950s.

Alex Wilkie: Yes, we certainly share an interest in how process theory can be employed to understand the multiplicities and becomings of studio life. On that note, I'm also interested in your approach to creativity, which draws on the work of A. N. Whitehead, as well as how your work informs an understanding of anti-creativity, something Andrew Barry points to at the end of his book *Political Machines* (2001) in relation to your IRCAM study and your argument about how cultural institutions routinely effect 'mobile stasis', stabilizing or resisting creative invention.

Georgina Born: From the start, Andrew and I were fascinated by the challenge of coming to some kind of judgement about what we're researching – a core problem for the sociology of art and science. What distinguishes the social sciences from the humanities is that the humanities start out with an *a priori* belief in value. Musicology, for example, hasn't changed its stance on this in the last 100 years: the analyst takes an established or neglected figure whose works are then read in order to vindicate, and elaborate an exegesis on, the value of their work. The sociology of art has dilly-dallied with this problem, often espousing value neutrality. My approach differs from both: I don't think the problem of value judgement can be dodged, and it has to be developed by a methodological hybrid. This begins by tracing ethnographically how the actors – musicians or artists – conceive of value and believe that their own work somehow makes a difference, or does something interesting. When you study cultural production, whether in an institution or a studio, you are confronted with people making stuff, say, composing music, and what their creative values are: what they think is significant in the recent history, say, of music, and how they locate their own work in relation to that. I've found this to be universal, if sometimes implicit, and it's something that any sociologist of art, music or culture must engage in eliciting.

To do this, I developed what I call an analytics of invention in three steps, which I can illustrate by way of IRCAM. First, as before, you understand the actors' own genealogy: the genre or genres that they see their practice as participating in and departing from. IRCAM espoused a particular post-serialist genealogy of musical modernism, a canon and a set of generic expectations with which its musician population broadly concurred. Second, you trace the actors' temporal ontology, their philosophical constructions of cultural–historical time – here I draw on the art philosopher and theorist Peter Osborne (1995). By tracing IRCAM's institutional discourse as well as that of my IRCAM subjects, it became obvious that the culture espoused a modernist temporal ontology, one oriented to the future and centred on innovation, the new, progress, rupture and so on. Third, you consider the actual output of creative practices: at IRCAM, the music being produced. By listening, it was possible to tell how the music being made there related to, built on or departed from IRCAM's modernist genealogy. In other words, this allows you to ask: how does this music relate to the genealogy the actors themselves have elected as the history of their musical practice? Does it introduce difference and do interesting things, moving this genre along, or not? But you can also assess whether the music actualizes the governing temporal ontology – by enacting 'the new', 'rupture', 'innovation' and so on – or not. In this way, as ethnographer, you form a subtle analysis, and on that basis a judgement, about the extent to which the music moves the genre along or simply prolongs it, and about whether it conforms, or not, to the actors' own understanding of history – in the case of IRCAM, its modernist expectations.

In my book, as a result of this approach, I came to the view that the sounds and aesthetic forms that characterized IRCAM music were continuous with the post-serialist lineage that had been around for decades: in my analysis, IRCAM music wasn't adding to this aesthetic lineage, wasn't moving it along. So music was being made, something was happening, but in a way that tended to reproduce the existing lineage or genre without new aesthetic interest. I summarized this situation, controversially, as a 'mobile stasis'. The point was that if modernist claims – to newness, rupture, innovation – were being made, then this was not evident, indeed it was contradicted, musically. I've theorized this since by pointing to four orders of time in music, arguing that you can also analyse the way a particular lineage or genre evolves, the rate and the kinds of aesthetic change that it embodies; on this basis, for any musical object or event, you can then see if it is continuous with the genre's curve or if it departs markedly from that curve. If it does depart, then the term 'inventive' might be justified. As I said, this is a hybrid method: it takes seriously researching the perspectives of the actors themselves: how they conceive of value, what they are trying to do; it then locates those aspirations within a wider ecology. It moves, finally, to the kind of interpretive judgement, of value, that is assumed by humanist scholarship – but only on the basis of the previous steps, and thus offers an enhanced interpretation.

One criticism that comes up is that this approach is thoroughly modernist, by valorizing difference as opposed to repetition in generic change. A quick retort is to point out that the movement between, or combination of, difference and repetition lies at the heart of all creative practice – indeed, of life itself. But a footnote in my post-Bourdieu paper counters this charge more elegantly, pointing out that the same method works for mass and popular culture – like popular music, or the television I saw being made at the BBC. First, one has to understand the temporal ontology that prevails in these production cultures, and in these fields there's no premium on innovation of a modernist kind. Rather, there's something more subtle going on: the attempt to produce difference, interest, that extends the form that exists but without any self-conscious 'innovation' or 'rupture'. So the best kind of mainstream popular music or great popular television seems to have this uncanny knack of producing a kind of difference, reinvigorating the genre and opening out new potentialities, new futures, without announcing itself as such, and certainly with no modernist dimension to it. In my BBC ethnography, I analyse this situation for the BBC's popular drama series and serials (Born 2005b: Ch. 8). The ontology that prevails in those cultures, in my ethnographic experience, involves a kind of involution: difference is wanted, but it's difference that conceals itself, by folding itself into the ongoing, self-propelling constellation of the genre. This is not modernist at all, and nor is my analysis of it.

Another example of how this hybrid method is useful in our MusDig work on digital art musics concerns recent eruptions of neo-avant garde and neo-modernist ontologies. This is evident in the writings of the speculative realists Ray Brassier and Robin Mackay about the work of sound artists Florian Hecker and Russell Haswell. Brassier and Mackay are energetically re-coining modernist ideas, reclaiming avant garde status for the work of these musicians. Now that's an interesting problem in itself: what do we make of people reiterating arguments made 50 or even 100 years ago? Then you listen to the music and observe the practices of these and other musicians, and you find what I call minor variation: practices that remix and depart from what's already been done, but in only minor ways. This fascinates me. I link it, partly, to the massification of these fields. Rather than seeing heroic departures of a modernist kind, then, I myself see what is happening globally in terms of populations or clouds of practices that are drifting, bifurcating, moving as a whole. There is certainly a tension, then, between how I'm analysing what's happening and the neo-modernist claims of exegetes like Brassier and Mackay.

Alex Wilkie: What's emerging here, then, is your preoccupation with temporality and the ways in which the modulations of practice, typically technical, and the performativity of artworks are themselves bound into the temporal tendencies of styles or certain historicities of aesthetic practice and sensibilities?

Georgina Born: Definitely, and to understand this, my researchers and myself can't help but use the concept of genre or something similar, like aesthetic formation. This is for two reasons. The first is that we see the same materials, the same technological and studio setups, being used in radically different ways and to very different aesthetic or musical ends. So here we need a notion of aesthetic trajectories, or of genre, because something is forming, or governing, how very similar material assemblages are being used aesthetically. The second point comes to what I just spoke about, the production of generic movement. To be Tardean about this, in our MusDig work on digital art musics we're seeing lots of imitation, as well as the hybridization of distinctive genres: that's how novelty or movement seem to occur, as well as what I spoke of as minor variation, sometimes budding off to form quite strongly bounded communities of practice, or genres, sometimes producing rather merged, shifting, boundary-less clouds of related practices.

Let's take the broad area of hacking, circuit-bending, glitch, noise and so on: a vast, emergent universe of practice in which the very definition of these practices is contested. Moreover, there's lots of overlap between them, and the adherents hang out together. Yet each scene has its own organic intellectuals – Nick Collins or Reed Ghazala for circuit-bending, Yasunao Tone or Merzbow for noise; they have their own historicities, their own genealogies. What I find now is that lots of practitioners who broadly come from somewhere in that space are taking it in new directions, in their practice, but in only a minor way – not radically distinctive ways. So there's a dynamic of change in which these minor variations take what are already inchoate genres, and take them in new directions, which are also inchoate.

To give an example: there's a musician who did his PhD at Goldsmiths, University of London in music, who is familiar with Atau Tanaka's and Bill Gaver's work and comes out of the electronic studio tradition at Goldsmiths. I encountered him as a member of LLEAPP, the Laboratory for Laptop and Electronic Audio Performance Practice, a scene that emerged among PhD students at British universities. Basically, it consists of these folk coming together to rehearse or perform collaborative improvisations, each of them bringing their individual setups, trying to hone a collective practice of performance in real-time. That's how I met him, and his project is to endow a game console-based setup, a take on circuit-bending, with a kind of loop-based recursivity in relation to its own sound production, by interlinking variables to produce something sonically very unstable and rich. I have to say that this is engaging; but in the broad scheme of all that's out there transnationally or on the net in this area, it amounts to a tiny intervention. When I probe what he thinks his practice is, he doesn't call himself a composer; maybe, he says, he's a researcher; is this practice music? It's unclear. His practice, and that of LLEAPP, is somewhere between rehearsal and performance, and in this sense there's an ebbing away of the distinction between preparation and performance, studio and live event, participation and audience. You can see how indistinct the boundaries between performance event and studio practice are becoming.

Recently I've turned to Hans-Jörg Rheinberger's (1997) work on experimental scientific systems to understand these processes. In Rheinberger's analysis of laboratory experimentation, he talks about the 'intrinsic' time and multiplicity of these systems which undergo 'continuing cycles of nonidentical reproduction', resulting in 'drifting, merging and bifurcating'. This fits perfectly what I'm observing. He identifies what he calls, with reference to Derrida, 'differantial' reproduction, the minute production of difference and deferring, which he argues gives experimental systems their generative power. I find this, by analogy, tremendously interesting for what I'm observing, which, as you discuss in your introduction, is far from the temporality of heroic modernism that is often claimed for – or imposed normatively on – art and artists.

Alex Wilkie: Of course, the elephant in the studio, and for studio studies, is aesthetics, which is often ignored and not accounted for, and which is certainly very different from representation in scientific practice. This connects strongly with everything you've been saying, and your interest in understanding practice in relation to genre.

Georgina Born: Yes, that's right. And let me offer another example. I'm very taken by Fernando Rubio's (2012) piece on Robert Smithson's 'Spiral Jetty'; it's very powerful. However, imagine the additional weight his analysis would have if he'd located Smithson in relation to the kind of artistic practices Smithson was bound up with: how his practice emerges from his relation to conceptual and post-conceptual art, the move beyond certain kinds of formalism. To grasp this, as one crucial mediation, would add to our understanding, not detract from Smithson's inventiveness, which lies in how he augments the potentialities in those lineages. Without this added historical or genealogical perspective, it seems to me, there's a kind of mystification of Smithson's practice when it's extracted from that analysis of his milieu.

What we're finding in our MusDig work ubiquitously is that accompanying the burgeoning new digital music practices are efforts, often contested, at remaking the musical past. At the time of my IRCAM study there was a very fixed, canonical understanding of twentieth-century music. But during the 1990s this began to crumble, and since then there's been an energetic revisionism that completely recasts late twentieth-century music. Brassier and Mackay, for example, are rewriting French music from the 1970s on, so that Xenakis becomes the most important figure while Boulez is denigrated, dethroned. In parallel, from a more mainstream standpoint, there's a collection called *Audio Culture* by Christoph Cox and Daniel Warner (2004): a revisionist account of music history from Varèse and Schaeffer to the 2000s that's been hugely influential. So there's a research challenge centred on questions like: what are the dominant genealogies? How do they bear on present practices? And how are these genealogies evolving or mutating in the present? But we also have to return to my reworking of Gell's Husserl, because what's happening in the present is at the same time a re-casting of the past and an envisioning of new futures – and all of these temporalities are bundled up in creative practices themselves, in the studio.

So one methodological point is that there *are* aesthetic canons: they are taught and institutionalized, they close down how people see things, and then they get blasted open again. And we happen to be at a historical moment in music where the canon is being blasted open. So, as ethnographers, we should analyse the canons that prevail. What are their contents? How do they persist? But we should also allow for fuzziness, for complexity. On this score, we developed a method where we asked musicians to describe the genealogy of their own practice. There's a prominent musician called Mark Fell, part of a duo called SND, a major international figure. I interviewed Mark and we became excited about reconstructing his aesthetic genealogy, what influenced him and got into his work. Having recorded hours with me, he wrote it up himself and put it online, adding illustrative tracks. By recovering artists' genealogies in this way, then, one produces a decentred account with multiple perspectives, and this adds complexity to the books and articles that are strenuously trying to reshape the canon by redrawing dominant aesthetic genealogies.

Alex Wilkie: I wonder, reflecting on my own work, how the 'genealogies' of design might be distinctive from those in art and music?

Georgina Born: My sense is that most fields of cultural production have their own genealogies. Take art–science, an emerging field that overlaps with bio-art, robotic art and so on. So does it even exist as a category? But actually, when you ask a range of practitioners, they disclose quite similar and recognizable landmarks in this putative field. And when I listened to the pedagogy, sitting in on classes in the art–science master's at UC Irvine, the genealogy is there in the teaching of histories and philosophies of the field; artist Simon Penny, directing the course, conveyed a rich and inventive genealogy of what one might imagine as the forerunners of such a field – from Duchamp, to early British cybernetics, to the Bauhaus, to A. Life, to what he called behavioural aesthetics (Born and Barry 2010). Interestingly, in Andrew Barry's current work on political geography and in his book on the Baku–Tbilisi–Ceyhan oil pipeline (2013), he's realized that he, too, needs to take account of genealogies – but here genealogies of political events, or of genres of political events. His point is that, when you're doing research on the politics of an oil pipeline, mired as it is in controversies, disputes, demonstrations, actions and so on, what you encounter are not entirely novel political events, but types or idioms, even genres, of event: event-forms, we might say, that themselves have histories that are being invoked, and at the same time remediated, in the present event. For Andrew, the political actions organised by Platform, the London arts and research collective,[3] for instance, invoke a genealogy of similar kinds of actions. This is to say that they are informed by, yet irreducible to, a history of such practices. So in design, even if it's not articulated as such, I imagine that there are genealogies, lineages, genres that cohere and that are broadly invoked in various ways in the teaching of design.

Alex Wilkie: So we come full circle, back to institutions and the relationship between the studio and the academy, practice and teaching. Here, practitioners in design and the visual arts often have a very different relationship to the academy, since universities don't typically offer studio space, compared with science, technology, engineering and maths disciplines, let's say, where technical facilities and resources are necessary. Studios are often elsewhere.

Georgina Born: Yes, but I would offer a slightly different view. Genealogies are not confined to the academy, or to institutions. One take on what you're saying is that the relation between art practice and its teaching, and art history, has never been close. The same is true in music – although arguably the work I do bridges the two, aspiring to be a kind of musical history of the present. Among my first attempts was the IRCAM study, though my BBC and art–science ethnographies were similar: pursuing a genealogical approach that complements the ethnography of contemporary practices, so as to feed the resulting analyses in an immediate and intimate way back to practitioners, opening a dialogue with them that is, precisely, open. This is very different from the relationship that prevails between contemporary art practice and art history, and you're absolutely right that this split is institutionalized in the difference between art schools and universities. The Slade at University College London is possibly one of the very few historical pivot points or crossovers between these domains. *A propos*, right now I'm reading a book on the history of computer art and how artists first got into using mainframe computers, and in the UK the Slade figures prominently. Why? Because during the 1960s it was artists at the Slade who could obtain easy and rapid access to mainframe computing.

This interview was conducted in Cambridge in October 2014

Notes

1 See http://musdig.music.ox.ac.uk: 'Music, Digitisation, Mediation: Towards Interdisciplinary Music Studies', a five-year research programme funded by the European Research Council and directed by Born.
2 The term genealogy here is not identical with Foucault's genealogy, although it shares certain premises with it, inasmuch as it is concerned with discerning, in relation to cultural production, the precursors of present practices in non-teleological and irreductive terms.
3 http://platformlondon.org.

References

Barry, A. 2001. *Political Machines: Governing a Technological Society*. London, New York: Athlone Press.

Barry, A. 2013. *Material Politics: Disputes Along the Pipeline*. Oxford: Wiley Blackwell.

Born, G. 1995. *Rationalizing Culture: IRCAM, Boulez, and the Institutionalization of the Musical Avant-Garde*. Berkeley, CA: University of California Press.

Born, G. 1996. (Im)materiality and sociality: the dynamics of intellectual property in a computer software research culture. *Social Anthropology*, 4(2), 101–116.

Born, G. 1997. Computer software as a medium: textuality, orality and sociality in an Artificial Intelligence research culture. In: Banks, M. and Morphy, H. eds, *Rethinking Visual Anthropology*. New Haven, CT: Yale University Press, pp. 139–169.

Born, G. 2005a. On musical mediation: ontology, technology and creativity, *Twentieth-Century Music* 2(1), 7–36.

Born, G. 2005b. *Uncertain Vision: Birt, Dyke and the Reinvention of the BBC*. London: Vintage.

Born, G. 2010a On Tardean relations: temporality and ethnography. In: Candea, M. ed., *The Social after Gabriel Tarde: Debates and Assessments*. Abingdon and New York: Routledge, pp. 230–247.

Born, G. 2010b. The social and the aesthetic: for a post-Bourdieuian theory of cultural production. *Cultural Sociology*, 4(2), 171–208.

Born, G. 2011a Music and the materialization of identities. *Journal of Material Culture*, 16(4), 1–13.

Born, G. 2011b. Music and the social. In: Clayton, M., Herbert, T. and Middleton, R. eds, *The Cultural Study of Music* (2nd edn). London: Routledge, pp. 261–274.

Born, G. 2013. Music: ontology, agency and creativity. In: Chua, L. and Elliott, M. eds, *Distributed Objects: Meaning and Matter after Alfred Gell*. Oxford: Berg, pp. 130–154.

Born, G. and Barry, A. 2010. Art–science: from public understanding to public experiment. *Journal of Cultural Economy*, 3(1): 103–119.

Bourdieu, P. 1996. *The Rules of Art: Genesis and Structure of the Literary Field*. Stanford, CA: Stanford University Press.

Brassier, R. 2009. Genre is obsolete. In: Attiarch, M. and Iles, A. eds, *Noise and Capitalism*, Donostia, San Sebastian: Arteleku Audiolab, pp. 60–71.

Connolly, W. E. 2011. *A World of Becoming*. Durham, NC: Duke University Press.

Cox, C. and Warner, D. 2004. *Audio Culture: Readings in Modern Music*. London: Bloomsbury Publishing.

Feld, S. and Fox, A. 1994. Music and language. *Annual Review of Anthropology*, 23, 25–53.

Gell, A. 1998. *Art and Agency: An Anthropological Theory*. Oxford, New York: Clarendon.

Goehr, L. 1992. *The Imaginary Museum of Musical Works*. Oxford: Clarendon.

Osborne, P. 1995. *The Politics of Time: Modernity and Avant-Garde*. London: Verso.

Pinney, C. 1997. *Camera Indica: The Social Life of Indian Photographs*. Chicago, IL: University of Chicago Press.

Pinney, C. 2005. Things happen; or, from which moment does that object come? In: Miller, D. ed., *Materiality*. London: Duke.

Pottage, A. 2001. Persons and things: an ethnographic analogy. *Economy and Society*, 30(1), 112–138.

Rheinberger, H.-J. 1997. *Toward a History of Epistemic Things: Synthesizing Proteins in the Test Tube, Writing Science*. Stanford, CA: Stanford University Press.

Rubio, F. D. 2012. The material production of the Spiral Jetty: a study of culture in the making. *Cultural Sociology*, 6(2), 143–161.

Schön, D. A. 1984The architectural studio as an exemplar of education for reflection-in-action. *Journal of Architectural Education*, 38(1), 2–9.

Skrebowski, L. 2009. Systems, contexts, relations: an alternative genealogy of conceptual art. PhD thesis, Centre for Research in Modern European Philosophy/History of Art and Design, Middlesex University.

Wilkie, A. 2010. User assemblages in design: an ethnographic study. PhD thesis, Goldsmiths, University of London.

Part 3

Displacements

10 Rediscovering Daphne Oram's home-studio

Experimenting between art, technology and domesticity

Laurie Waller

Introduction

The home-studio is a hybrid conjoining two sites – the domestic dwelling and the artistic laboratory[1] – that have often been counterposed in social studies of invention. In trajectories of invention, these two sites often occupy opposing poles: artistic experiments are conducted in the studio and the artefacts they produce are later domesticated in society.[2] In such trajectories, home and studio appear, if not antithetical to one another, then minimally, as social contexts that are distinguished by their proximity to, or distance from, experimental practices.[3] In this chapter I explore whether, and in what ways, the home-studio invites us to reconsider the role of domestic settings in processes of

Figure 10.1 Daphne Oram working with the Oramics Machine
Source: publicity image for 'Oramics to Electronica' exhibition.

invention.[4] I suggest that two consequences follow the choice to investigate the home-studio as the conjoining of artistic laboratory and domestic dwelling: first, the social significance of the studio is more than that of simply serving the production of culture; second, the home is no longer simply circumscribed and differentiated as a social context, such as the private sphere, marked by its distance from experimental practice. The home-studio, I argue in this chapter, does not simply site invention in a context of everyday life, but also incorporates into studio experiments various practices, procedures and materials that might otherwise be dismissed as uninventive modes of domesticity.

This chapter takes as its focus the home-studio of the electronic musician Daphne Oram, founded in the late 1950s, in which the composer attempted to invent new 'drawn-sound' composition techniques and build a machine to realize these. Oram envisaged the electronic music studio as a 'sound-house', a setting of unbounded sonic experimentation, and in this chapter I elaborate how the composer attempted to realize this vision for her home-studio. Central to Oram's home-studio project was the drawn-sound machine that Oram collaborated with an engineer to build, and which she named the Oramics Machine. But Oram largely failed to demonstrate drawn-sound as an innovation in her own lifetime; her own sound-house was never completely realized. In this chapter I explore how Oram's attempt to create a home-studio can be appreciated as an experiment that was at once artistic, technological and domestic. I suggest that if we treat the home-studio as only a setting of cultural production, if we ignore the domestic experiment of the home-studio, then Oram's work appears a well intentioned but largely unsuccessful experiment: in terms of musical composition or electro-mechanics alone there seems little to recommend the Oramics Machine as an innovation. Taking seriously the proposition that Oram's home-studio was a setting of invention, I argue that Oram's development of the Oramics Machine was an experiment in both cultural production and domestic practice.

Rediscovering the home-studio

This chapter begins in an exhibition about Oram's home-studio in London's Science Museum, an institution that holds in its collections some of industrial history's most celebrated inventions.[5] Called 'Oramics to Electronica', the exhibition centres around the Oramics Machine that Oram built in her home-studio, and is accompanied by displays about two other British electronic music studios from the same historical era: the BBC's Radiophonic Workshop and the Electronic Music Studios Ltd.[6] In the publicity image for the exhibition (Figure 10.1), Oram is shown composing with the Machine, drawing wavy lines onto strips of film that run across the its surface: the Oramics Machine, we are told, was the vehicle for Oram's ambitions to compose with graphical techniques. Founding the Oramics studio at her home, a converted oast house in rural Kent called Tower Folly, Oram initially worked with her brother to construct early prototypes of the Machine. Alongside the relics of industrial history in the surrounding galleries of the Science Museum, the Oramics Machine appears very noticeably 'home-made' in its construction: the frame is assembled from repurposed metal shelving, a wooden cabinet housing one part of the machine is labelled 'commode', and a broom handle is jammed in one side of the Machine. In comparison with the celebrated industrial heritage we find in the Science Museum, the Oramics Machine appears to have a somewhat less glorious history: publicity for its exhibition even going so far as to highlight that the Oramics Machine was left forgotten and rusting in a barn in rural France until it was acquired by the Science Museum in 2008 (Mugan 2011). On one side of its exhibition case, we are told that the Oramics Machine will never work again, and this seems corroborated when we look inside the case at the dishevelled device from which wires hang off, the circuitry of which is exposed and corroded, and a switch appears labelled 'do not switch'. And yet, though it existed largely in obscurity prior to the exhibition (for a discussion of the role of this exhibition in 'reviving' Daphne Oram in electronic music history see Reynolds 2012), the Oramics Machine is nonetheless foregrounded over the inventions of two studios widely credited as key players in the development of electronic music in Britain. Despite its seeming poverty as a historically recognized invention that never left the four walls of Oram's home-studio, the Oramics Machine takes the centre stage of an exhibition in an institution whose name has become synonymous for many with displays of technical pedagogy and the celebration of liberal progress.[7]

In an email conversation with one of the curators working on the exhibition, we discussed the significance of the Oramics Machine for the Science Museum, the curator elaborating their personal view of the exhibition:

> Was the Oramics Machine important as an invention? Maybe not, but it is important in the sense that it says so much about the inventiveness and creative minds that were involved in electronic music in those early years. And it's a nice counterbalance for the idea that it's a masculine story involving knobs, dials and an emotionless process. I think museums should talk about dead-ends quirks and failures a lot more. They are part of the history of Science, Technology, Engineering and Medicine and can help us see the big stories in a different, more diverse and balanced light.
> (Personal communication from a curator, 10/09/2012)

The recently rediscovered Oramics Machine is, it seems, not on display in the Science Museum by virtue of its recognition as an artistic or technological innovation. In fact, to this curator it matters little if the Oramics Machine fails as a historically significant invention. Instead, the curator proposes the Oramics Machine as a device with which to investigate the invention of electronic music in the collaborations between musicians and engineers that developed at studios like Daphne Oram's.[8]

An artist's mechanical wreck displayed in a temple of the high-tech, the rediscovered Oramics Machine invites us to investigate processes of studio invention beyond the conventions of cultural production and technological innovation. Somewhere between experimental proposition and material product, the Oramics Machine is an object that never left Oram's home-studio and which remains seemingly incomplete: part idea, part thing. In the vernacular of studio studies, the Oramics Machine might be said to be closer to a studio *maquette* (see Hennion, chapter 5 in this volume) than to a fully realized cultural product. As a mediator of the experimental work undertaken in Oram's studio, the Oramics Machine is not a domesticated invention in the sense that would have enabled it to be replicated and circulated beyond the studio. Never successfully disentangled from the setting in which it was materially developed, the Oramics Machine is an object that, in its exhibition, carries Oram's home-studio with it. In what follows, I argue that we would fail to appreciate the ways in which the Oramics Machine mediated the composer's attempt to create a laboratory for drawn-sound if we were to enforce analytic separations between the Oram's artistic aims, the studio's technological infrastructure and the home as a domestic context. Instead, I suggest the Oramics Machine is better conceived as an experimental artefact that mediates between artistic, technological and domestic modes of practice. Accepting the invitation of the Science Museum's curators to investigate invention beyond the conventions of cultural production and technological innovation, I ask how and to what extent the development of the Oramics Machine can be said to be experimental, not only as musical and electro-mechanical practice but also as domestic practice.

Daphne Oram's sound-house

The Science Museum's curators seem convinced that Daphne Oram's home-studio can reveal to us something of the processes of invention in electronic music history generally, and give us insight into the developments that reshaped the contemporary sound world. And indeed, Oram was clearly an individual at the heart of developments in electronic music in Britain. As an electronic musician and an employee at the British Broadcasting Corporation (BBC), Oram founded the Corporation's Radiophonic Workshop in 1958 with the aim of creating an electronic music studio comparable with others in Paris and Cologne, and to experiment with the respective *musique concrete* and *Elektronische Musik* techniques these studios had developed (Niebur 2010). With its beginnings in the creation of sound effects for radio dramas, the Workshop subsequently also became renowned for the music and jingles it produced for flagship BBC radio and television programmes, such as the theme tune for the cult British television series 'Doctor Who'. In the BBC's own history of the Radiophonic Workshop (from which Oram is largely absented),[9] the studio is celebrated as the setting in which engineers and composers worked together, often on tiny budgets, to innovate musically and technically, inventing new kinds of sound and music for consumers of the broadcast media (Briscoe and Curtis-Bramwell 1983). Entering the BBC in the 1942 as a junior programme engineer, for which she gave up a place to study at the Royal College of Music, Oram continued to pursue her ambitions in musical composition by using empty radio studios to work on electronic music compositions outside working hours. According to recent biographers (e.g. Manning 2012), Oram's particular interest in drawn-sound developed while at the BBC, where she encountered an oscilloscope for the first time, an instrument that visualizes a sonic frequency, and inquired whether the process could be reversed to create sound with graphical techniques. However, Oram's vision for the Workshop differed greatly from the BBC's, leading to her departure after less than a year working there. Leaving the Corporation behind, Oram sought to pursue her ambition to create a machine that could control sound graphically, setting up her own studio in Tower Folly, the converted coast house where she lived in the rural English countryside. After receiving a grant from the Gulbenkian foundation to build the Oramics Machine, Oram later employed an electrical engineer named Graham Wrench. Despite having few sources of funding for her work (Oram received a handful of commissions for advert and film soundtrack beyond the Gulbenkian grant), Oram nonetheless pursued the development of the Oramics Machine with Wrench over a number of years in an attempt to realize her drawn-sound ambitions. Beginning work on the Oramics Machine in the early 1960s, the first composition to be recorded using the Machine, called 'Contrasts Essconic', was completed in 1968 (Grierson and Boon 2013). The Oramics Machine's slow realization now appears perhaps even more exaggerated within a decade of electronic music history that saw the invention of the synthesizer and a new intensity of artistic experimentation in an emergent counter-culture (Pinch and Trocco 2004).

Oram's vision for the electronic music studio was an experimental one. On the exhibition case housing the Oramics Machine in the Science Museum's exhibition is a quotation from *New Atlantis*, a utopian novel written by the sixteenth-century natural philosopher Francis Bacon. Described in a caption as 'Daphne Oram's favourite quotation',[10] the text describes the fictional setting of the 'sound-house' in which experimenters push the limits of sonic possibility:

> Wee have also Sound-houses, wher wee practise and demonstrate all sounds and their Generation. Wee have harmonies and lesser slides of sounds. Wee make diverse tremblings and Warblings of Sounds [...] Wee have also diver Strange and Artificall Eccho's. We have also means to convey Sounds in Trunks and Pipes, in strange Lines and Distances.

In the early days of the BBC's Radiophonic Workshop, Oram had pinned the quotation to the wall as a statement of intent for the studio (see discussion in Wilson 2011). As a setting of unbounded sonic experimentation in which to 'practise and demonstrate all sounds and their generation', it's not hard to see why Oram found the 'sound-house' quotation so compelling as a vision for the electronic music studio.

And yet, if it was the sound-house that Oram sought, then there appears something paradoxical in Oram's move from the BBC Radiophonic Workshop to her home-studio at Tower Folly: surely the BBC's well equipped and professionally staffed Workshop constituted *de facto* a much better sound-house than the poorly resourced and isolated setting of Tower Folly? Surely, in the composer's mind, these studios were not meant to be comparable as experimental settings? Isn't Oram's move from the BBC to Tower Folly a move away from this (broad) experimental vision of the studio for a very specific focus on developing a single compositional technique in drawn-sound? There seems something almost comical in the suggestion that this under-resourced historic craft site (become bourgeois living quarters) could provide the setting for a cutting-edge and high-tech experimental electronic music studio. In hindsight, knowing that Oram largely failed in her lifetime to demonstrate drawn-sound as an innovation, it seems unrealistic to suppose that Oram ever seriously imagined that her rudimentary home-studio at Tower Folly would ever have competed in experimental terms with other, much better funded electronic music studios at the time. Tower Folly might have provided the site for the composer's amateur foray into new composition technique perhaps, but is it really possible to make a serious comparison between Oram's home-studio and other electronic music studios like the Radiophonic Workshop as a settings of sonic experiment?

One way to characterize Oram's move from the Radiophonic Workshop to Tower Folly as one of experimental progression is to consider the electronic music studio as the context that enabled or constrained Oram's drawn-sound ambitions in particular ways. Certainly, the Radiophonic Workshop became more of a service-oriented department within the BBC than Oram had originally envisioned it would be (Niebur 2010), and it is likely that Oram felt she could not pursue her goal of creating drawn-sound in such an environment. We might speculate on this basis that Oram's move from the Radiophonic Workshop to the home-studio was because the latter offered a site of experimentation free of the constraints of the corporate studio (see for instance Born's 1995 discussion of musical stasis at IRCAM); the 'freehand' modes of composition that Oram sought to develop in the Oramics studio largely incompatible with the bureaucratically arranged forms of experimentation that organized the BBC's studio. In artistic terms, we might propose that the composer was freer from corporate obligation at Tower Folly. But beyond the few (distinctly negative) freedoms that Oram may have gained at Tower Folly, there seems little else to render it in any way comparable with other serious electronic music studios as a context for sonic experiment. And indeed, even in these very limited terms, it is not clear that Oram's move to Tower Folly could easily be construed as one of the composer's liberation from organisational constraints: as several commentators have highlighted that, with little money or income-generating activity, Oram lived an extremely frugal life which on occasion descended into relative poverty, considerably limiting her prospects for developing new forms of electronic music (BBC Radio 3 2008). Moreover, it would be a mistake to think that Oram saw her experimental Oramics studio as comparable only with other electronic music studios.[11] If the home-studio was only the context for Oram's drawn-sound work, then there appears little (beyond the composer's freedom from corporate forms of organization) to recommend it as an experimental setting.

In her lifetime, Oram largely failed to demonstrate that her electronic music studio was anything like the electronic music sound-house she had envisioned. But despite this, I think the concept of the sound-house can nonetheless enable us to appreciate Oram's home-studio as another kind of experimental setting. Drawn-sound may have been, for Oram, principally a musical invention, but in Oram and Wrench's collaboration to build the Oramics Machine at Tower Folly, the development of drawn-sound became an experiment that also involved electro-mechanical practice and, I argue in this chapter, domestic practices. Might we re-appropriate the concept of the sound-house to describe Oram's electronic music studio both as a setting of sonic invention and as an experimental domestic setting? Deploying the concept of the sound-house in this way, I suggest, permits us to value Oram's home-studio as a setting of sound experiment without being obliged to draw a conclusion that, because the Oramics Machine never made it out of the studio, the experiment necessarily failed? In re-appropriating the concept of the sound-house, I'm not trying somehow to rescue Oram from experimental failure: in terms of musical composition, for instance, we can maintain that the Oramics Machine still appears far from an experimental success. But this version of the sound-house concept, I suggest, might enable us to appreciate more clearly that Oram's work in developing the Oramics Machine was a manifold experiment in which domestic registers of practice were significant. Beyond evaluating successes and failures, considering Oram's home-studio as a sound-house invites us to appreciate Oram's collaboration with Wrench at Tower Folly and the development of the Oramics Machine as an experiment that was at once artistic, technological and domestic.

The Oramics Machine

Oram's (1972) only published book, *An Individual Note: Of Music, Sound and Electronics*, presents the composer's own retrospective account of the development of the Oramics Machine. Here, Oram describes how in developing Oramics – Oramics was the hybrid name that Oram gave to her home-studio, the Oramics Machine, the drawn-sound technique and the philosophy informing it – she aimed to extend, and 'transduce',[12] the composer's individuality. Oram contrasted her new Oramics drawn-sound approach with the dominant approaches of *musique concrete* and *Elektronische Musik*, the approaches that had informed the work of the Radiophonic Workshop throughout the 1960s (Niebur 2010). In developing the Oramics Machine,

Oram sought to invent a 'machine-with-humanising-factors' (Oram 1972: 97–107) to counter what she describes as the increasing reliance of electronic music composers on machines. In the work of composers like Boulez – whose total serialism attempted to rationalize modern musical composition and purge it of its romantic antecedents (Born 1995) – Oram saw the domination of the composer by abstract, mechanical rules, and in the increasing use of aleatoric techniques of computer music Oram feared that composers were too dependent on machines and were compromising their individuality. Drawn-sound, then, was Oram's attempt to recalibrate the relations between human composers and the machines and techniques they used. Following a discussion about the precedents for drawn-sound (in painting, photography and singing), Oram offers the following specification for the Oramics Machine:

> We will certainly require these facilities:
>
> 1 Freehand drawing of all instructions.
> 2 Facilities for drawing, separately, the instructions for each parameter.
> 3 A monitoring system to allow immediate, or almost immediate, 'feedback' of the result.
> 4 Easy access to the separate parameter instructions so that, after monitoring, alterations can be made and the results re-monitored.
>
> (Oram 1972: 96)

Based on this cybernetic-inspired 'feedback' model of the Oramics Machine, Oram goes on to describe how the use of freehand graphical techniques will facilitate the emergence of the composer's individuality in a dialectical and iterative process through which the composer's energies are transduced and realized as sound. We do not have to embrace wholeheartedly Oram's highly eclectic influences to recognize the way in which the composer's aim to invent drawn-sound took her well beyond the concerns of musical composition. The account of the Oramics Machine found in *An Individual Note* is *post-hoc*, and hence appears at times to present the electro-mechanical design of the Machine as if derived and constructed unproblematically from Oram's compositional and philosophical aims.[13] Various commentators have since questioned whether the Oramics Machine was ever fully realized to the particular specification that Oram presents in this text (Hutton 2003, Manning 2012). But, even if Oram's ideas about the Oramics Machine ran ahead of its material realization, her vision of the machine-with-humanizing-factors nonetheless highlights the way in which this artefact was envisioned as an invention for recalibrating relations between composer and machine.

The Science Museum's exhibition stages the Oramics Machine as an instrument that mediated an experimental collaboration between a music composer and an electro-mechanical engineer. In the display, the Oramics Machine is comprised of two central components:[14] (i) its programmer,[15] and

(ii) its wave-form scanners.[16] The programmer was designed so that Oram could draw shapes onto 35 mm film strips running across it, each strip assigned to a different parameter and processed with photoelectric sensors. The frame of the programmer is made from repurposed Dexion, an industrial system for producing light metal shelving. Both 35 mm film and Dexion were mass-produced materials and relatively cheap to acquire, and (in contrast to Oram's account in which design followed artist specification) their use in the Oramics Machine has been subsequently characterized as more likely a matter of expediency, as materials that met Oram's immediate practical needs, rather than a prior design choice (Mullender 2011). A similarly resourceful inventiveness is suggested by the Machine's electro-mechanical design, which would seem to evidence Wrench-the-*bricoleur* as much as it does the engineer. The photoelectric sensors that read the shapes Oram drew onto the film are particularly conspicuous in the case display of the Oramics Machine as they hang limp and corroded from the programmer's Dexion frame. In an interview for a music technology magazine, Wrench describes the unorthodox engineering practice of repurposing ordinary transistors to create the Machine's photoelectric sensors:

> We had so little in the way of components in those days. Transistors had only recently appeared on the general market, so they were still pricey. I needed to use light-sensitive photo-transistors but they were far too expensive, at almost a pound each. This was at a time when a good wage was about £25 a week! But I started experimenting and discovered that I could take apart the ordinary transistors. Scraping off their covering of paint turned them into photo-transistors, so I made my own.
>
> (Marshall 2009)

Wrench's description of the choice to repurpose ordinary transistors to create the Oramics Machine's photoelectric sensors makes clear that this was not only a theoretical determination of electro-mechanics, but also involved calculations that are more often the preserve of home economics. In Wrench's account, thrift in consumption, the budgeting of income and re-using existing materials were all significant considerations in building the Oramics Machine's programmer.

Traces of the particular biographies of Oram and Wrench also appear in a key component of the Oramics Machine, namely its wave scanners, which were designed to read hand-drawn wave-forms that Oram drew onto glass slides. The wave scanners are comprised of two cathode ray tubes that scan the shape of the drawn wave-forms, both controlling the pitch of the Machine's oscillators and producing the timbre of the sound. This very particular electro-mechanical design of the wave scanners can be attributed in large part to the particular expertise of Wrench, who had worked with radar technology during his service in the Royal Air Force.[17] And, what is perhaps most striking about the wave scanners, certainly when we see them

Figure 10.2 Daphne Oram inserting glass slide with drawn wave-form into wave scanners housed inside a commode
Source: publicity image for 'Oramics to Electronica' exhibition.

somewhere like the Science Museum, is the faded white wooden container, formerly a piece of storage furniture in Oram's house, used to house the electrical components. The contrast is stark: the once stylish and delicate piece of domestic furniture is presented with its doors and top open to reveal the bright yellow cathode ray tube scanners and corroded circuitry. The cabinet's open top section makes visible the exposed circuitry that tuned the oscillators, below which are Oram's handwritten notes E, A, D, G: 'it's tuned like a guitar' one sonic artist noted.[18] The particular social identities of Oram and Wrench (both breaking with convention in their musical and engineering practices) are materialized in the unique electro-mechanics of the wave-scanners and their casing in a piece of furniture, along with traces of the domestic setting and the economic necessities the shaped their collaboration in the pursuit of drawn-sound.

Something between unattainable aspiration and laboured materialization, the Oramics Machine assembles the Oramics home-studio in the particular people (Oram and Wrench), place (Tower Folly), time (the 'long' 1960s), materials (repurposed and mass-produced), knowledges and practices (musical and engineering). This very particular assemblage is, on one hand, evidence that the Oramics Machine was, in Oram's lifetime, never effectively demonstrated as an innovation, either technological or artistic, such that it could have circulated beyond the studio setting. On the other hand, its handcraft materiality seems to be precisely what establishes the Oramics Machine as the worthy centrepiece of an exhibition about invention in early British electronic music. In the Oramics Machine, we are confronted with traces of the collaboration between Oram and the engineer Wrench in Tower Folly. Their design choices for the Machine reveal as much about the biographies of these individuals, the conditions in which they worked together and the economics of their collaboration as they do about musical and electro-mechanical invention. It is in this way that the Oramics Machine demonstrates how drawn-sound provided the medium for an experiment that was at once artistic, technological and domestic. Valuing the Oramics Machine as an experimental domestic artefact – as opposed to evaluating it against models of innovation that equate success with tame domestication – offers a way to understand Oram's home-studio as an experimental setting, beyond the conventions of cultural production and technological innovation. More than a site of artistic invention, I have used the sound-house to advance a conception of the electronic music studio as a manifold of experimental practice. And it is in this sense, I suggest, that we might appreciate how Oram's experiments with drawn-sound could also be said to be characteristic of the inventive work undertaken in early electronic music studios.

Conclusion

The home-studio is a setting of domestic experiment. The years of work that Oram and Wrench put into developing and modifying the Oramics Machine at Tower Folly was also a labour of attempting to create a 'sound-house', an electronic music studio where the composer could experiment freely with sound. In her lifetime, Oram largely failed to demonstrate the Oramics Machine as an innovation in electronic music. Now we find a different kind of sound-house demonstrated in the Machine. In the Science Museum's rediscovery and exhibition of the Oramics Machine, we are confronted with an artefact that never ascended to the status of a studio product, an artefact that never successfully 'left' the studio, but which nonetheless materializes Oram's home-studio as a setting of experiment. The Oramics Machine may yet enter the canon of electronic music history as an overlooked innovation, but if it does, it will almost certainly not be as an invention that facilitated the composer's free exploration of sound in the way that the synthesizer did. Instead, I agree with the Science Museum curator's proposition that, if the Oramics Machine is significant as an invention, it is insofar as it reveals something about the experimental practices in early electronic music studios, and specifically those particular to the home-studio. Approaching the Oramics Machine as a studio assemblage, we find that domestic work was, along with musical composition and electro-mechanics, a key register of practice in Oram's experiments with drawn-sound.

This point perhaps becomes clearer if we consider its alternative. Had I limited the discussion of Daphne Oram's home-studio only to the question of the modes of cultural production that developed at Tower Folly, the Oramics Machine would appear only as a well intentioned failure: it may have been a pioneering vision but technological innovations moved too fast for Oram, who was overtaken by the industrial development of synthesizers and computers; machines that could facilitate musical composition more efficiently than the Oramics Machine, and which thereby rendered Oram's work at Tower Folly an eccentric pastime of little consequence. Treating the Oramics studio as only an artistic laboratory leaves us with little to say about the significance of Oram's work, which largely never made it out of the lab. But when we approach the Oramics studio as a setting of domestic experiment, then quite a different story appears. In this perspective Oram was not simply a competitor within the 'creative economy' of electronic music studios, but rather an artist whose experimental domestic practices have participated in developing new economies of creativity. We find experimental modes of domesticity in the Oramics Machine's thrifty electro-mechanics, the repurposed materials, the composer's adaptive machine specification; all traces of Oram and Wrench's collaboration at Tower Folly. Exhibited in the Science Museum, the Oramics Machine is an artefact that challenges our existing conceptual vocabularies for describing invention; vocabularies that largely separate out science from art, experimentation from domestication, technology from craft. This exhibition of the Oramics Machine is not simply 'revivalist', as if we could already name the Machine's cultural significance, but more obviously a proposition that this artefact reveals something about studio life which often goes unaccounted for in models of invention (not least those that would tell us the Science Museum is where we find the most domesticated cultural artefacts). If there is a common theme, then, that is obviously shared between the Science Museum's historical exhibition about electronic music studios and my own sociological account of the home-studio, it is in challenging accounts of invention as a cultural production that would circumscribe both the home and the museum as repositories of domesticated artefacts that are removed from experimental processes of invention.

In this chapter I've discussed little about the contemporary relevance of the home-studio. Why is London's Science Museum now showcasing the home-studio as a setting of invention? One answer might relate to the contemporary proliferation of the home-studio. Particularly in the case of music, there exist many contemporary studies that document the 'rise' of the home-studio via themes relating to changes in modes of cultural production: that is, in terms of the multiplication of the arenas of artistic experimentation, the inclusion and participation of new actors and the 'democratization of technology' (see discussions in Taylor 2001, Théberge 1997). If such accounts of the development of this curious hybrid – both dwelling and laboratory – provide insight into the contemporary processes through which culture is produced, then, following the argument I make in this chapter, they might also be said to propose changing relations between the home and culture. If social theory has often told us that the existence of the home is a necessary condition prior to the production of authentic culture (for instance, classically as the shelter in which man can retreat from the world and deal with life's necessities before performing his art in public), then the investigation into the home-studio reminds us that there is little pre-cultural about the home. To narrate the 'rise' of the home-studio, then, might mark not only an expansion in our understanding of domestic experimentation, but also a diversification in the cultural practices through which homes are made. To be 'at home' in the studio would not only signify an artist's comfort in their place of work, but also describe an accomplishment of mediators like Oram, whose work has established the domestic experiment as a plausible genre of cultural invention.

Acknowledgements

I would like to thank Ignacio Farías, Michael Guggenheim, Noortje Marres and Alex Wilkie for their comments on earlier drafts of this chapter. I would also like to thank the Daphne Oram Trust and the Science Museum for assisting me in collecting the material that informed the research.

Notes

1 The term laboratory as I use it here is in the deliberately loose sense, meaning simply a setting of material creativity. For a discussion of the studio as the artist's laboratory see Alpers (2005).
2 The domestication of novelty has often been described as a process of taming, in which practices of private consumption in the home have served as paradigmatic. Silverstone and Hirsch's (1994) empirical studies of the domestication of new technology and media illustrate clearly why the use of novel artefacts in the home is not always simply a process of taming, but can also be understood as a process that remakes the home in particular ways.
3 The notion that the home is antithetical to experimental practice can be found throughout social theory. We find one account of the antithesis between these settings in classical social theory, in which it is the former – the home-as-shelter – that enables man to experiment freely with his art in public arenas. Here the domestic is a space of retreat from the world; a setting in which the individual deals with life's necessities in order to prepare for his public engagements and lasting interactions. The home conceived as the private sphere of necessity entails, as Hannah Arendt (1958) noted, that nothing new or lasting can be fabricated in it.
4 There are many precedents for treating the home as an experimental setting. Studies in disciplines ranging from interaction design, to political theory and feminism, to science studies have highlighted the very varied experimental capacities with which homes can be equipped. For instance, as a laboratory (Shapin 1988), a setting of demonstration (Marres 2012) or of technical expertise (Wajcman 1991), or as a testing site for new devices (Michael and Gaver 2009).
5 It might be legitimately asked, why start a discussion of the home-studio in a museum exhibition where we are at once already one remove from the studios themselves? The museum might seem a strange decision if we want to highlight the experimental character of the domestic setting, since there is no shortage of cultural production that has led us to believe that in museums we will encounter the most domesticated cultural objects, those that have been tamed as the furniture of

the social world or that have passed into history (for instance, Adorno 1967, Baudrillard 1995). On this basis, it is not unreasonable to doubt that a technology exhibition can tell us much at all about the inventive life of music home-studios. By contrast, it is precisely because starting in the Science Museum puts us at the 'wrong end' of linear trajectories of invention that I attempt to highlight what is overlooked by approaches to the studio that consider it only as a site of cultural production.

6 Due to space constraints, in this chapter I do not discuss the Electronic Music Studios Ltd, a British studio best known for producing early synthesizers used by pop groups such as Kraftwerk and Roxy Music. The Oramics exhibition, as I argue below, is particularly interesting because it foregrounds Daphne Oram's home-studio over two that are more broadly recognized and credited with particular innovations in electronic music.

7 The Science Museum is a national institution founded from the machines assembled for the Great Exhibition of 1851, which celebrated advancements in industrialism as evidence of evolutionary progress of civilization and the accomplishments of monarchal rule and Empire (for discussion see Bennett 1995, Stocking 1991).

8 The curator's proposition about the Oramics Machine might, in this sense, be said to be continuous with the findings of studio studies in highlighting that, in music studios, the distinctions between technology and art are much less determined than social theory, musicology and aesthetics have often allowed. Empirical studies of studios ranging from the high-tech/high-culture studios like IRCAM in Paris (Born 1995), to the early American and British electronic music studios (Pinch and Trocco 2004), and to studies of pop music studios (Hennion 1989), have highlighted the difficulty of enforcing clear-cut distinctions between the 'artistic' and the 'technical' on the actors, practices and artefacts we find in these settings.

9 Oram's absence from the BBC's formal history of the Radiophonic Workshop has been discussed by several authors (Marshall 2009; Niebur 2010).

10 Oram describes Bacon as the originator of the approach to sound of which her own Oramics philosophy is the most contemporary manifestation (Oram 1972: 64–65). Several of my Goldsmiths colleagues who work on digitizing Daphne Oram's archive have raised with me the significance that Bacon's sound-house quotation held for Oram, who reportedly reproduced many copies for her teaching work. Her archive, for instance, also holds an early print edition of the *New Atlantis.* Furthermore, as Wilson (2011) discusses, Oram later 'updated' Bacon's sound-house for her own version in a manifesto titled *Atlantis Anew.* Though Oram is no orthodox Baconian, the experimental imagination of the sound-house was evidently one that resonated with the composer's musical aims.

11 Wilson (2011), for instance, reports that Oram was, amongst other things, deeply interested in the concept of 'higher sense perception' developed in the 1970s by American neuroscientist Shafica Karagulla, as well as an emerging discipline called 'archaeoacoustics' (the use of acoustics as a methodology to study archaeology). Wilson reports that Oram wrote to Karagulla offering to make her Oramics studio the European outpost of the latter's Higher Sense Perception Research Foundation. Oram's vision of electronic music studio as a sound-house was, it seems, as a setting of heterogeneous modes of sonic experimentation, exceeding those of musical composition alone.

12 In *An Individual Note* Oram appropriates the term 'transduction' from electronics and acoustics and uses it to create a highly idiosyncratic philosophy of compositional individuality in the 'vibrational universe' (Wilson 2011). The influences of *An Individual Note* are a highly eclectic and idiosyncratic mixture combining, amongst other things: contemporary music criticism, didactic explanation of

electronics theory and musical theory, and a highly idiosyncratic metaphysics that draws on sources from Western classical tradition (Greek myth, Latin etymology) and Eastern spiritualism (ancient Chinese symbolism, for example). By synthesizing all of these aspects into a coherent philosophy Oram created the blue-print for a 'machine-with-humanising-factors' that could enhance, rather than diminish, the composer's individuality.

13 The book's publication in 1972 occurring significantly after Oram had completed the majority of work on the Oramics Machine.

14 This account of the Oramics Machine as comprised principally of a programmer and wave-scanners is that presented in the Science Museum's exhibition, but it is also found in Oram's and other accounts of it (Manning 2012, Oram 1972).

15 The programmer is the most iconic of the two components, comprising the film strips onto which Oram is pictured drawing. Like the black-and-white keys of a contemporary keyboard synthesizer, Oram used the programmer to control the pitch, the volume and the application of vibrato to the sound that the wave-scanners produced.

16 The wave-scanners were designed specifically to read the idiosyncratic shapes that Oram drew onto them: Oram's graphical approach an attempt to bring precision to the definition of the wave shape that was lacking in the geometrically defined sine, square and triangle waves of standard oscillators used in electronic music.

17 On the influence of Wrench's background in the British Air Force see Marshall (2009) and Manning (2012). The notion that sound technologies are shaped by earlier advances in the military existence of modern societies was perhaps most forcefully argued by Kittler (1999), who advanced a kind of military–technological determinism in his discussion of sound media. That the Oramics Machine was developed by Oram in collaboration with an air force engineer repurposing radar technology could very easily be interpreted as further confirmation of Kittler's thesis. However, in this chapter I argue that such determinism would leave us poorly equipped to account for the Oramics Machine as an experiment of the home-studio, since we would have already determined that its inventiveness lies in technology. By contrast, in this chapter I argue that, once we consider the home-studio as a domestic experiment, then the question of technical practice is no longer easily separable from the other modes of practice that we find there. In this sense, the juxtaposition of Wrench's military background with Oram's imaginative compositional background marks the particularity of the Oramics Machine as an artefact that mediates not only between different practices, but also between different biographies.

18 See video of the sonic artist who discovered the Oramics Machine, Mick Grierson, receiving the Machine as it is delivered to the UK from France: http://vimeo.com/21310959 (accessed 20 September 2014).

References

Adorno, T. W. 1967. Valéry Proust museum. In: Weber, S. and Weber, S. trans., *Prisms*. Cambridge, MA: MIT Press, pp. 173–187.

Alpers, S. 2005. *The Vexations of Art: Velázquez and Others*. New Haven, CT: Yale University Press.

Arendt, H. 1958. *The Human Condition*. Chicago, IL: University of Chicago Press.

Baudrillard, J. 1995. *Simulacra and Simulation*. Ann Arbor, MI: University of Michigan Press.

BBC Radio 3. 2008. *Wee Have Also Sound-Houses*. London: BBC. www.bbc.co.uk/programmes/b00ct1y1.

Bennett, T. 1995. *The Birth of the Museum: History, Theory, Politics.* London: Routledge.
Born, G. 1995. *Rationalizing Culture: IRCAM, Boulez and the Institutionalization of the Musical Avant-Garde.* Berkeley, CA: University of California Press.
Briscoe, D. and Curtis-Bramwell, R. 1983. *The BBC Radiophonic Workshop: The First 25 Years.* London: British Broadcasting Corporation.
Grierson, M. and Boon, T. 2013. The Oramics Machine: the lost legacy of British electronic and computer music? In: Weium, F. and Boon, T. eds, *Material Culture and Electronic Sound.* Washington, DC and Lanham, MD: Smithsonian Scholarly Press/Rowman & Littlefield.
Hennion, A. 1989. An intermediary between production and consumption: the producer of popular music. *Science, Technology & Human Values*, 14(4), 400–424.
Hutton, J. 2003. Daphne Oram: innovator, writer and composer. *Organised Sound*, 8(1), 49–56.
Kittler, F. 1999. *Gramophone, Film, Typewriter.* Stanford, CA: Stanford University Press.
Manning, P. 2012. The Oramics Machine: from vision to reality. *Organised Sound*, 17(2), 137–147.
Marres, N. 2012. *Material Participation: Technology, the Environment and Everyday Publics.* New York: Palgrave Macmillan.
Marshall, S. 2009. Graham Wrench: the story of Daphne Oram's optical synthesizer. *Sound on Sound* (February). www.soundonsound.com/sos/feb09/articles/oramics.htm.
Michael, M. and Gaver, W. 2009. Home beyond home: dwelling with threshold devices. *Space and Culture*, 12(3), 359–370.
Mugan, C. 2011. Science Museum to display legendary Oramics Machine. *The Independent*, 19 August. www.independent.co.uk/arts-entertainment/music/features/science-museum-to-display-legendary-oramics-machine-2340020.html (accessed 15 June 2012).
Mullender, R. 2011. Silent light, luminous noise: photophonics, machines and the senses. PhD thesis, London College of Communication, University of the Arts London.
Niebur, L. 2010. *Special Sound: The Creation and Legacy of the BBC Radiophonic Workshop.* New York: Oxford University Press.
Oram, D. 1972. *An Individual Note: Of Music, Sound and Electronics.* Great Yarmouth: Galliard.
Pinch, T. and Trocco, F. 2004. *Analog Days: The Invention and Impact of the Moog Synthesizer.* Cambridge, MA: Harvard University Press.
Reynolds, S. 2012. What's behind the reissue boom in 'outsider electronics'? *Frieze Magazine*, 145. www.frieze.com/issue/category/issue_145.
Shapin, S. 1988. The house of experiment in seventeenth-century England. *Isis*, 79(3), 373–404.
Silverstone, R. and Hirsch, E. 1994. *Consuming Technologies: Media and Information in Domestic Spaces.* London: Routledge.
Stocking, G. 1991. *Victorian Anthropology.* New York: Free Press.
Taylor, T. D. 2001. *Strange Sounds: Music, Technology, and Culture.* New York: Routledge.
Théberge, P. 1997. *Any Sound You Can Imagine: Making Music/Consuming Technology.* Hanover, NH: Wesleyan University Press.
Wajcman, J. 1991. *Feminism Confronts Technology.* University Park, PA: Pennsylvania State University Press.
Wilson, D. 2011. Daphne Oram: the woman from New Atlantis. *The Wire*, 330, 28–35.

11 The studio in the firm

A study of four artistic intervention residencies

Ariane Berthoin Antal

Seeking new spaces in which and with which to work, and new opportunities to influence society, some artists have been crossing the cultural divide between the world of the arts and the world of organizations by engaging in artistic interventions in companies. The first documented experiments of this kind started in the UK and the USA in the 1970s and 1980s; they have multiplied since 2000, particularly in Europe (Stephens 2001, Berthoin Antal 2009). This phenomenon could be interpreted as yet another form of flight from the 'private place, an ivory tower perhaps' of the studio (Buren 1979 [2010]: 156).

Many different kinds of organizations outside the artworld are bringing in artistic interventions; in this chapter I draw on an example in a French company that I studied over a three-year period. From January 2008 to July 2010 the company hosted four residencies, during which the artists (including one collective) spent five months working in the heart of the modern business district of Paris. Each residency closed with an exhibition and a catalogue.[1] The case offers the possibility of discovering whether there is a single model or multiple ways of using the studio in the firm for research, production and exhibition. In addition it provides a basis for learning how the actors from the world of the arts and the world of business identified and responded to the curatorial needs associated with the studio in the firm.

The chapter starts by introducing the context; the following empirical section describes how each artistic intervention residency thereby redefined anew the space and practice of a studio in the firm. The chapter then outlines the curatorial approach used to accompany the artists (and employees) in crossing the divide between the world of the arts and the world of the organization. It closes with a reflection on the possibilities of mutual learning processes.

Contextualizing artistic interventions in organizations

Artists' engagements in non-arts-based organizations take many forms, lasting from a few hours to years, with all kinds of art, and different degrees of participation by members of the organization (Darsø 2004, Berthoin Antal 2009, 2014). A significant differentiator is whether the primary intention is to work with employees on issues in the organization by drawing on artistic sensibilities and practices, or rather to create art *in situ* that is destined to be recognized by the artworld. The latter, which I characterize as 'artistic intervention residencies' (Berthoin Antal 2012), essentially entails relocating the studio into the firm. Artists who undertake such residencies nourish their creativity by interacting with the space and the people who work there. They take the risk of exposing themselves and their processes to the gaze and questioning of employees, thereby offering people outside the artworld the unusual opportunity to discover artistic practices.

Artistic intervention residencies in organizations raise various questions about studio practice. How do artists go about developing and realizing their ideas in the studio in the firm? As the French artist Daniel Buren pointed out in his seminal essay problematizing the studio, 'the studio is a place of multiple activities ... production, storage, and finally, if all goes well, distribution' (Buren 1979 [2010]: 157). Other artists and curators add the preparatory phase before production, when the studio is 'the place where lightning supposedly strikes' (Storr 2010: 62), which may entail 'puttering' (Smith 2010: 28), reflection: 'I reflect, make notes, begin to order my thoughts and in time bring things into shape' (Lawson 2010: 121), or active research (Billier 2006, Farías chapter 12 in this volume). Grabner describes the post-modern studio as 'ad hoc and fractured, no longer the sole site of artistic enterprise' (2010: 4). To what extent does the studio in the firm replace or complement artists' use of other studio spaces for research, production and exhibition?

The movement of the studio into the firm not only affects the artists, it also has implications for other actors and functions in the artworld. While the traditional studio is 'a filter which allows the artist to select his work screened from public view, and curators and dealers to select in turn that work to be seen by others' (Buren 1979 [2010]: 157), the studio in the firm implies new curatorial roles. Building on Becker's (1982) discussion of the editing function in the artworld, Acord (2013) highlights the meaning-making role of curators for the preparation of an exhibition. However, if employees may gaze upon the artist at work before the art is exhibited, the meaning-making role of curation starts much earlier than the moment of installation. Given the current discussion about the changing nature of curation, in which 'curating becomes a wide-reaching category for various organizational forms, co-operative models, and collaborative structures within contemporary cultural practice' (O'Neill 2010: 8), the studio in the firm offers another context to explore. What kind of constellation of actors is emerging to fulfil the curatorial needs in this setting?

The literature on artistic interventions in organizations has addressed the phenomenon from many angles, but has not yet considered the company as a studio space in which artists engage in research, production and exhibition under the gaze and questioning of employees. Scholars studying post-studio practices triggered by Buren's (1979 [2010]) challenge to the modern studio have explored many sites, but have not attended to the studio in the firm.

Organizational scholars have identified the multiple roles that intermediaries play in connecting the world of the arts with the world of organizations (Berthoin Antal 2012, Grzelec and Prata 2013, Johansson Sköldberg and Woodilla 2014). The analysis here takes a different perspective by relating to the artworld's discussion about the 'curatorial turn' (O'Neill 2007). This chapter therefore offers something new to both bodies of literature by examining four artistic intervention residencies in a company to see how artists create and use studio space there, and to discover new possibilities for curatorial constellations.

The case of the *Résidence d'artistes* programme at Eurogroup Consulting

Eurogroup Consulting is a Paris-based strategic management consultancy. At the time under study the company had 35 partners and some 500 consultants in France. They have particular expertise in financial services, manufacturing and utilities, and the public sector, and work with partner operations in 20 countries.

The idea of the *Résidence d'artistes* programme at Eurogroup Consulting was sparked off when Julien Eymeri, a consultant, happened to be seated next to an artist during a dinner in Paris. Despite their initial assumptions that they shared nothing in common, over the course of the meal their discussion grew into curiosity about what might happen if members of their two very different worlds participated in a process of mutual discovery. Julien left the dinner inspired to propose the idea to his company. His later conversations with artists and with people who had worked with artists in organizations persuaded him that it was worth embarking on a process whereby artists and their practices might 'hold up a mirror' to the company and enable the members to see themselves and their work in new ways. He also believed that interactions with the artists and their work might bring fresh perspectives on the societal context in which the company was operating and in which its employees were living and working.

Julien recommended to his board that the company commit itself to a residency programme over a period of two years, with four residencies, each lasting about five months, which would create new situations and new works. He intended to focus on visual art with conceptual artists, and he did not want Eurogroup Consulting employees to settle on one idea of what that means in terms of artistic process or product. By gaining commitment to a four-part programme from the outset, he also wanted to avoid pressure on the first residency to prove it was worth having an artist in the organization. The artists would work regularly in the company during their residency, with access throughout the organization, and employees would be able to meet with them easily and see work-in-progress.

The first residency began in January 2008, shortly after the company had moved into new office quarters in one of the tall towers in La Défense.

Evidence of the ability to work under the gaze of an organization was one of the elements that played a role in selection of all the artists. Other criteria were that the artists must be exhibiting their work in the artworld, and that their motivation for the residency should somehow relate to, or reflect on, the nature of consulting and/or the space in which consultants worked.

I started studying the project just after the first residency had ended, and continued half a year after it was completed in order to understand the experience from the perspective of the different stakeholders involved in the project: employees, the participating artists, the project organizers, and advisors from the artworld. I conducted individual and group interviews, observed interactions in context, designed a web-based survey for all employees after the programme ended, and reviewed documentation prepared by the company and articles by journalists in the business and art media (Berthoin Antal 2011).

Four versions of the studio in the firm

The artist chosen to launch the programme was Igor Antic (January–June 2008). The second was Renaud August-Dormeuil (October 2008–February 2009), followed by Barbara Noiret (April–October 2009). For the final residency in the programme, Eurogroup invited three artists, the Collectif 1.0.3 (February–July 2010). The artists decided how and where to create their studio in the firm for research, production and exhibition.

Igor Antic: please disturb the artist in his studio

Igor had already been an artist-in-residence in 10 other organizations, but this was his first experience in a private company, 'I believe that art is research. I came to Eurogroup knowing practically nothing.'[2] He spent the first four months of his time as a 'free electron', walking around, talking with people throughout the organization and attending meetings. 'I decided to dive into the company, be with the consultants and with their clients to understand how they work.'

He noticed similarities between their worlds. 'As an *in situ* artist, I study the situation and place, then I propose an artwork taking this into consideration. I come with nothing, and start from there. The consultants do almost the same. They start a mission and have to understand the problem in the context very quickly.' However, here similarity ended. He found their use of language and materials very different from his own, and he did not understand them. Igor realized that 'if I try to understand things the way they understand them, it will never work, it is too different, our training is too different'. He therefore decided 'to rely on my intuition, and I tried to understand how they use their intuition in their work'. The differences in sense-making processes and timeframes were particularly stark. 'Imagine, sometimes they asked me to summarize what I had seen/understood in a meeting. That is impossible! We artists need time to reflect, to digest, then to transform that into a result with form, and *then* we have something to share with others.'

Among the questions that arose from his observations were: 'How does a human being function, use his or her creativity in a different job?' 'What do consultants talk about when they are not talking about work?' He wanted to reveal the human side of things in the organization, and the 'collective subconscious of the company', a term he discovered in a management text. One of his research methods was to write an email to all the employees inviting them to send him Powerpoint slides (a ubiquitous tool in consulting) about their life in Eurogroup Consulting. Another was to invite consultants for coffee to talk about their understanding of 'vision', a term he realized they used completely differently from how he used it as an artist. He also collected some of the drawings that consultants produced on flipcharts during meetings.

After the first four months of roaming around the organization, Igor turned one of the meeting rooms on the 22nd floor into his production studio, near the coffee bar around which people congregate several times a day. Igor hung a sign on the door '*prière de déranger*' (please disturb), so the studio was accessible and employees could come and see him working with different materials, although they did not discover the final form until the works were unveiled at the *vernissage*.[3] Each piece plays with the codes of the organization and invites the viewer to re-examine them, such as the series of photographs of the coffee grounds that remained in the cups, accompanied by 'visionary' texts he constructed using phrases from the conversation, and the installation of framed flipcharts with names he invented from consultant terminology. As Igor explained to a journalist, ascribing the view that 'an artist is by nature a bit subversive', his intention is to 'project a deforming mirror of what he captures' (*Capital Privé Magazine* 2008: 9, my translation).

In summary, the first artistic intervention residency in the consultancy began by transforming the whole organization into a studio as a space of exploration and exchange, before claiming one room as his production studio. There, he spent the last month of his residency creating works that reflect on the organization as a whole. The production studio implies a boundary demarcation that needs to be counteracted with a sign inviting members of the organization to be part of the studio in the firm. Igor's final exhibition space was the meeting area that employees use informally for coffee breaks and into which they also bring customers.

Renaud Auguste-Dormeuil: temporary annex of the artworld

Renaud was the only artist who arrived with a specific idea for an artwork to be created during the residency. He immediately converted the meeting room with the most spectacular view across Paris into his studio, in order to address the theme of disappearance by 'erasing' Paris by night. He combined research and production in his studio in the firm as he studied the glittering lights of Paris each night and experimented with different ways of eliminating them from view, one by one. The first step of production was to transform the bright room into two small, dark spaces, leaving just a seat in the middle for a single viewer to look at the scenery, which the artist progressively blacked out with two dots (he discovered in his research that one dot did not suffice to dupe the two-eyed observer). Renaud's studio in the firm offered employees a constantly changing experience of the artwork-in-progress and, as such, the exhibition overlapped with his research and production.

One of the reasons that Renaud was particularly attracted to this residency was that it offered him the opportunity to engage with people who know little about contemporary art. He had a political agenda of wanting to interest people in it:

> Usually I wait in my atelier for things to come to me, then I produce my art and send it out to be exhibited out there. And usually people come to me and say 'I like your work and want to exhibit it.' Here, for the first time, I have the opportunity to show my art to people who are not won over already.

He had no idea what would happen, and felt vulnerable exposing himself and his work process for an ambitious project he was not sure he would succeed in creating. Renaud discovered that many conversations sparked by the experience of being in his studio in the company were meaningful. 'They ask good questions, like the ones I am posing in making the project,' and they talked about many themes, such as taste, mental images and fear of failing. People wondered, 'Why do you take the risk of doing something that might not work out?'

Renaud's choice of the meeting room was a conscious challenge to the organizational culture in several ways. He wanted 'to impose the art object into the workplace and get people thereby to talk about the question, the sense of art', evoking Dirié's (2011: 34; my translation) characterization of the studio as 'a space temporarily annexed to the artworld'. In addition, he wanted people to enter into the space alone, because in the company people tend to work in groups, enter the meeting room in groups, and share their ideas in groups. He challenged them to suspend this norm and build their own impressions individually first, then give words to them and speak about them, defend their own point of view, rather than immediately having a collective experience:

> When I suggest that they should enter the room alone, it is about breaking with the social model of collegiality in the company, and getting the individual point of view to come back. I am present to explain to people that what they are doing is significant.

In response to my question about whether he felt that it was working, he responded 'Yes! People are talking about the room, not about me. They are asking questions about the art object, not about my presence.' Another challenge to the organizational culture was double-sided, combining a way of differentiating himself from the first artistic intervention residency with a mirroring to the consulting company about its own approach:

> Yes, I did want to take power by taking that meeting room, acting differently from Igor. That is violent in their work and in the company: a way of establishing power. Consultants do that too, they go into other companies, take over space and tell people what to do.

The *finissage* date for 'Black Out' was determined by the moon's cycle.[4] Even though employees had seen the work emerging over the five months of the artistic intervention residency, the artist still felt it as 'the moment of unveiling, when he accepts to be naked'. The work-in-progress that the employees experienced in the meeting room that had been metamorphosed into a studio became an ephemeral artwork. What remains is a negative photograph of the scene, which the artist produced in an external studio after the residency. The artist explained that by 'destroying Black Out and leaving only a different imprint from what people had experienced, I am appealing to the story, the word, the intimate. To talk about Black Out, people will only be able to refer to their memories' (Dirié 2011: 34; my translation).[5]

In summary, Renaud had started his research before entering the organization, then he immediately declared one room to be his studio as a space for research, production and exhibition in parallel. His choice was a conscious provocation to the organization, and his studio practice was essentially a temporary annex of the artworld in the firm. Like Igor, he invited employees to cross the boundary he had erected by declaring the space to be his studio, but the invitation to individuals was a conscious contravention of the organization's norm for using the room for group meetings. The studio served as exhibition space for experiencing his ongoing process and as a catalyst for conversations beyond its boundary.

Barbara Noiret: portable studio

Barbara always works *in situ*. Before being chosen by Eurogroup, she had focused on sites of memory, such as historical sites and chateaux. She did not want to be labelled as someone who only works on the past, so she welcomed the opportunity to work in a new, very modern building, where people are trying to go further in their thinking and develop new ideas for the future. In addition, she was attracted to this residency:

> because I am also interested in nomads, the idea of nomads, and the consultants move all the time. They have several projects at a time, and they work at the clients' offices, and when they come here they have their

materials in lockers and when they come they can choose to work anywhere in the building.

She drew a parallel between their working mode and her own: 'I am also a nomad, I have never had a studio, I work in new places each time.'

Like Renaud, Barbara was aware of being compared with her predecessors in the programme. 'For them it is important to position me in relation to what they already know.' She pointed out similarities and differences from the outset. 'In fact, I am a bit like Igor, starting without projects. The difference is that I will put in place ephemeral installations, like a projection and a performance (for example with musicians and dancers), and film them.'

During her artistic intervention residency, Barbara did not ask for a specific space for her studio. She enacted the 'nomadic' by making the entire organization her studio. By entering spaces, she discovered the cultural codes relating to the use of space and language in the organization. For example, she learned how nomadic consultants establish their place because she 'was about to sit down at an empty place at the table, but someone said that the place is occupied. Each one knows where they are going to sit. Their place.' In discovering the codes for herself, she revealed them to the members of the organization. She was struck by the visual vocabulary people were using at a meeting. 'I commented on that in the meeting, showing them how they had used different images when they had spoken. They were surprised because they had not been aware. They were really interested in my observations, so my presence was also revealing for them.' She sees herself 'as an intermediary between the person and his or her environment, to create links and reveal things'.

In fact, meetings turned out to be one of her primary portable studio spaces for research. She made audio or visual recordings, focusing the camera on what others were not attending to. For example, instead of capturing people's faces, she focused on the objects on the table and how hands reached out to them. She challenged herself to work in a new way, putting herself in the same production mode and time frame as the consultants: after every meeting, she sent them an email with a kind of 'report', usually an image she created of an aspect of the situation that had struck her. For example, noticing how the consultants worked through their lunch breaks, she created a montage of a sushi-box inside the screen of a notebook computer. Employees responded. Some said they remembered the lunch meeting, others said the image was a sad comment on the reality of their working life. And sometimes people saw something she had not noticed. For example, someone said the picture reflects that they 'feed' their computers. After another meeting she spliced the recording of the conversation and surprised the participants by the formulations they had used. She was constantly collecting and producing impressions in the organization, exhibiting them on her screen and those of the employees. Much of this material went into her final exhibition in enlarged formats. All the research and production was done on-site, except for the montage of a film, when she worked with a colleague in his technically equipped studio. Rather than limiting her *vernissage* to the meeting area on the 22nd floor where the first two had been held, Barbara spread it over two floors, because she wanted to exhibit in the space where people work, and in spaces that had inspired the works.[6]

In summary, Barbara, like Igor, transformed the whole organization into a place of study, research, exploration and inspiration. Like Renaud, she combined research and production throughout the residency, but in a portable studio rather than a fixed location: her studio was wherever she took her laptop computer in the firm, and sometimes in clients' offices. Unlike the two artists who had preceded her, she did not retreat to a fixed and bounded space to produce her works. Her portable studio in the organization served as a production site, with the same types of technology and communication infrastructure as the employees use for their work. She worked in external studios when she needed some specialist technical support (e.g. film production and large-format printing). She exhibited her work throughout the duration of the residency, like Renaud. Unlike him, however, she showed the outcomes of her reflections rather than revealing the process, and she used the employees' computers rather than the organization's walls for these works by sending pieces to employees as email attachments. Barbara's final exhibition covered more organizational space than the first two, spanning two floors, and it added an aural dimension with a sound installation and performance.

Collectif 1.0.3: multiple studios in the firm

Anne Couzon Cesca and twin brothers Arnaud and François Bernus formed the Collectif 1.0.3 straight after graduating from art school, eight years before starting their artistic intervention residency at Eurogroup Consulting. They were wondering 'how to re-distinguish ourselves', so one rationale for undertaking the programme was the opportunity to explore novel ways of working as a collective: together and separately. At first all three came to the company daily, 'Being together is also a way of protecting each other, being safe.' After a month they 'felt protected in Eurogroup' and took turns coming in one at a time. They conducted their research together, developed ideas together, and then decided who would realize an idea.

Every week they sent emails around hinting where the next ephemeral sculpture would pop up, perturbing the consultants, who expect clear, concise messages. The artists contrasted their approach to that of their predecessors, which they heard about from people in the organization who had experienced the earlier residencies: 'Igor and Barbara's work was clear, simple, evident to understand, it was easy for people to project themselves into it. Ours is more complex, and we want to be enigmatic.' They enjoyed veiling some of their work. 'We tell them without telling them that we are working on a cartography that will be a kind of portrait of them. We have shown fragments, which they do not understand. At the *vernissage* the curtain will be raised.'

Besides their studio on the 16th floor and the weekly new studio spaces they suddenly occupied to create their ephemeral sculptures, the Collectif 1.0.3 used additional external studios. There were several reasons for working in other studios. One was that the three artists shared the residency stipend from Eurogroup Consulting, and worked on other projects in parallel to supplement their income. Also, one explained, 'I have to work at home first, I can't start here straight away, have to warm up to it.' Third was the need for equipment that was not available onsite.

The employees engaged with the process and output of the Collectif 1.0.3 in various ways. They often took pictures of the ephemeral white booklet sculptures with their mobile phones, sometimes then using the image on their computer. One day, a kind of scarecrow sculpture appeared across the hall from the artists' studio space, made anonymously by some employees. I discovered who they were and asked about it. They told me that they had envied the fun they saw the artists having working together, and decided to try to respond in kind. In another case, a consultant offered to advise them on how to improve their ability to 'align their intention and their practice', after watching the Collectif 1.0.3 perform '*Conférence équitable*' halfway through their residency. The artists were delighted, because they had wanted to ask the consultants to consult for them, but did not want to ask outright. So they decided to film him advising them and they integrated the footage in the *vernissage*. Another kind of engagement came from a receptionist who had has 'a fantastic memory for faces and participated in the process as a game, looking for matches' when she learned about the project that involved changing faces on banknotes.

The topic of what work and identity looks and feels like in the consulting world and the artworld was in the air throughout the four-part artistic intervention residency programme. By the time the Collectif 1.0.3 arrived, there were many points of comparison. These artists pointed out that:

> we have a certain definition of work. It is important for all artists to do it seriously. We used to try to prove that 'this is art.' But that has changed. Now we have to show that 'this is work!'

Referring back to their predecessors, they observed:

> Barbara sent her emails to show to people that she was working, and how she was working. Renaud was not seen at work, because he worked mainly at night. Although his room was open. Actually, he was totally opposed to proving that he was working. We play with the idea of having to provide proof.

Several comparisons emerged in the conversations, The artists characterized their style of working as 'not the direct kind of development along a line that they are used to, it is more 'tentacle-like'. We irrigate ourselves from everything and we irrigate everywhere.' They explained that being an artist 'is like sinking your hands into murky water, where you cannot see what is in there, and then little by little trying to create some sense from it', adding that 'our work translates the tensions and the challenges we feel people are experiencing here'. A key difference between the work of consultants and of artists raised by some employees related to the concept of vocation. 'The consultants say that they do not have a vocation. They see us as courageous for having chosen to pursue our vocation.'

The Collectif 1.0.3 was prolific.[7] The *vernissage*, which was held in the meeting area on the 22nd floor, showed seven works, including photographs of two of the ephemeral white booklet sculptures.

In summary, the Collectif 1.0.3 enacted multiple studios in the firm and outside. They used a dedicated studio space in the firm as a base but, unlike the first two studios, this one was boundaryless. In addition, their practice also entailed engaging in research, production and exhibition all over the company and throughout their residency. They offered employees the opportunity to gaze on ephemeral performances of the risky process of creating ephemeral sculptures, claiming space on various floors for these exhibitions during the residency. Furthermore, they used external studio space for warming up and for some of their research and production.

Curating the artistic intervention residencies

Artists who dare to cross the boundary into the world of business by engaging in artistic intervention residencies take risks in both the world of the organization and the world of the arts. By working in the studio in the firm, they leave what Buren (1979 [2010]: 157) characterized as the 'private place' over which they preside. While they make themselves vulnerable by exposing themselves and their creative process to the gaze and questioning of employees, they cannot count on being protected or understood in their own world. Artists and art critics express concern that artists who are paid for their work in a company are selling out to the corporate world. One of the artists reported, 'some artists say that artists who work with companies are corrupt'.

When Julien negotiated with the board to launch the residency programme, he devised an approach to address this two-sided problem that can be characterized in cultural and organizational theory terms as fulfilling the functions of an intermediary (Negus 2002, Maguire and Matthews 2012, Berthoin Antal 2012). Looking at what he did from the perspective of literature in the artworld, the terminology shifts from 'intermediary' to 'curation'. This case therefore offers the opportunity to study an experiment with a curatorial approach to the whole process of temporarily embedding the artists and their studios in the firm. It can be seen as an example of an emergent curation that 'engenders new practices, new meanings, values and relations' (O'Neill 2010: 6). However, the literature on curation still focuses on what happens in the artworld, and those writers do not envisage curation of relations between artworks and spaces in the firm, let alone between artists and employees during the processes of research, production and exhibition (O'Neill 2010, Smith 2012, Acord 2013).

Julien addressed the challenge by working with an art critic and curator, Clément Dirié. They put in place a framework to address the needs of the artists as members of the artworld. Another cornerstone of his approach was that he suspended the dominant logic of his world by rejecting an instrumental relationship with the arts in the residency programme. An instrumental stance would have been normal in his company, and is indeed a constant (problematic) theme in the discourse on artistic interventions in organizations (Berthoin Antal and Strauß 2013). Julien wrote contracts that gave the artists *carte blanche* to develop their ideas.

All the artists emphasized having experienced the freedom and support that this approach offered them in the heart of the business world. They felt that they were 'taking a risk, and the organization too. Here at Eurogroup we sensed that they were willing to accept the possibility that things might not work, might fall flat.' They appreciated the way time and value were framed around the residency in the company, in contrast to the way these aspects are often treated in society today: 'It is vulgar, simply vulgar, to try to get value too quickly, with no courage. You have to let things grow and emerge with more distance.'

The tandem curatorial approach that Julien and Clément put in place held moments of irritation for the two worlds. For example, the *vernissages* in the company brought together employees, corporate customers, gallery owners and art critics. Transforming the 22nd floor into a gallery disturbed the space the employees knew as their work space, while it brought members of the artworld into the heart of business space. The situation turned everyone there into insiders of one world, and yet also outsiders to the other world.

The artists moved on to new projects after their time in Eurogroup Consulting, having added to their repertoire of methods and to their portfolios. Julien and the board decided to stick to the original plan of four residencies and did not extend the programme. But the artistic intervention residencies left traces of their presence in the company in the memory of employees and in the form of artworks that continue to spark questions and feed conversations (Bessière 2013).

Concluding reflections

Artists' residencies in non-artistic organizations offer artists the opportunity to make new choices about their studio practice. The four examples in this case confirm that there is a 'considerable extension of the definition of the artist's studio' (Billier 2006: 28), which 'can be dematerialized or relocated' (ibid.: 22). They show how each artist defined and opened the boundaries for their studios in the firm differently, as well as how differently they distributed or combined their processes of research, production and exhibition in their various studios inside and outside the firm over the course of their residencies.

One model entailed conducting research throughout the firm before confining production to a dedicated space for production in the firm; another model was to reformat one space for research and production as well as viewing of the artwork throughout the residency. The third was a portable studio, in the form of a notebook computer, for research, production and distribution of the artwork. The fourth model was multiple temporary studios distributed throughout the firm, many of which served for research, production and ephemeral displays. Two of the artists combined their studios in the firm with external studio spaces, partially in order to use special technical equipment, partially in order to retain their 'safe' art space. These cases therefore also illustrate the emerging phenomenon of artists working in larger studio networks. If so much variety is possible within a single firm, how many more possibilities must there be still to be tried (and studied) in an era that has been characterized as 'the fall of the studio' (Davidts and Paice 2009)?

These cases are interesting because they are not just about new places to observe artists at work; they are about the interactions between members of two worlds at work (Billier 2006). Artistic intervention residencies stretch the concept of artists-in-residence because they entail engaging with the employees in their context, trying to understand their codes and playing with them. The process is as important as the outcome, and both kinds of stakeholder take risks in revealing themselves personally and professionally to each other. When artists leave their private studio to work in the studio in the firm, under the gaze and questioning of employees, they cannot 'disguise themselves and conceal their process' (Storr 2010: 62). Similarly, employees experience the vulnerability that comes with having their organizational practices challenged, taboos revealed, codes broken and professional masks removed. It is this special kind of mutual risk-taking that lays the groundwork for learning with and from each other across the cultural divide in an artistic intervention residency.

Afterwards, the artists return to their own world, while the employees remain in their work space with traces of the experience to remind them of the questioning that underpinned the creating of which they were a part. The traces the artists leave behind can take various forms: the studio space, the visible artworks and the stories they engender. After the departure of the artists, the rooms revert to their former use, but the spirit of the studio space can stay alive, 'the not knowing part and always being surprised' as Bruce Nauman describes it (2010: 66, see also Berthoin Antal 2013). The experience of engaging with the artists can continue to reverberate in conversations in the organization among those who experienced the artistic intervention residency – and beyond. When newcomers come with questions about the objects, employees may find themselves becoming storytellers with the curiosity-laden and provocative voices of the artists ringing in their ears, thereby renewing the learning process.

These cases also suggest that the studio-in-the-firm requires more curatorial attention than the installation of the artworks at the end of the residency. The approach taken in this artistic intervention residency develops the current discourse around the curatorial turn in two ways: it extends the process and the agents. First, rather than focusing primarily on the closing exhibition, curation started at the beginning of the process that brought the world of the arts into the world of the organization, accompanying the artists and the employees along their new journey. Second, the process entailed sharing the curatorial role between members of both worlds, rather than entrusting it entirely to the art expert. The knowledge and sensibilities of the representative of the world of the organization were as significant those of their partner from the world of the arts. Might such process orientation and partnerships enrich curation in art organizations as well as in the corporate setting? The past decade has brought much pressure on art organizations to learn from business, with the problematic expectation that imposing the norms and practices from business will improve arts management (Chong 2010). The experience in this project suggests that shared learning journeys are likely to generate more valuable insights and energy for change than the current preaching down one-way streets.

Notes

1 The catalogues documenting each residency, as well as a fifth one reflecting back on the whole programme, can be downloaded from the website created for the residency programme. Media clippings are also available there: www.eurogroupconsulting.fr/vous-et-nous/nos-engagements/notre-residence-dartistes.
2 Unless otherwise indicated, the quotations are from my interviews, and I have translated them from the original French.
3 See the catalogue: www.eurogroupconsulting.fr/sites/eurogroupconsulting.fr/files/document_pdf/catalogue-igor-antic-eurogroup-consulting.pdf.
4 From my notes about that night: The Tour Eiffel was still visible, only the top had been blacked out. He had left the Tour itself visible as an orientation. When I was in the room, I tried to figure out how I was supposed to sit in order not to see, which is an amusing exercise – where did the artist need me to sit in order not to see Paris/to see his achievement? The artist is not present but is making me shift from right to left, up and down, a bit like a puppeteer.
5 See the catalogue: www.eurogroupconsulting.fr/sites/eurogroupconsulting.fr/files/document_pdf/catalogue-renaud-auguste-dormeuil-eurogroup-consulting.pdf.
6 See the catalogue: www.eurogroupconsulting.fr/sites/eurogroupconsulting.fr/files/document_pdf/catalogue-barbara-noiret-eurogroup-consulting.pdf.
7 www.eurogroupconsulting.fr/sites/eurogroupconsulting.fr/files/document_pdf/catalogue-collectif-1-0-3-eurogroup-consulting.pdf.

References

Acord, S. K. 2013. Art installation as knowledge assembly. Curating contemporary art. In: Zembylas, T. ed., *Artistic Practices. Social Interactions and Cultural Dynamics.* London and New York: Routledge, pp. 151–165.

Becker, H. S. 1982. *Art Worlds.* Berkeley, CA: University of California Press.

Berthoin Antal, A. 2009. *Research Report: Research Framework for Evaluating the Effects of Artistic Interventions in Organizations.* Gothenburg: TILLT Europe. www.wzb.eu/sites/default/files/u30/researchreport.pdf.

Berthoin Antal, A. 2011. Manifeste, corporel et imprévisible: L'apprentissage organisationnel de la Résidence d'artistes. In: *La Résidence d'artistes Eurogroup Consulting, Retrospectif*, Puteaux, France: Eurogroup Consulting, pp. 10–19.

Berthoin Antal, A. 2012. Artistic intervention residencies and their intermediaries: a comparative analysis. *Organizational Aesthetics*, 1(1), 44–67.

Berthoin Antal, A. 2013. Art-based research for engaging not-knowing in organizations. *Journal of Applied Arts and Health*, 4(1), 67–76.

Berthoin Antal, A. 2014. When arts enter organizational spaces: implications for organizational learning. In: Meusburger, P. (series ed.) and Berthoin Antal, A., Meusburger, P. and Suarsana, L. (vol. eds), *Knowledge and Space: Vol. 6. Learning Organizations: Extending the Field.* Dordrecht, the Netherlands: Springer, pp. 177–201.

Berthoin Antal, A. and Strauß, A. 2013. *Artistic Interventions in Organisations: Finding Evidence of Values-Added.* Creative Clash Report. Berlin: WZB. www.wzb.eu/sites/default/files/u30/effects_of_artistic_interventions_final_report.pdf.

Bessière, J. 2013. *Etude retrospective pour évaluer l'impact résiduel dans le temps des démarches artistiques sur l'organisation. Le Cas d'Eurogroup Consulting* [Retrospective study to evaluate the residual impact of artistic interventions on the organization: the case of Eurogroup Consulting], Master's thesis, Université Paris Dauphine.

Billier, D. 2006. The artist's studio: from local to global. In: Billier, D., Froehlicher, T. and Joly, J.-B. eds, *Work Spaces in Art, Science and Business.* Stuttgart, Germany: Merz & Solitude, pp. 14–28.

Buren, D. 1979 [2010]. The function of the studio. In: Jacob, M. J. and Grabner, M. eds, *The Studio Reader. On the Space of Artists.* Chicago, IL: University of Chicago Press, pp. 156–162. (Originally published in French in 1971; translated by Thomas Repensek, *October*, 10 (Fall 1979), 51–58).

Capital Privé Magazine. 2008. Un artiste en immersion chez Eurogroup [An artist immersed in Eurogroup], *Capital Privé Magazine*, 6, 9.

Chong, D. ed. 2010. *Arts Management*, 2nd edn. Milton Park, New York: Routledge.

Darsø, L. 2004. *Artful Creation. Learning-Tales of Arts-in-Business.* Frederiksberg, Denmark: Samfundslitteratur.

Davidts, W. and Paice, K. 2009. Introduction. In: Davidts, W. and Paice, K. eds, *The Fall of the Studio. Artists at Work.* Amsterdam: Antennae, pp. 1–20.

Dirié, C. 2011. Présentation des Residences d'artiste Eurogroup Consulting. In: *La Résidence d'artistes Eurogroup Consulting, Rétrospectif.* Puteaux, France: Eurogroup Consulting, pp. 30–39.

Grabner, M. 2010. Introduction. In: Jacob, M. J. and Grabner, M. eds, *The Studio Reader. On the Space of Artists.* Chicago, IL: University of Chicago Press, pp. 1–14.

Grzelec, A. and Prata, T. 2013. *Artists in Organisations: Mapping of European Producers of Artistic Interventions in Organisations.* Creative Clash Report. Gothenburg, Sweden: TILLT Europe. www.creativeclash.eu/wp-content/uploads/2013/03/Creative_Clash_Mapping_2013_GrzelecPrata3.pdf.

Johansson Sköldberg, U. and Woodilla, J. 2014. Mind the gap! Strategies for bridging artists and organizations in artistic interventions. In: Bohemia, E., Rieple, A., Liedtka, J. and Cooper, R. eds, 19th DMI: Academic Design Management

Conference. Design Management in an Era of Disruption London. Boston, MA: Design Management Institute, 538–561.

Lawson, T. 2010. Thomas Lawson. In: Jacob, M. J. and Grabner, M. eds, *The Studio Reader. On the Space of Artists.* Chicago, IL: University of Chicago Press, pp. 121–122.

Maguire, J. S. and Matthews, J. 2012. Are we all cultural intermediaries now? An introduction to cultural intermediaries in context. *European Journal of Cultural Studies*, 15(5), 551–562.

Nauman, B. (2010). Setting a good corner. In: Jacob, M. J. and Grabner, M. eds, *The Studio Reader. On the Space of Artists.* Chicago, IL: University of Chicago Press, pp. 63–67.

Negus, K. 2002. The work of cultural intermediaries and the enduring distance between production and consumption. *Cultural Studies*, 16 (4): 501–515.

O'Neill, P. 2007. The curatorial turn: from practice to discourse. In: Rugg, J. and Sedgwick, M. eds, *Issues in Curating Contemporary Art and Performance.* Bristol and Chicago, IL: Intellect, pp. 13–28.

O'Neill, P. 2010. The politics of the small act. Interview with Paul O'Neill. *ONCurating.org* (The Political Potential of Curatorial Practise), 4 (10), 6–10. www.on-curating.org/files/oc/dateiverwaltung/old%20Issues/ONCURATING_Issue4.pdf.

Smith, M. 2010. Recipe: Perfect studio day. In: Jacob, M. J. and Grabner, M. eds, *The Studio Reader. On the Space of Artists.* Chicago, IL: University of Chicago Press, pp. 28–29.

Smith, T. 2012. *Thinking Contemporary Curating.* New York: Independent Curators International.

Stephens, K. 2001. Artists in residence in England and the experience of the year of the artist. *Cultural Trends*, 11(42), 41–76.

Storr, R. 2010. A room of one's own, a mind of one's own. In: Jacob, M. J. and Grabner, M. eds, *The Studio Reader. On the Space of Artists.* Chicago, IL: University of Chicago Press, pp. 49–62.

12 Studio operations

Manipulation, storage and hunting in desert landscapes

Ignacio Farías

In May 2013, I embarked on a four-week road trip with the German artist Mirja Busch through the American southwest. The trip was the key juncture in an artistic project on which she worked for about two years and which, at some point, we began to call the Tracing Land Art project. Each day we spent many hours working at different outdoor locations in Nevada, Arizona, New Mexico and Utah, making temporary interventions in the landscape with different objects and documenting these in various media. An inordinate part of our time, however, was spent driving a recreational vehicle (RV) along an 8600-kilometre route whilst engaging in all sort of domestic and mundane activities: cooking, cleaning, buying groceries, moving stuff around, finding the way, taking pictures, silently looking through the window, engaging in long conversations – about the places we'd visited, about our relationship, about where to stop next, about my upcoming ethnography of a video game company, about the concept behind the Tracing Land Art project, about the activities of the day before, about the exhibition resulting from the trip, about follow-up projects, and so on. We also profusely discussed the practical difficulties and challenges resulting from working on-site and on-route, especially when contrasted with Mirja's work in the studio. We spent long hours talking about the romanticized ways in which Land Art artists established an opposition between the studio and the site, and began to think about the various continuities and similarities between studio-based and site-specific work.

It is important to note that at practically no point during, before or after the trip could my role be accurately described as involving participant observation or observing participation. These notions are misleading here, as they often imply the application by a researcher of a research agenda that is not shared with the research subjects. In fact, if there was a research agenda shaping the trip, then it would concern the affordances of sites of historical land art and contemporary experiences of landscape; an agenda in which we were collaboratively engaging. Collaboration certainly does not involve taking a different role – a Science and Technology Studies (STS) scholar trying to act as a visual artist – but rather bringing in one's own capacities and skills to a collective project. Writing scholarly articles, however, was certainly not on the agenda. If writing was to be part of the project, we imagined it would involve texts for some kind of travel-log art book. For this purpose we kept an audio diary, which recorded our ongoing discussion of daily events. How, then, to write and understand a scholarly account of Mirja Busch's artistic practice of working on-site on a road trip in the USA?

To begin addressing this question, it is helpful to consider Tim Ingold's (2008) distinction between ethnography and anthropology as two very different ways of engaging and producing accounts of the world. Ethnography, he argues, is the art of describing 'the lives of people other than ourselves' (ibid.: 69). This would involve writing *about* Mirja Busch's artistic practice, producing an account based on, first, having accessed a different world and, second, turning away from it to write *about* it. Anthropological writing, certainly informed by ethnographic records, involves instead a form of thinking *with* someone based on the experience of being *with* sharing a common world. Shaped as a collaborative dialogue, the anthropological challenge would then be one of corresponding, that is, not writing about others or from their point of view, but *for* them. Writing *for* someone involves 'speaking well' of someone's practice, in the sense proposed by Isabelle Stengers, which involves an ethico-political commitment with its becoming (López 2012). The issue then is not whether our accounts are descriptive or explanatory, empirical or theoretical, qualitative or quantitative, but whether they add or subtract reality to/from the objects of research. Accordingly, as Maria Puig de la Bellacasa (2011) has observed, writing thus becomes shaped by a speculative commitment towards producing scientific accounts capable of articulating and thickening the reality of a practice.

This chapter explores and unfolds this commitment in three steps. First, it addresses and discusses the art-historical account of the studio/site bifurcation in contemporary art discourses. This is not introduced as a template or as a context against which to understand Mirja Busch's practice, but as one key art historical articulation reconfigured in and by her practice. Second, it describes the efforts by both Mirja Busch and myself to perform two key studio operations in desert landscapes, namely the manipulation of the objects and conditions affecting visual interventions, and the careful storage and transportation of a heterogeneous collection of things. Rather than analytically unpacking the socio-material assemblages shaping her practice, this section focuses on the care invested in performing these operations. Finally, this chapter provides a speculative account about the specific temporalities shaping her work on-site, exploring the figure of the hunter to capture the relationship between process and event.

The studio/site bifurcation

We are confronted with an apparent paradox: while the possibility of studio studies is based on the analytical extrapolation of the artist's studio as the prototypical site of creative production, since the late 1960s the artist's studio has been the subject of radical critiques by influential visual artists in Europe and especially the USA. The timing of this critique is worth considering, as its articulation broadly coincided with the spread and mobilization of an idealized vision of artistic work in management texts as a means to criticize industrial modes of organizing work (Boltanski and Chiapello 2006). Taking into account this 'artistic critique' of industrial capitalism, the inflationary use of the notion of the studio can't come as a surprise, especially with regard to designating a variety of sites dedicated to cultural production, reimagining workshops, ateliers, offices as spaces for individual self-realization, creativity and imagination. In *The Invention of Creativity*, Andreas Reckwitz (2012) describes the late-modern process by which the arts, once a differentiated system of cultural practices and semantics, became unbounded, rendering the production of affective attachments into the model for the most various fields of activity, especially the cultural industries and the creative economy. The visualization in Figure 12.1 of the spread of the terms 'studio' and 'creativity' can be interpreted along these lines: the graphic shows, over the course of three-and-a-half centuries, the slow institutionalization of the studio as the ideal workspace of visual artists. Since the 1960s, there is a significant increase in the use of the term, which coincides with the invention and expansion of 'creativity'. Seen from this perspective, the dissemination of the studio as a workplace model can be seen as part of a more general trend towards what might be called, not without a critical undertone, the 'creativization' of work practices (cf. Osborne 2003).

Interestingly, as this 'artistic critique of industrial work' became articulated and the studio emerged as a workplace ideal, the exact opposite movement occurred in the visual arts, leading to what, following Jones (1996), one could call an 'industrial critique of the artist studio'. It is important to keep in mind that this was by no means the first time that the studio was displaced as the fundamental space of artistic creation. In the late-nineteenth century, for example, various developments, especially photography, compelled painters to work outside the studio: 'Cézanne and his contemporaries were forced out of

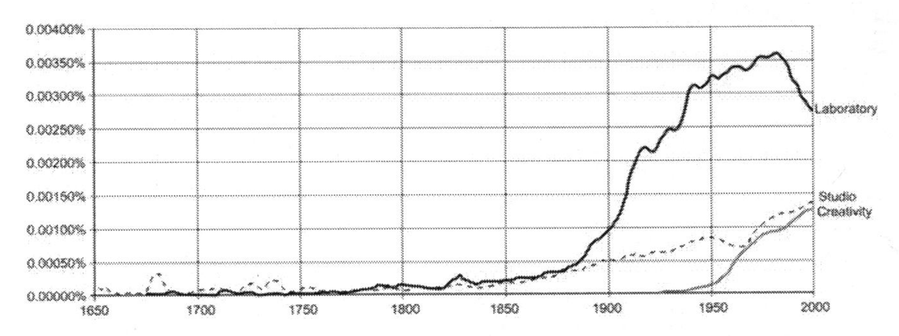

Figure 12.1 Use of terms 'studio', 'creativity' and 'laboratory' in English books (smoothing: 3 years)
Source: Google Books Ngram Viewer, https://books.google.com/ngrams.

their studio by the photograph. They were in actual competition with photography, so they went to sites' (Smithson 1996: 188). In that historical moment, the move out of the studio was also enabled by new mobile painting technologies such as portable tube colours and specially outfitted studio boats (cf. Jones 1996: 16). The industrial critique of the artist studio, as we will see, was different. It certainly involved the exploration of new modes of work, but perhaps more strongly than before it was also based on a radical critique of the artist studio.

Following Jones (1996), whom I read closely here, the specificity of this critique needs to be sought first in the North American post-war romance with the studio. The key development had been the success of abstract expressionism, which performed the studio as the space of an isolated genius. In the 1950s, the artist studio in the big city, especially in New York, was not yet a locus from which to discover and join an artistic scene or even community, but rather an austere, isolated space in an unwelcoming environment. But isolation was recast as intrinsically connected with the act of painting. As the painter Philip Guston put it:

> when you start working, everybody is in your studio – the past, your friends, enemies, the art world, and above all, your own ideas – all are here. But as you continue painting, they start leaving, one by one, and you are left completely alone. Then, if you are lucky, even you leave.
>
> (cited by Jones 1996: 11)

Connecting with the early nineteenth-century European romanticism, which imagined the 'spontaneous brushstroke' not as labour, but as a gratuitous, expressive and playful activity, abstract expressionism reconfigured the artist's studio as a place of affective creation rather than one of organized production. This involved, in turn, a radical depoliticization of artistic expression, as the preference for abstract pictorial languages made evident, as well as the capacity of the studio to establish a clear demarcation between the private world of the artist and the public world of political life. Accordingly, the studio was reconfigured as a conduit for the sublime, which 'is located entirely within the artist' (Lawrence Alloway, quoted by Jones 1996: 53).

Jones' thesis asserts that the disenchantment of this romantic studio configuration was shaped by the entering of the machinic in the visual arts foregrounding a new 'technological sublime'; a fascination with the capacities of technology to reinvent aesthetic registers and modify what is to be a human, a collective, what is to think and to create. Jones underscores two displacements resulting from this new technological sublime. First of all, an iconic displacement took place, by which the machinic and the technological were rendered into subject and media of new art forms (cf. Century 1999). A good example of this, to which I return in the next section, is the Center for Advanced Visual Studies (CAVS) founded at MIT in 1967 by artist Gyorgy Kepes, and dedicated to artistic research and experimentation in large-scale collaborative projects at the boundaries of art and technology. Especially with artist Otto Piene as its director, the CAVS became known for art experiments with robots, sky art performances, laser light installations etc. Second, the technological sublime had performative effects, as it involved a redefinition of artistic practices to resemble more complex industrial processes. The isolated genius in the studio was radically challenged by a new figuration of the artist as 'manager and worker in a social space, or engineer of a decentred and dispersed "post-studio" production' (Jones 1996: 9). Two key examples here are Frank Stella and Andy Warhol, who invoked the industrial in different ways. In Frank Stella's case there is a celebration of delegation: a figuration of the artist as an office manager capable of organizing, coordinating and controlling a distributed process of production. In the case of Andy Warhol, the studio is refigured as a mechanized space referred to as a proletarian 'factory', as an executive management office focused on 'business art business', as well as a social space for cultural happenings and distributed creativity curated by the artist.

Arguably, the most radical case is the practice of Robert Smithson, who attempted to overcome the studio altogether, 'dispersing artistic production into multiple sites and producers that could no longer be easily unified into a central, "authorizing" source' (Jones 1996: 345). For Smithson, 'the studio – even if it was mechanized, managerial or proletarian – was still centralized, and thus still linked to modernism' (ibid.: 355). Warhol's factory and Stella's office were 'confined to unitary objects made in an interior, centralized space' (ibid.). With Smithson, the industrial critique of the studio also becomes a postmodern one, a critique of the idea of the author and of the studio as the centre of synthesis (cf. Wilkie and Michael, Chapter 2 in this volume). The displacement was, however, not literal, as Smithson kept working spaces that he would call his studio. The 'nonstudio' was rather a theoretical statement, 'indicating that the studio would be denied sole importance as the site of creation or meaning' (Jones 1996: 271). Instead of the modern topology of the studio and the gallery, Smithson proposes a different, alternative topological system, based on the distinction of the site and the non-site:

> The site, in a sense, is the physical, raw reality – the earth or the ground that we are really not aware of when we are in an interior room or studio or something like that [...] I decided it would be interesting to transfer the land indoors, to the nonsite, which is an abstract container.
>
> (Smithson 1996: 178)

The distinction site/non-site is, however, asymmetrical, for the artworks that Smithson calls 'nonsites' refer to and stand for the site, which in the context of the gallery is the absent source of authenticity and meaning of the nonsite artwork. In Smithson's words: 'The site is the place where a piece should be but isn't' (cited by Kaye 2000: 91).

With Smithson, site-specificity becomes a key quality of a post-studio approach to artistic work. The key principle is that the identity and meaning of an artwork lies in the relationship with the place or situation where it was created, so that 'to move the work is to destroy the work', as the American sculptor Richard Serra put it (ibid.: 2). This proposition does not just question the 'white cube' as an ideal exhibition space in which artworks unfold in an autonomous system of references, but also the studio as the workplace of an isolated genius. For the French artist Daniel Buren (1979), author of foundational writings for site-specific art, the fundamental problem of the modern art system was that artworks would move only between these two places, the studio and the white cube, so that studio artists had to either adapt their work to the sterility of the white cube or accept that when artworks leave the studio and are presented in the gallery or the museum, they would lose their truth and authenticity. Only site-specific works could then truly unfold, making apparent their connection to the complex spaces of inception.

Beyond this, site-specificity has been also a crucial principle in the rise of a relational aesthetics during the 1990s, where the site is increasingly imagined as shaped by human encounters and social participation (Bourriaud 2002). Artistic work increasingly takes place in social settings, or rather interstices, and becomes a strategy for intervening and even inventing socio-political relationships. In all these cases, 'site specificity arises precisely in uncertainties over the borders and limits of work and site' (Kaye 2000: 216). More importantly, site is about questioning the modernist idea of a single author, who conceives, creates, is in control, and eventually authorizes an artwork.

The studio/site bifurcation has been extremely productive for the invention of new artistic languages, repertoires and imaginaries (cf. Davidts and Paice 2009), but can be misleading if understood as describing two opposing spatio-temporal configurations of art making. Especially problematic is the suggestion that site-specific art is more authentic, original and ultimately better than studio-based art. Instead, the critique of the studio can be understood as part of the institutional critique of the museum and gallery system (O'Doherty 1976), and as an ingredient of critical thought and reflection about authorship and commoditization rather than a practical rejection of the studio as a workplace. One could even argue that since the 2000s the studio has again gained centrality in artistic discourses and imaginaries that portray it as a kind of laboratory in which to conduct 'experimental' artistic research.

In Berlin, this trend has become particularly apparent as successful artists cannot just afford large studios, but also buy and convert old industrial buildings, as well as get vacant land in the city centre to build tailor-made studios. The most famous example is perhaps Olafur Eliasson's large multi-disciplinary studio at a former brewery, in which studio members also work independently on ideas for commissions, which are then presented to and negotiated with the artist, as though he were a client for whom they work (see Ursprung 2008). Remarkably, when rejecting my request to conduct ethnographic research, Eliasson's studio director wrote: 'As you will probably understand, we are happy to have [the] studio continuously balancing between measures of demystification and re-mystification' (email exchange, 13 January 2009). There are, indeed, many other examples of this re-mystification and reconfiguration of the studio. One is Katharina Grosse's tailor-made painting studio, featured in a book about new relationships between studio and painting. Others could include artists as diverse as Jonathan Meese, who has a series of videos that portray him working in the studio performing painting as a playful and divine act of creation (Ullrich 2009); Elmgreen & Dragset, who converted an old pump station into what they call a 'thinking space' (Wenk und Wiese Architekten 2011); and Reynold Reynolds, who in recent years has been exhibiting in galleries and museums his own filmmaking studio process (Farías 2012).

Be that as it may, the key point is that the studio/site bifurcation is rather limiting when it comes to understanding the situated practices of art making, deviating our analytical attention from the key operations shaping those practices to the spatial containers within which they supposedly unfold. A good set of lessons on how to avoid a false opposition between the studio and the site can be taken from science studies, where laboratory-based science is construed not as the opposite of field-site science, but as a configuration within a continuum shaped by similar type of epistemic operations. In an article about botanists' research on the Amazonian forest/savannah border and the intermixing of both ecosystems, Bruno Latour presents an important argument about how knowledge making is based on rendering of the research site into an open-air laboratory. Pushing the argument to the extreme, Latour suggests that 'For the world to become knowable, it must become a laboratory' (Latour 1999: 43). More recently, other authors have put forward more nuanced versions of this claim by grasping the continuities and discontinuities between labs and field sites. A major contribution in this regard is Thomas Gieryn's (2006) discussion of the Chicago school of urban studies as constantly going back and forth from an understanding of Chicago as lab and field, and thus moving back and forth between detached and immersed modes of knowing epistemic objects, which are seen as either made in the neutral space of the lab or found in unique places. Fabian Muniesa and Michel Callon discuss a somewhat similar distinction between laboratory and *in vivo* experiments in economics, stressing that even if they involve different forms of experimentation, they differ along the same parameters: the material display of the sites, the nature of the manipulations imposed on the object of experimentations, and the forms of demonstration. In this manner, Muniesa and Callon (2007) offer a symmetrical analysis of laboratory and *in vivo* experiments, in the sense that they avoid mobilizing different conceptual repertoires for each form of experimentation.

Inspired by such developments in science studies, the following section attempts to go beyond the studio/site bifurcation and demonstrate how key studio operations are performed in site-specific artistic engagements. Given this, I propose an alternative definition of the studio, one that does not figure it as an architectural type or as a built space, but as an interiority resulting from the execution of specific operations. Hence the key empirical question is not what is a studio, but *when*, that is, in relation to which practices, does a spatial configuration – within four walls or in the open air – *become* a studio.

27 desert days: performing an itinerant open-air studio

The Tracing Land Art project was a more or less a logical development in Mirja Busch's continued sculptural engagement with landscapes since 2008, as land art was one of the most influential sculptural movements from the late 1960s, foregrounding a new topology in the art world beyond the studio and the gallery. Interestingly, while the most important land art works were known for involving spectacular landscape interventions, they were mostly conceived as 'impermanent antimonuments' (Wallis 2010: 26) made to remain isolated in deserts and abandoned areas of difficult access. The result was a quite powerful tension between huge material interventions and a constant sense of absence, as these were works that could not be exhibited and condemned, as it were, to a temporary existence or to a slow but unavoidable transformation, or even destruction, by natural forces and geological processes. Taking this into account, Mirja's Tracing Land Art project involved visiting key sites of historical land art and making *in situ* artistic interventions that critically engage with the spectacular way these sites are represented in the art world, as well as with the strict physical and legal policing of these works. Apart from this, the project involved searching for sites in which to make visual interventions and compositions with both self-made and found objects. Some of the resulting works, shown in a solo show entitled *27 desert days* at the Berlin gallery L'Atelier-ksr, included the photographic work *A Highway Performance* that shows an incomplete geometrical pattern made with found rocks, which fails to be completed by the moving trucks in the horizon, and addresses the deep entanglement of landscape experiences and transport infrastructures, as well as the audio installation *Sound Sites*, which features recordings of the ambient sound, mostly wind, of well known earth works. As these examples make apparent, Mirja's practice outside the studio offers a fitting example of how artists typically work on-site, while making ironic references to the romantic imagination of sites in land art discourses.

Notably, the Tracing Land Art project didn't just unfold in the approximately 50 sites along the 8600-kilometre route, where interventions or performances were tried out, made and documented. Two other spaces were also of extreme importance for the project. The first was the archive of the former CAVS at MIT, the institution where, from the late 1960s onwards, environmental art developed. Just before the trip, Mirja spent three months in the archive, researching the common origins of Land and Environmental Art, as well as about different documentation strategies used to make present

Figure 12.2 A Highway Performance
Source: © Mirja Busch.

otherwise absent works. In a public talk, reflecting on this archival research, Mirja explained that:

> visiting the archive was like going to a place that establishes connections to many sites out there in the desert; sites that I was looking for and could connect with through records and documents. The archive was thus a site containing all these other sites in a virtual form.
>
> (8 March 2014)

The second key spaces were Mirja Busch's studios. In Cambridge, she transformed the living room of a small flat into a place for cutting, pasting, building and painting various elements for the trip. In her studio in Berlin, processes of reviewing, ordering, selecting and further transforming the visual materials collected during the road trip took place; processes that involved writing texts, building objects, preparing a solo show, etc. In the same talk mentioned above, Mirja reflected upon her practice in both the archive and the studio as off-site work constituted by reference and in continuity with the on-site work that occurred during the trip.

The distinction between working on-site/off-site is interesting here as it emphasizes the continuity between the different locales in which the works were realized. Instead of taking 'site' to determine the way in which an artistic practice unfolds, and opposing this to studio practice, the 'site' appears here as the subject and material with which the artist works, either directly or at a distance. Distinct from the studio/site bifurcation, which refers to the spatial contexts *within* which artistic practices unfold, the on-site/off-site distinction highlights different ways of working *with* sites. Accordingly, it provides a good starting point to think about the spaces of artistic practice not as physical and neutral containers, but as active relational configurations. As I will show in what follows, this allows me to explore studio-like configurations and operations attuned to manipulation, storage and hunting in and of desert landscapes.

Manipulation

The Tracing Land Art project is the most recent of a number of project trips made by Mirja to what might be desribed as extreme or inhospitable landscapes, such as high-altitude landscapes in the Andes and the Alps, or salt deserts and other desert regions of the Americas, North and South. In all these places, Mirja's work has mainly consisted in making interventions with materials and objects, experimenting with perspective, spatiality and optical illusions, such as the two-dimensional flattening of space. Landscapes are thus carefully chosen and explored with regard to their capacity to enable the controlled manipulation of visual compositions.

Interestingly, the landscapes chosen are predominantly white or monochrome flat landscapes, in which experiments with light, colour and three-dimensionality are possible under more or less stable conditions. Considering some of the resulting works (see Figure 12.2), it is possible to describe her exploration of white landscapes as a strategy to recreate a white cube, work with its affordances, while breaking with its artificiality. But this displacement of the white cube is an aesthetic operation performed by accomplished works only. Paying attention to the actual practices of making them, it becomes evident that these landscapes are performed as settings not just for visual experimentation, but also for the repetition of experiments and manipulation of the materials involved.

Different landscape materials, however, place considerable constraints on both the reproducibility and manipulability of visual experiments. Consider, for example, the case of snow landscapes. One of the main problems is the fact that every single intervention leaves indelible traces on the landscape, be it footsteps or marks made by the installed artefacts, so that in most cases corrections cannot be made at the exactly same location, but a few metres away, introducing slight but often consequential changes in the visual compositions, as framing, horizon, perspective and other atmospheric conditions vary.[1] In other places, such as the Uyuni salt desert in Bolivia, the manipulability of visual compositions was constrained by material properties and processes that significantly change the appearance of the salt desert over the year. When we visited it, almost its entire surface was made up of geometrical salt formations produced by erosion. Instead of a stable white landscape, in which experiments under neutral conditions are possible, these geometrical

Figure 12.3 Working on the Uyuni Salt Desert
Source: © Mirja Busch.

formations dominated every possible framing. During the various days working at the salt desert, different strategies were tried out to manipulate these salt formations, from simply stepping on them to flatten them, to using a broom to sweep them from the ground. When such interventions were insufficient to achieve the desired conditions, the location was changed. What started as a days-long travel to the Uyuni salt desert became a number of hours-long travels within the salt desert, searching for spots where erosion advanced at a different pace and where salt formations would be less salient or more malleable.

As this suggests, Mirja's practice working on-site can hardly be interpreted along the lines of the studio/site bifurcation discussed above. Rather, her practices resonate with the seventeenth-century pre-romantic formatting of the artist studio as a house of experiment. Its history has been wonderfully reconstructed by Svetlana Alpers (1998), who demonstrates how the painter's studio was born out of the same experimentalist spirit that led to the invention of the laboratory. Figure 12.1 suggests that during the seventeenth-century, the studio had even more currency than the laboratory, which became highly prominent only in the late nineteenth century. In the seventeenth century, however, painters such as Velázquez and Jan Vermeer, influenced by the camera obscura, configured the studio as a key instrument or setting for experimenting with light as a medium, and where light effects could not be just better perceived, but also controlled, manipulated and artificially created. In Alpers' account, this particular disposition and application of the studio would shape the historical evolution of the artist's studio more generally.

Accordingly, the studio needs then to be conceived as a space created for and through the operation of manipulating both objects and environmental conditions. Etymologically the term studio refers not primarily to a type of place, but to the activity of studying or inquiring. The first appearances of the term in early modern Italy designated radically different places, such as the 'social spaces of educational establishments (Pisa University was known as *lo studio*, for example)' (Hughes 1990: 34) or 'a small room set aside for solitary reading or writing, an ancestor of the study found in a modern middle-class home' (ibid: 35). This diversity suggests that the studio configuration, rather than the necessary effect of an architectural typology, involves the execution of certain practices. Whether this occurs between four walls or out in the open is of secondary importance.

Such an understanding of the studio as the result of operations of inquiry through manipulation allows us to clearly distinguish it from the master's workshop, which, as Sennett (2008) has suggested (see also O'Connor, Chapter 7 in this volume), is a place of collective learning oriented towards skilful, quality craftsmanship. In contrast, the studio is a place not of learning and implicit knowledge, but of study and experimentation via a targeted attempt at arranging, maintaining and transforming the socio-technical and atmospheric factors influencing material processes of inquiry. It is important to notice that these arrangements also include mundane activities, such as cleaning up or ordering tables and objects, while work on a particular project occurs. This is, to a certain extent, a matter of course for practitioners, but these apparently meaningless and non-creative practices are crucial in making the studio or the site function as an 'experimental' setting.

Storage

The practical continuum of working off-site and on-site can also be explored by following the objects, materials, tools, sketches, notes and inscriptions transported back and forth between the studio and the sites. In the case of the Tracing Land Art project, archival research at MIT did not just involve learning about the common origins of land and environmental art and about different documentation techniques. More importantly, the engagement with archived projects was oriented to the generation of ideas and visual concepts for Mirja's own work. Sketches, concepts, diagrams, maps, project titles, long lists of possible interventions at a particular site, etc. filled a bulging yellow notebook. Many of these ideas were prototyped and built, mostly with cardboard and other light materials, in her improvised home-studio. This was also the place where a wide range of material artefacts, ranging from bought or found industrially manufactured objects to self-made visual elements that seemed necessary for the trip, were accumulated and stored. Mirja's practice of working off-site involved building a heterogeneous collection of visual and textual inscriptions, tools, artefacts and materials which, properly packed, joined us in our trip to yet unknown sites. This was certainly not the first time Mirja would take with her such heterogeneous materials on her travels, including those made under the most precarious conditions.

During the trip, some of these elements influenced the selection of sites where visual interventions and compositions were to be tried out. However, rather than searching for an imagined site, where one such element would be installed, Mirja, and increasingly also myself, let the landscape afford interventions with some of the transported items; a process with varying success.

Figure 12.4 Storage space in the vehicle
Source: © Mirja Busch.

Beyond this, many sites elicited ideas for interventions and compositions with found materials, such as rocks (see Figure 12.2) or industrial garbage, and with other visual elements self-made *in situ* or rapidly obtained at the next town store. Interestingly, almost half of the elements carefully transported along the 8600-kilometre route were never used. Some didn't leave their boxes within the RV, others were taken out of the boxes but didn't leave the RV, and others, at a given moment, made it outside the RV but were not installed or tried out. One quick conclusion that can be drawn here would point to the difficulty of anticipating off-site the terms of the on-site engagement with properties and capacities of the landscape. This, however, wouldn't take into account the fact that, from the beginning, when these things start to be made and accumulated, Mirja knows very well that many of them will never be used. This has been the case in many other art-project trips, and yet they are made and cared for during a long and difficult route. Thus, rather than pointing to the impossibility of complete anticipation, it is crucial to understand the function played by materials, objects, tools, models and references, even if they are not used for any particular site intervention.

One way of addressing this is taking seriously the more quotidian interactions with these elements. During the trip they were stored in the back of the RV, a space that each day had to be reorganized to enable different activities, such as cooking, eating and sleeping. Each time, the small interior needed to be tidied and rearranged, inevitably leading to constant interactions with the materials. Whether they had already been used, lost their currency, or their usefulness remained uncertain was not relevant in such domestic rearrangements of the RV space, which required taking equally into account each stored element. Each was thus a constituent of a domestic ecology or background within or against which experiments were conducted, interventions documented, works made. As such, these elements acquired important capacities to affect Mirja's work. First, they functioned as a material memory, a mobile archive, whose sheer presence reminded of possibly forgotten possibilities, ideas and concepts. Second, the simultaneous presence of the stored elements relativized the distinction between the old and the new. Third, their material proximity and intermingling made fluid the boundaries between different concepts, ideas or works.

Seen from this perspective, it becomes evident that storing stuff is a key operation configuring the settings of art production, as it produces (somewhat excessive) heterogeneous material ecologies capable of opening up unexpected possibilities. If there is anything that characterizes most architectural spaces called studios, it is that they are full of stuff: materials, tools, sketches, models, works – old and new, well maintained and deteriorated, etc. The studio is not only an experimental space but also, and crucially, a repository (Jacob and Grabner 2010). Taking seriously the huge effort made by Mirja to maintain a storage resource while working on-site and on-route provides an important way to further undo the studio/site bifurcation. Working on-site is seen not as an opportunity to escape, but rather as a practice that requires reassembling the studio as a reservoir and inventive archive, even if only in reduced and provisional form.

A matter of time

One reason why the studio/site bifurcation misses the specificity of working on-site is that it asserts difference to be grounded in the spatial container of practice. In the previous sections I have argued that the key operations shaping spaces of art making are not fundamentally different when working on-site or off-site. In both engagements, it is possible to encounter the more or less controlled manipulation of the environmental conditions of experimental practices, as well as the storage of stuff. One could also point to practices of boundary-making oriented at protecting artistic practices from unwanted exposure, premature critique or distracting stimuli. Whereas the four walls of a studio enable a precise control over which and when impulses come in, and which and when works come out, the long detours made by Mirja and myself to avoid touristic and other crowded places can also be understood as attempts at performing an isolated, protected workspace. Certainly, all these various operations can be realized in the 'secluded' space of the studio more radically and consistently than in the context of a road trip through the desert, although this is a relative, not a categorical difference.

To conclude, it seems crucial to pay more attention to the temporalities of different artistic practices (see Born and Wilkie, Chapter 9 in this volume), foregrounding the eventful temporality of Mirja's work on-site. A productive entry point to think about time is the metaphor of prey, used by her from time to time during the Tracing Land Art project, for instance at the end of a day of work when suggesting we have a look at the 'day's prey'. Interestingly, she has never used this metaphor to talk about her work in the studio: a spatial setting where the creation of artworks is defined less by single events than by slow and subtle processes of growth – or where artworks can also cease to grow, and slowly, but very slowly, die (see also Farías 2012). Accordingly, one could think of the temporality of her studio-based practice as rather equivalent to that of organic or agricultural processes, where change can be observed only over long stretches of time. Eventually a product can also be harvested, but the process involves a slow maturation. Slowing down decision-making processes becomes thus an important principle of her studio practice, even if momentarily exhibitions or other deadlines can lead to an acceleration of things.

The metaphor of the prey, figuring the artist as a hunter, who needs to learn to see the environment and respond skilfully to unpredictable events, points to a process with very different temporalities. As the exhibition title *27 desert days* suggests, the project involved a long-term immersion in the landscape, a process of becoming attuned with its changing colours, forms, lights, affordances and opportunities, as well as 'acquiring the skills for direct perceptual *engagement* with its constituents' (Ingold 2000: 54). The metaphor of the prey speaks of long hours on the hunt, attentive to the slightest differences in the environment, even though nothing seems to happen. But this is precisely what hunting is all about, as it is based, as Ingold (2000) observes, on a fundamental trust in the occurrence of an encounter with the prey. This trust is not equivalent to being confident that something will happen, confidence that is based on knowledge about certain systemic or structural regularities and thus requires no personal engagement. Trusting the environment is rather an active and personal act of being in the presence and engaging with it. Being on the road searching for punctual opportunities to realize visual interventions is thus very different from the processes of cultivation and growth shaping her studio practice. It involves rather a process shaped by unpredictable encounters, in which the hunter needs to act *with* the prey. The project faced Mirja several times a day with such sudden encounters, moments in which specific visual compositions reveal themselves as possible, and which required her to react quickly, making punctual decisions over whether and how to intervene in the landscape while knowing that there is no turning back, no second chance under exactly the same conditions. Working on-site thus involved a succession of unique encounters with the landscape, which at the same time are embedded in a quite different temporality, moments 'in the unfolding of a continuing – even lifelong – relationship between the hunter and the [prey]' (ibid.: 71).

Acknowledgements

I would like to thank Mirja Busch for having first drawn my attention to contemporary practices of art making and the possibility of studio studies. I would also like to especially say thank you to Alex Wilkie for supporting the writing of this chapter from beginning to end, and to Noortje Marres and Nina Wakeford for enthusing and challenging comments on a previous version.

Note

1 In scientific laboratories, the repetition of experiments also confronts the problem of difference resulting, for example, from the 'ageing' of technical devices, as Knorr-Cetina (1999) has discussed for particle sensors.

References

Alpers, S. 1998. The studio, the laboratory, and the vexations of art. In: Jones, C. A. and Galison, P. eds, *Picturing Science, Producing Art*. New York, London: Routledge, pp. 401–417.

Boltanski, L. and Chiapello, È. 2006. *The New Spirit of Capitalism*. New York: Verso.

Bourriaud, N. 2002. *Relational Aesthetics*. Paris: Les presses du reel.

Buren, D. 1979. The function of the studio. *October*, 10 (Autumn), 51–58.

Century, M. 1999. *Pathways to Innovation in Digital Culture*. Report published by the Centre for Research on Canadian Cultural Industries and Institutions. Montreal: McGill University.

Davidts, W. and Paice, K. eds. 2009. *The Fall of the Studio: Artists at Work*. Amsterdam: Valiz.

Farías, I. 2012. The artist studio as a cyborg machine. Paper presented at Department of Arts and Cultural Studies. University of Copenhagen. http://podcast.hum.ku.dk/mediaviewer/?objectId=839.

Gieryn, T. F. 2006. City as truth-spot. *Social Studies of Science*, 36(1), 5–38.

Hughes, A. 1990. The cave and the stithy: artists' studios and intellectual property in early modern Europe. *Oxford Art Journal*, 13(1), 34–48.

Ingold, T. 2000. *The Perception of the Environment: Essays on Livelihood, Dwelling and Skill*. London: Routledge.

Ingold, T. 2008. Anthropology is not ethnography. *Proceedings of the British Academy*, 154, 69–92.

Jacob, M. J. and Grabner, M. eds. 2010. *The Studio Reader: On the Space of Artists*. Chicago, IL: University of Chicago Press.

Jones, C. A. 1996. *Machine in the Studio. Constructing the Postwar American Artist*. Chicago, IL: University of Chicago Press.

Kaye, N. 2000. *Site-Specific Art: Performance, Place and Documentation*. London, New York: Routledge.

Knorr-Cetina, K. 1999. *Epistemic Cultures: How the Sciences Make Knowledge*. Cambridge, MA: Harvard University Press.

Latour, B. 1999. *Pandora's Hope: Essays on the Reality of Science Studies*. Cambridge, MA: Harvard University Press.

López, D. 2012. Transiciones hacia otra(s) teoría(s) del actor-red: agnosticismo, interés y cuidado. In: López, D. and Tirado, F. eds, *Teoría del Actor-Red. Más allá de los Estudios de Ciencia y Tecnología*. Barcelona: Amentia Editorial, pp. 157–186.

Muniesa, F. and Callon, M. 2007. Economic experiments and the construction of markets. In: MacKenzie, D. A., Muniesa, F. and Siu, L. eds, *Do Economists Make Markets? On the Performativity of Economics*. Princeton, NJ: Princeton University Press, pp. 163–189.

O'Doherty, B. 1976. *Inside the White Cube: The Ideology of the Gallery Space*. Berkeley, CA: University of California Press.

Osborne, T. 2003. Against 'creativity': a philistine rant. *Economy and Society*, 32(4), 507–525.

Puig de la Bellacasa, M. 2011. Matters of care in technoscience: Assembling neglected things. *Social Studies of Science*, 41(1), 85–106.

Reckwitz, A. 2012. *Die Erfindung der Kreativität*. Frankfurt am Main: Suhrkamp.

Sennett, R. 2008. *The Craftsman*. New Haven, CT: Yale University Press.

Smithson, R. 1996. *Robert Smithson, the Collected Writings*. Berkeley and Los Angeles, CA: University of California Press.

Ullrich, W. 2009. Das Atelier als 'Tal der Lächerlichkeit': Jonathan Meeses Inszenierung. Paper presented at the Conference Wo entsteht die Kunst? Das Atelier seit Caspar David Friedrich, Greifswald.

Ursprung, P. 2008. From observer to participant. In Olafur Eliasson's studio. In: Engberg-Pedersen, A. and Eliasson, S. O. eds, *Studio Olafur Eliasson: An Encyclopedia*. Cologne: Taschen, pp. 10–19.

Wallis, B. 2010. Survey. *Land and Environmental Art*. London, New York: Phaidon.

Wenk und Wiese Architekten2011. Pumpwerk Neukölln. *Arch+*, 201/202, 138–141.

Afterword – studio studies

Scenarios, supplements, scope

Mike Michael

On reading the chapters in this collection, one can't help but be impressed by the variety of case studies, the wealth of theoretical perspectives and the richness of the empirical material. Yet studio studies is still in its infancy – there is still work to be done in delimiting its scope and demarcating its domain. The work presented here collectively suggests a number of avenues, and in this essay I pick up on some these in an attempt to draw out a number of themes that seem to me to be particularly interesting to pursue.

In what follows, I trace out three broad themes. First, I suggest one possible expansion of the setting of 'studio studies'. More specifically, I ask what gain there might be in placing studio studies in relation to longstanding discussions about risk and technoscience, but also to processes of aestheticization and what I call epistemic-ization. Second, I develop some thoughts on the heterogeneities evidenced in studio practice that are described in the present studies. In particular, I suggest that we can draw on Serres, Latour and Whitehead to sketch a common, though always provisional, vocabulary for theorizing the human–non-human and actual–virtual heterogeneities that seem characteristic of studio practice. I tentatively propose the notion of pre/pro-positional figures as a means of addressing these heterogeneities, but also of tackling the (temporary) sense of creative completion or 'satisfaction' that also marks studio practice. Finally, I explore what it means to think 'studio studies' through the idiom of 'interdisciplinarity'. Baldly, can studio studies encompass the methodologies and discourses of both social scientific and studio practices? I point to Isabelle Stengers' vision of an 'ecology of practices' as one (idealized) mechanism whereby divergent practices can at once move closer toward each other while maintaining their differences to produce some kind of interdisciplinarity.

Inevitably, the suggestions and scenarios I present are all too schematic, but the modest hope is that they supplement the emerging scope of 'studio studies' so ably delineated in this volume.

Studio, science, setting

Many of the essays here struggle, in one way or another, with the question: What is a studio? Studios seem to be easy to exemplify yet difficult to pin down. As Farías and Wilkie (chapter 1 in this volume) stress in their introduction, the studio comes in very many different forms, and they make great inroads into setting out a number of empirical and analytic strategies through which to explore 'the' studio. Thus to engage with the studio means 'closely studying the situations in and through which distributed creation processes take place'.

This recommendation is, as they note, concerned with getting away from the studio as a tightly demarcated space. I shall return to this point below. Here, however, I want to reflect briefly on the suspicion that 'studio' is a term applied in a proliferating number of domains. So I prefixed 'studio' with things chosen by and large at random from my domestic setting as I sat thinking about an entrée into this essay. Obviously there are photo, nail and hair studios, but Google also listed dental studios, bread studios, a flour studio, fireplace studios and sofa studios. There was also doorknob studio, though this turned out to be the moniker for a designer's website. There was, however, no tablecloth studio.

At first glance, and picking up on the hint in Grimaud's Chapter 4 (this volume) on the precipitous spread of the 'on-board' camera, one might ask whether this indicates some sort of 'studio-fication' of the contemporary world. Just as it has been said that society has become a laboratory (e.g. Krohn and Weyer 1994; Beck 2000), perhaps we are witness to a society that is becoming a studio writ large. While this is doubtless fanciful, it does point to a difference between the studio and the laboratory, a difference that concerns the issue of risk. The idea of 'society as a laboratory' is intimately tied to risk – the risks of conducting experiments whose impacts are so widespread that they can pose major threats to large swathes of society. These risks come in various forms: epochal environmental dangers, prospective biotechnological dangers (the slippery slope – e.g. Mulkay 1997), or the generic dangers of technoscientific hubris (e.g. Turney 1998). It is harder to imagine a studio-fication of the social world having similar potentially catastrophic consequences (cf. Wilkie 2013).

But perhaps this misses the mark. A supposed 'laboratorization' does other things too – it is part of a larger and longer moment. To the extent that the scientific laboratory has had a role in the disenchantment of the world – in its conversion to a chronic concern with, let's say, 'matters of fact' – it has also been instrumental in its 'epistemic-ization'. By epistemic-ization I simply mean to connote that our grasp of the world is routinely mediated through expert knowledge and abstract systems, and therefore relations of trust (e.g. Giddens 1991; Wynne 1995). We might ask whether the studio is a component in a later development – the 'aestheticization' of everyday life (see Featherstone 1991; also Lash and Lury 2007). Here, commodities (not least the products of studios) have become equivalent to, as Lury once put it, 'works of art, images or signs, to be engaged with via processes of fantasy, play, daydreaming and image-making' (Lury 1996: 77–78). Ironically, this brings us back to risk. Studios mediate practices of consumption: the products and images that they foster contribute, in more or less direct ways, to environmental risks, after all.

Yet this, too, is too simplistic. After all, aesthetics are not foreign to scientific practice, and the 'scientific citizen' is also a consumer who both consumes scientific knowledge (not least in terms of its aesthetic qualities) and uses scientific knowledge to inform their consumption 'choices' (Michael 2006). On top of this, we have maybe been too enthusiastic in linking laboratory science to an abstracted 'epistemic-ization'. Science comes in many forms and the practices of different disciplines reflect very different 'epistemic cultures' (Knorr-Cetina 1999). This point simply reflects Hennion's serious quip that we should make a 'studio of studios' (Chapter 5) in order to attend to the diversity of the studio form. In sum, I am suggesting that the contrast between laboratory and studio that informs much of the discussion in this volume risks simplifying the differences amongst labs and studios, and simplifying the ways in which they interdigitate in relation to more extensive assemblages that can become territorialized around risk or particular forms of consumption (to echo Georgina Born's argument that studio needs to be read through longer lineages, Chapter 9). Although the emphasis in the present volume is rightly on the micro-study of studios, this does not exclude a more 'expansive' analytic (once all the usual provisos have been put in place, of course).

Stuff, signs, satisfaction

Without exception, the chapters in this volume are keen to stress the distributedness of the studio. Most obviously, we can note the complex institutional settings within which a studio is situated (the university and the corporation for Wilkie and Michael; the firm for Berthoin Antal); the specific links between the studio and other 'discrete' spaces (Waller's domestic space; or O'Connor's hot-shop); or the peculiar interconnections that studios forge or negotiate with various actants (the local government officials described by Houdart; or the references collected spontaneously by creative professionals in Ariztía's case study).

But for all this distributed-ness, with its confluence of flows and gathering of relations – this concrescence of prehensions, as Whitehead (1929) would frame it – there is usually some sort of 'creative accomplishment' that 'punctuates' this movement and combination of various types of stuff and signs. Amongst the rich arrays of stuff that are discussed in this volume, we can point to skilled and sweating bodies (O'Connor), particular reconfigurations of space (Berthoin Antal), paper, wood, cardboard and glue (Houdart, Waller), microprocessors (Wilkie and Michael), or headphones and screens (Ash). Amongst the streams of signs that the authors have documented, we can note the creatives' references (Ariztía), the atmospheric fug of aggression (Ash), the metaphors of 'day's prey' (Farías), or the accounts of studio genealogy (Born and Wilkie). Of course, the distinction between stuff and sign – the material and the representational – is by no means so hard and fast, as Latour (1990, 1992) showed many years ago. The crucial insight is that these 'prehensions' come together to generate 'meaning' understood heterogeneously:

> in its original nontextual and nonlinguistic interpretation: how a privileged trajectory is built, out of an indefinite number of possibilities; in that sense, semiotics is the study of order building or path building and may be applied to settings, machines, bodies and programming languages as well as texts …
>
> (Akrich and Latour 1992: 259)

There are a number of points to raise here. First, there are limitations around what can comfortably enter a particular concrescence. Not everything can go with anything in the emergence of an actual occasion (such as glassblowing, brainstorming or model-building) or an actual entity (such as a prototype, a *maquette* or a sculpture). This is the teleological element in Whitehead's event-thinking: some elements are more central than others in the building of a specific path or order, more relevant to attaining what Whitehead calls 'satisfaction'. In relation to 'the' studio, satisfaction can be translated into the 'feeling' that something creative has reached some sort of completion or fruition – a 'satisfactory' accomplishment of creation (even if that accomplishment concerns the opening up of new possibilities – see below).

Putting this another way, we might say that only some relations are feasible in the 'creative' making of meaning (conceived heterogeneously). On this score, we can turn to Michel Serres and his call for a 'philosophy of prepositions'. Over the years he has developed a range of what we might call prepositional figures – the parasite, Hermes, angels – that have allowed him to explore the complex, topological intertwinings of heterogeneous elements (e.g. Serres 1982a, b1995; Serres and Latour 1995). Putting Whitehead and Serres together, we might ask if there are, peculiar to studios, classes of prepositional figures that can serve in the pulling together of particular relations. What comes immediately to mind is the figure of the 'user'. To be sure, the user is highly malleable and multiplicitous (see Wilkie 2010). Nevertheless, in its specificity across the studios presented in the present volume, can it comprise a mechanism by which to trace what relations can feasibly become a part of a studio? For instance, how does the client–user shape what 'references' are viable (Ariztía) or how does the practitioner–user afford some architectural relations over others (Houdart)? Needless to say, within and amongst studios there are many other candidates for the position of 'prepositional figure'. However, the suggestion here is whether the 'user' (or some similar term) is special to studios – or especially useful in analysing the specificities of studios.

Now, for Serres, prepositional figures are not confined to the making of orders or paths; they are also seen as disruptive – instrumental in the process of dis-ordering (having said that, it is also worth noting that their role in the fracturing of relations might, further down the line, yield more complex orderings). In other words, rather than close down a nexus of relations, new relations might open out and come into view, simultaneously rendering a sort of 'dis-satisfaction'. We have seen numerous moments of 'dis-satisfaction' throughout the volume: the tinkering with models (Houdart), the arguments over screens and headphones (Ariztía), the intransigence of the Oramics machine (Waller), the seeming redundancy of an artist's mobile 'collection of resources' (Farías). Each of these objects, for differing reasons, has a hand in 'proposing' potential relations to, respectively, local government officials, 'appropriate' gamers, bricolaged technologies, potential landscape-prey.

The use of the term 'proposing' is quite deliberate: it refers to the possibility that studios are populated not only with 'prepositional figures', but also with 'propositional figures'. Drawing on Latour, a proposition addresses those 'occasions given to different entities to enter into contact. These occasions for interaction allow the entities to modify their definitions over the course of an event' (Latour 1999: 141). In other words, a proposition points to the new relations that can be crafted. In this respect, Latour is echoing Whitehead (1929: 185–186) who writes that a proposition is 'a hybrid between pure potentialities and actualities'. In addition, these propositions are constitutively hybrid: they 'are not statements, or things, or any sort of intermediary between the two. They are, first of all, actants' (Latour 1999: 141).

This double heterogeneity of propositions (combining human and non-human, the actual and the potential – see Halewood and Michael 2008; Michael and Rosengarten 2012) is clearly present in Farías and Wilkie's, and Born and Wilkie's, referencing of Rheinberger's (1997) work. However, the idea of a 'propositional figure' finds its most forceful expression in Antoine Hennion's advocacy of an 'anthropology of *maquettes*', and its ideal typification in the form of the maquette. Hennion (Chapter 5 in this volume) says:

> The *maquette* is an empirical materialization of the plurality of things [...] *Maquette* is half an image made thing, half a thing made image, and it gives life to these images. Then I can be between the two. I am in front of a material thing, which is not really yet the object. Producing this kind of intermediary object, intermediary between, well, between these kinds of layers of virtualities – although virtualities is probably a too strong word [...]

So, it would seem that the maquette encompasses the not-as-yet, while also being rooted in the actual here-and-now – it is actual and potential. It is a propositional figure *par excellence*, heterogeneously composed of various elements while opening out onto numerous, though delimited, potential relations. Ironically, it is the very 'dis-satisfaction' of the propositional figure that indexes its 'satisfaction': a good actual *maquette* gathers to itself new potentially productive relations. The questions that follow in the wake of the maquette as propositional figure include: What else within a studio environment might take on this role? Is there anything peculiar to the studio propositional figure that distinguishes both it and the studio from other work settings?

Then again, taking the discussion of prepositional figures into account, perhaps we would do better to seek pre/pro-positional figures within studios. A pre/pro-propositional figure is one that at once captures the nexus that underpins the actuality of studio practice while also tracing the potentialities of that practice. What are the sorts of pre/pro-positional figures that might help us schematize a programme of studio studies?

By way of an initial illustration of a pre/pro-positional figure, we might point to the 'cultural probes' (Boehner et al. 2012) used in what is sometimes called the speculative design tradition (Michael 2012). These are devices designed to be playful, ambiguous and provocative in ways that enable their users to develop new ways of thinking about technologies. A good example is the *Listening Glass* which comprises a mundane drinking glass along with a set of instructions (that invite the user to press the glass against a wall and to record unusual house sounds) and a marker pen (for recording an account of those sounds on the glass itself). The cultural probes are composed of heterogeneous elements that include the physical components but also aesthetic and utilitarian parameters. Together, these 'pre-positionally' interrelate – concresce – in a moment of 'satisfaction' where the designers are 'satisfied' that the cultural probe will do a particular job (provide insight into how people engage with their domestic environments). By the same token, cultural probes are designed 'pro-positionally' to draw in new and unexpected associations. The *Listening Glass* is thus also a means of enabling its user – and the designers – to access the complex, ambiguous, diffuse, inchoate and unfolding relations that *potentially* constitute a household.

Study, society, symmetry

The chapters in this book, in the main, comprise studies *of* the stuff and signs, as well as the practitioners and practices, that constitute studios. Of course, there are cases where this has been questioned, notably in Farías' evocative chapter on his travels *with* an artist, and memorably in O'Connor's depiction of the *shared* corporeality of glass-blowing. These latter hint at the possibilities of interdisciplinary relationships between the social science work on display in the present chapters and the practices documented by that work. Now, Born discusses interdisciplinarity, and Wilkie and Michael touch on it in passing, but in both cases this refers to the way interdisciplinarity manifests itself in others' projects (art–science; the Culture Lab). Instead, we might ask whether there are prospects for 'collaboration' across social science and studio disciplines. Phrased in the vocabulary of the preceding section, we could ask whether we can propose pre/propositional figures through which to explore the possibilities of *joint* work.

On the face of it, this might seem strange – after all, are not the 'objects' of the social sciences and the various studios depicted in these pages rather different? If the 'objects' of the former include spatialization, temporalization, atmo/spheres, corporeality, perspectivism, overflowing, amongst the 'objects' of the latter are glass and fire, stones and landscapes, transistors and circuit boards. Yet, unsurprisingly, this bald contrast belies the similarities amongst the concerns of both social scientists and studio practitioners. It is now commonplace to acknowledge 'a crisis in empirical sociology'. Sociology's once pre-eminent position as the source of valued commentary on contemporary societies has been catastrophically undermined by the proliferation of (especially digital) methods outside of the academy (e.g. Savage and Burrows 2007). In light of this, we might ask whether the practices present in the studios do not entail something akin to social scientific method.

We can elaborate on this along two lines. First, we can turn to the insights of actor–network theory (e.g. Latour 2005), which insisted that we understand scientists and technologists as heterogeneous engineers (Law 1987). Scientists and technologists draw together all manner of heterogeneous elements in forging their objects – elements that include 'the social'. Of the many things that can fall under the rubric of 'the social', for present purposes we can note the local 'models' of the social that inform technoscientific work, models that address which colleagues are trustworthy; what regulatory bodies are amenable; what funders are willing. In parallel, technoscientists also take into account the sort of society that is willing to 'consume' their scientific knowledge or technological artefact. Thus, when technoscientists raise expectations (e.g. Brown and Michael 2003), they are also making assumptions about what sorts of expectation are 'raise-able' within particular social constituencies. The point is that studio practitioners are likely to operate with similar 'models of the social'. The obvious question that follows is: How are these 'models' derived? In this volume we can detect a number of 'methods', ranging from the explicit (e.g. market research) to the intuitive (e.g. a sense of what precipitates environmental critique). Following Savage and Burrows (2007: 888) we should not 'bemoan [these practitioners'] limited awareness, their instrumentalism' – from their perspective these 'methods' generally are productive and effective. Rather, and in the spirit of actor–network theory's tenets of radical symmetry and free association, we could seek to freely associate with studio practitioners and aim to treat their 'models of the social' in ways symmetrical to our own.

A second way to examine the idea of interdisciplinary collaboration is through the performativity of social method (Law 2004). Social scientific practices are performative insofar as they variously constitute the 'world' that is engaged – a world which is, according to Law, in flux, unfolding, open. We might also add that not only is the 'world' enacted through method, but so too is the social scientist (and their method) enacted by the 'world'. That is to say, out of the research event (whether that be interviews, focus groups, ethnography, archival work), researched *and* researcher co-emerge (Michael 2012). As such, in the studies reported here, can we identify narrative vestiges of these mutual enactments? No doubt this will be difficult: after all, these processes of co-emergence are likely to be happening at an affective level that is not necessarily subject to direct articulation.

Isabelle Stengers' (2010) idea of an 'ecology of practices' might be especially helpful in this respect. For her, in the cosmopolitical meeting of different 'practitioners' (who might be expert or lay), such practitioners bring valuable knowledge and perspective that is always already 'situated', entailing both a responsibility to their object of knowledge and commitment to the standards of their specialist community. Put very crudely, the critical element in this ecology is that such an ecology is open to change: any practitioner's practice can be responsive to another's, and any object of knowledge can emerge anew through the process of negotiation. At the same time, such a process is not an unproblematic 'synthesis' of practices (see Wilkie and Michael, Chapter 2 in this volume), but a dynamic in which practitioner differences are preserved: any synthesis is therefore also a continued, if shifted, differentiation. On top of this, there is no 'outside' from which to comment on interdisciplinarity or collaboration – each of these is enacted from within divergent practitioner commitments (which might nevertheless be partially connected). One hope, then, is that 'an ecology of practices' offers a skeletal framework through which to begin to articulate the mutual affective changes and tensions that tacitly mark studio studies, and to express the complex topologies of contact between social science and studio practices.

As a tangential (and superficial) example of what I'm getting at, we can turn to a collaboration between designers and social scientists on the issue of energy demand reduction. The ECDC project – short for Energy and Co-Designing Communities, which is itself short for Sustainability Invention and Energy Demand Reduction: Co-Designing Communities and Practice – involved the design of probes and prototypes through which to explore the emerging ways in which people understood the practices of 'energy demand reduction' and related practices around 'community' 'futures' and 'information' (Gaver et al. 2015). Amongst some of the designers and social scientists, there seemed to be a more or less common theoretical vocabulary (e.g. actor–network theory), a common research object (energy demand reduction) and, in time, common materials (photographs, probe returns, participant recordings). However, these were routinely treated in different ways. For instance, at certain points in the project, the designers tended to see these incoming materials in terms of their potential *connection* to other materials (from design and art history, various popular and technical sources) and their contribution to the emergence of new design artefacts (prototypes), while the social scientists tended to view these in terms of data to be *analysed* and related to theory. In a sense, these practitioners had to negotiate the meaning of these materials by way of their disciplinary community commitments. Any tensions were partly dealt with by a mixture of deferral (to the other's expertise) and divestment (the partial shedding of one's usual framing and the partial take-up of the other's perspective). Here we have an ecology of practices in which materials/data were enacted in different ways which, nevertheless, began to 'resonate' with one another. Certainly for one social scientist (me), the treatment of materials in the designers' studio in ways that seemed to be connective, or additive (as opposed to analytic), was both a challenge and a revelation, both threat and promise (Michael in press).

In this all-too-scant illustration of how an 'ecology of practice' might play out in the context of a collaboration between designers and social scientists, perhaps we can divine a more ambitious hope for studio studies. Can we imagine a studio studies that is constitutively interdisciplinary in the way described above, and as such, a medium through which to expand not only the empirical horizons of the social sciences more generally, but also their conceptual, methodological and affective horizons?

References

Akrich, M. and Latour, B. 1992. A summary of a convenient vocabulary for the semiotics of human and nonhuman assemblies. In: Bijker, W. E. and Law, J. eds, *Shaping Technology/Building Society*. Cambridge, MA: MIT Press.

Beck, U. 2000. Risk society revisited: theory politics and research programmes. In: Adam, B., Beck, U. and Van Loon, J. eds, *The Risk Society and Beyond*. London: Sage.

Boehner, K., Gaver, W. and Boucher, A. 2012. Probes. In: Lury, C. and Wakeford, N. eds, *Inventive Methods: The Happening of the Social*. London: Routledge.

Brown, N. and Michael, M. 2003. A sociology of expectations: retrospecting prospects and prospecting retrospects. *Technology Analysis and Strategic Management*, 15(1), 3–18.

Featherstone, M. 1991. *Consumer Culture and Postmodernism*. London: Sage.

Gaver, W., Michael, M., Kerridge, T., Wilkie, A., Boucher, A., Ovalle, L. and Plummer-Fernandez, M.2015. Energy babble: mixing environmentally-oriented internet content to engage community groups. In: *Proceedings of the 33rd Annual ACM Conference on Human Factors in Computing Systems*. New York: Association for Computing Machinery, pp. 1115–1124.

Giddens, A. 1991. *Modernity and Self-Identity*. Cambridge: Polity.

Halewood, M. and Michael, M. 2008. Being a sociologist and becoming a Whiteheadian: concrescing methodological tactics. *Theory, Culture and Society* 25(4), 31–56.

Knorr-Cetina, K. 1999. *Epistemic Cultures: How the Sciences Make Knowledge*. Cambridge, MA: Harvard University Press.

Krohn, W. and Weyer, J. 1994. Society as laboratory: the social risks of experimental research. *Science and Public Policy*, 21(3),173–183.

Lash, S. and Lury, C. 2007. *Global Culture Industry: The Mediation of Things*. Cambridge: Polity Press.

Latour, B. 1990. Drawing things together. In: Lynch, M. and Woolgar, S. eds, *Representations in Scientific Practice*. Cambridge, MA: MIT Press.

Latour, B. 1992. Where are the missing masses? A sociology of a few mundane artifacts, In: Bijker, W. E. and Law, J. eds, *Shaping Technology/Building Society*. Cambridge, MA: MIT Press.

Latour, B. 1999. *Pandora's Hope: Essays on the Reality of Science Studies*. Cambridge, MA: Harvard University Press.

Latour, B. 2005. *Reassembling the Social: An Introduction to Actor–Network Theory.* Oxford: Clarendon Press.

Law, J. 1987. Technology and heterogeneous engineering; the case of Portuguese expansion. In: Bijker, W., Hughes, T. P. and Pinch, T. eds, *The Social Construction of Technological Systems.* Cambridge, MA: MIT Press.

Law, J. 2004. *After Method: Mess in Social Science Research.* London: Routledge.

Lury, C. 1996. *Consumer Culture.* Cambridge: Polity.

Michael, M. 2006. *Technoscience and Everyday Life.* Maidenhead: Open University Press/McGraw-Hill.

Michael, M. 2012. Toward an idiotic methodology: de-signing the object of sociology. *Sociological Review*, 60 (S1), 166–183.

Michael, M. in press. Speculative design and digital materialities: idiocy, threat and com-promise. In: Ardevol, E., Pink, S. and Lanzeni, D. eds, *Designing Digital Materialities: Knowing, Intervention and Making.* London: Bloomsbury.

Michael, M. and Rosengarten, M. 2012. HIV, globalization and topology: of prepositions and propositions. *Theory, Culture and Society*, 29(4–5), 93–115.

Mulkay, M. 1997. *The Embryo Research Debate: Science and the Politics of Reproduction.* Cambridge: Cambridge University Press.

Rheinberger, H.-J. 1997. *Toward a History of Epistemic Things: Synthesizing Proteins in the Test Tube.* Stanford, CA: Stanford University Press.

Savage, M. and Burrows, R. 2007. The coming crisis of empirical sociology. *Sociology*, 41(5), 885–899.

Serres, M. 1982a. *Hermes: Literature, Science, Philosophy.* Baltimore, MD: Johns Hopkins University Press.

Serres, M. 1982b. *The Parasite.* Baltimore, MD: Johns Hopkins University Press.

Serres, M. 1995. *Angels: A Modern Myth.* Paris: Flammarion.

Serres, M. and Latour, B. 1995. *Conversations on Science, Culture and Time.* Ann Arbor: Michigan University Press.

Stengers, I. 2010. *Cosmopolitics I.* Minneapolis, MN: University of Minnesota Press.

Turney, J. 1998. *Frankenstein's Footsteps: Science, Genetics and Popular Culture.* New Haven, CT: Yale University Press.

Whitehead, A. 1929. *Process and Reality: An Essay in Cosmology.* New York: Free Press.

Wilkie, A. 2010. User assemblages in design: an ethnographic study. PhD thesis, Goldsmiths, University of London.

Wilkie, A.2013. Prototyping as event: designing the future of obesity. *Journal of Cultural Economy*, 7(4), 476–492.

Wynne, B. E. 1995. The public understanding of science. In: Jasanoff, S., Markle, G. E., Peterson, J. C. and Pinch, T. eds, *Handbook of Science and Technology Studies.* Thousand Oaks, CA: Sage.

Index

Page numbers in **bold** refer to figures.